Current Research in
Comparative Communism

Lawrence L. Whetten

The Praeger Special Studies program—
utilizing the most modern and efficient book
production techniques and a selective
worldwide distribution network—makes
available to the academic, government, and
business communities significant, timely
research in U.S. and international economic, social, and political development.

Current Research in Comparative Communism

An Analysis and Bibliographic Guide to the Soviet System

Praeger Publishers   New York   Washington   London

PRAEGER SPECIAL STUDIES IN INTERNATIONAL POLITICS AND GOVERNMENT

Library of Congress Cataloging in Publication Data

Whetten, Lawrence L
    Current research in comparative communism.

    (Praeger special studies in international politics
and government)
    Bibliography
    1. Communism—1945-   —Bibliography.
2. Communism—Russia—Bibliography.   3. Communism—
Europe, Eastern—Bibliography.   4. Communism—1945-
—Research.   I. Title.
Z7164.S67W47   [HX44]   016.33543   76-19553
ISBN 0-275-23550-5

BT. app. 1-28-77

PRAEGER PUBLISHERS
111 Fourth Avenue, New York, N.Y. 10003, U.S.A.

Published in the United States of America in 1976
by Praeger Publishers, Inc.

Printed in the United States of America

PREFACE

The purpose of this volume is to provide a guide for the study of change in the Soviet system, or comparative communism as it is now called. It consists of several parts: The first outlines the research design used in advanced university seminars; it may be of use to the students in devising their own approach to examining change over time and space. The second section is a survey of the methodological trends in comparative communism that also may assist students in coming to grips with one of the most complex methodological challenges in contemporary social science. The third part includes an altogether too brief overview of the evolution of the principal themes in communism, emphasizing the evolution that has occurred since the proclamation of Marx's first model for societal progress. A fourth section contains a short discussion of the key problem areas that have emerged in the Soviet system in which change and reform are occurring as the societies move from the mobilization to the modernization stage of development. This section points out those problems that tend to be more hazardous to socialist societies than to other countries at similar levels of development. The final part is a selected bibliography of contemporary literature in the field of change in domestic polity within the Soviet system (which is confined to the USSR and the East European states, minus Albania but including Yugoslavia, because of its unique innovative impact of creative Marxism).

It is important to note that this study is not intended to be a comprehensive presentation of the work to date in the field of comparative communism. It is intended to be merely representative, selective and illustrative.

I wish to acknowledge my gratitude for advice and assistance provided by Stanley Riveles, and Peter Berton, and for research assistance by James Simon, Edward Shannon, and Dorothy Griffith. I am, of course, deeply indebted to the pioneering work already undertaken in the field and cited below.

CONTENTS

PART

I

CHANGE IN THE
SOVIET SYSTEM

Explaining communist behavior has been a main concern of policy makers and students of communism alike. Whatever term one chooses as most appropriate, polycentrism or national communism, the phenomenon of autonomous development, generated by internal conditions and external environment, has been apparent for some time. Yet, the implications for the academic study of communism have taken some time in germinating. Only during the last five or ten years has there been a sustained effort to develop methods of comparison between communist states, on the one hand, and other countries at similar levels of economic, social, and political development, on the other. In the past it was normal to assert the unique character of totalitarian communism. Presently, students tend to assume a range of similarities among states and then to account for the differences.

The problem remains, however, to devise a methodological design that will facilitate a systematic examination of both the conventionally accepted similarities and the presumed differences, one that could take into account variations within a single society on individual functional areas over time and could also explicate the reason for change among like-minded societies.

A project was originally developed to serve the dual purposes of providing a teaching vehicle and a research undertaking on the scope and nature of change in the Soviet system. The project was designed to afford a sufficiently elaborate framework for systematic investigation and yet remain simplistic enough to be conducted in a series of advanced seminars.

The basic assumption behind the project was that socialism is fundamentally progressive or change-prone. While propelled by self-adduced historic progressions, policy and conceptual changes have not always followed the Marxist prescription. Progressions have usually resulted from a mixture of ideological aspirations and operational imperatives which at times have generated contradictions or policy errors. Thus, the Soviet system can be characterized as innovative within the context of certain ideological and traditional constraints in its political culture. The project was not designed, however, merely to confirm socialist change or to verify the existence of national communism. It was intended to provide greater insight into the nature of innovation and its relationship to the larger picture of leadership and fraternalism, modernization pressures and traditional constraints, conceptual cross-fertilization, and ideological single-mindedness within the dynamic Soviet system.

The project was also not envisioned as a demonstration of the compatibility of areas studies with comparative politics, nor to justify and rationalize

3

the intellectual rigor of the study of comparative communism. The project intentionally side-stepped debates on these issues and merely presumed the relevance of both the nomothetic and ideographic approaches to the investigation. The present state of the nomothetic art was examined and appropriate analytical tools were employed as guides for posing germane questions and deducing appropriate generalizations. Ideographic techniques were also used by confining the primary data to only original communist documentation and contemporary historical analyses of events, actions and policies that influenced change during each particular period.

It was also assumed that gaps would occur in data collection, especially since only communist sources were to be used. Adequacy could vary from one line of inquiry or component of domestic policy to another and from one society to another. Yet differing degrees of closedness could be compensated for by degrees of openness on the same components in other countries and by the level of fundamental similarity among the societies under investigation. The degree of similarity between Romania, East Germany, and the Soviet Union on social structures, political institutions, and legal practices renders comparison of differences simpler to manage than, for example, between West Germany, France, and Great Britain, despite the abundance of empirical data available on the latter in those fields. Thus, it was assumed that the persisting problem of the data gap could best be minimized by the use of case studies on the vertical plane, plus cross-national comparisons on a horizontal level, which would increase the total number of case studies and introduce appropriate comparisons. Furthermore, only through repeated team efforts could recurring data gaps be offset in such an ambitious undertaking.

In attempting to analyze the present state of the Soviet system and identify indicators of future trends, the investigation was confined to the scope and nature of change in only domestic policy of the Soviet Union and the East European states, minus Albania. Nine lines of inquiry and their respective or subcategories were compared over time and space (see Table 1).

Sub-Lines of Inquiry for Change
in Domestic Policies or Concepts

1.   Economic development and political change: partial revolution and economic growth

      Economic planning
      Price structure
      Macroeconomic levels (taxes, interest rates, and so on)
      Management principles
      Organization
      (USSR, Hungary, CSSR, DDR, Yugoslavia)

2. Postindustrial society: political stability and social change during the second industrial revolution

   Nature of socialism
   Social welfare
   Individual incentives
   Mobilization versus modernization
   Social striation
   (USSR, Hungary, CSSR, Yugoslavia)

3. Man and society: alienation, collectivization, and class struggle

   Class struggle
   Social collectivization
   Alienation
   Family
   Minorities
   (USSR, Poland, CSSR, DDR, Yugoslavia)

4. Communist elites: revolutionaries, bureaucrats, technocrats . . . composition and authority

   Bureaucracy
   Technocrats/specialists
   Party cadre
   Interest groups
   (USSR, Hungary, CSSR, DDR, Yugoslavia)

5. Collective leadership and institutional interest groups: centralism and influence manipulation

   Leading role of party
   Political succession and accretion of power
   Governing process—legislation versus direction
   Election process—representation
   Interest aggregation
   (USSR, Hungary, CSSR, DDR, Yugoslavia)

6. Ideology and political culture: revolutionary and traditional values

   Traditional value
   Revolutionary ideals
   Individual motivation

Education
Youth groups
(USSR, Romania, CSSR, DDR, Yugoslavia)

7.   Culture and socialist morality: personal expression and societal
     responsibility

     Artistic policy
     Censorship control
     Dissent
     Nationalities
     Russification
     Socialist morality
     (USSR, Poland, CSSR, DDR, Yugoslavia)

8.   Law and public discipline: the development of citizens' rights and
     the role of contracts

     Source of law-legislative process
     Judicial system
     Criminal process
     Social correction
     Resolution of conflicts of interest
     (USSR, Romania, CSSR, DDR, Yugoslavia)

9.   Agriculture: property relationships and investment priorities

     Ownership
     Organization
     Management
     Investment
     Social conditions and incentives
     (USSR, Poland, Hungary, DDR, Yugoslavia)

The baseline for comparison for each subsystem was drawn whenever possible
from the theoretical definition or conceptualization of ultimate goals or opti-
mum operations as conceived by prerevolutionary Marxist writers. Changes were
identified at appropriate historical intervals, for example, war communism and
NEP, and so on; from official publications; and, whenever possible, criticisms
and defense of policy changes were analyzed. When original data were not available the reasons for policy changes were adduced from secondary sources. After
1945, the variations that had been identified in Soviet policy on each subcategory were compared with those in European countries that indicated the
sharpest deviation.

Thus, on each subcategory three to four independent variables were examined over time.

Several levels of analyses were then employed. Each line of inquiry was aggregated horizontally over time to determine the extent and nature of change in that specific area and then over space to assess the degree of national variation. All lines were subsumed vertically at each historic period to ascertain those factors that induced change and their impact of the evolution in communist policy. The horizontal aggregations of change and variations on specific subcategories were then subsumed vertically and inputted along with the vertical subsummations about historical factors into an overall analysis of the nature of change in the Soviet system. Highly qualified generalizations were the final output.

For simplicity's sake, a crude matrix can be constructed to illustrate the methodological format:

Historic Periods

	Pre-revolutionary	War Communism	NEP	
Lines of Inquiry Economic Development	degree of change severe moderate negligible			aggregations of degree of change
subsume factors influencing change				generalizations about the level of change: when, why and how much

Any attempt to quantify policy change is highly schematic and can only be intended to demonstrate that certain changes at selected times have been more or less influential than others. In turn, this demonstration can illustrate whether a correlation exists between the relative importance of individual change and total subsystem development. This methodological schema then employed aggregative and correlation analytical techniques only in their crudest forms. Factor analyses of individual changes were confined to general terms rather than details. Only limited use was made of developmental, decision-making, or organizational theories.

Specifically, the final subsuming addressed at least the following questions: When was the time of greatest conformity to and greatest deviation from the original conceptualization of appropriate policy? Was there a discernible movement to the left or right or were there cyclical shifts? Did severe changes in policy result in conceptual shifts? Were modifications or abrogations of various ideological parameters attempted? In which lines of inquiry did the correlation between policy imperatives and ideological guidelines deteriorate or remain constant over time? What were the reasons for change at each interval, for example, national emergency, political rivalry, and so on? What was the impact of each change on general development, for example, greater stability or precedents for continuing oscillations? To what extent have severe oscillations in, for example, education or party structure, and less drastic modifications in cultural and agricultural policies been rationalized? Do inconsistencies persist between lines of inquiry or contradictions within any subcategory that domestic critics insist require further changes? When were changes the result of subsequently acknowledged policy errors and when were they the product of desired improvements? What is the correlation between severity of change in any area or subcategory and the impact on the total system? Is there a perceptible linkage between change in one area and modifications in others? Finally, what is the relationship of change in Soviet domestic policy and the development of the socialist commonwealth? To what extent is the ever-changing Soviet model universally applicable and how wide is the latitude for autonomous national growth? What are the perceived and anticipated levels of Soviet tolerance for deviations in national communism? And to what extent is Soviet policy influenced by the East European experience in creative Marxism? Thus, what are the prospects for accelerating or reinforcing the development of national communism in Eastern Europe?

Several caveats should be emphasized at this juncture. As outlined, the project is clearly exhaustive and beyond the capability of a series of seminars. The problem was reduced to manageable proportions by a process of selectivity. The most intensive effort was concentrated on those subcategories in each line of inquiry and historic periods that appeared to have the most significant bearing on change in domestic policy and for which there was the greatest amount of relevant resource materials. Those subcategories that received less attention, however, were not discarded because of the tentative and somewhat arbitrary selection and their secondary importance to the overall analyses. The weakness of the selection process was that no accurate means existed to ensure that the ruling elites under study followed the same preferences established for the project in their domestic policies, or to determine whether these priorities themselves were subject over time to varying weights. In other words, was it safe to assume that agriculture, industry, or education were allocated a relatively consistent percentage of resources and attention based on requirements for political consolidation and societal mobilization? Could it also be assumed that expansion in some sectors experienced during the evolution to modernization was the product of total national efforts and of reallocations within those sectors, and not the result of deliberate shifts in priorities among sectors? Planning documents, national budgets, and declaratory statements did not provide the outsider sufficient confidence to determine whether percentage point fluctuations in planning goals, for instance, were valid reflections of changes in preferences related to various domestic policies. Studies couched in such stringent qualifications cannot provide the bases for model or theory building about the general nature of societal change.

They can offer, however, limited insight into the evolution of social change within the Soviet system. Generalizations deduced from each line of inquiry were compared and analyzed to determine their accuracy, relevance, completeness, similarity, uniqueness and variation. The conclusions drawn from the study were useful in illuminating critical junctures, persisting weaknesses or sensitivities, and continuing preferences. More important, they underscored the necessity for greater methodological refinement and more intensive vertical development before model and theory building can be undertaken. Indeed, even conceptualizations about the nature of change and comparative communism are hazardous at this stage in the development of the discipline.

STATE OF COMPARATIVE COMMUNISM STUDIES

It is appropriate to survey briefly the state of the art of communist studies in order to ascertain the nature and orientation of the present transition, identify the contending nomothetic approaches, and determine their relevance to on-going research. In the past ten years communist studies have been modified from what was commonly known as "Kremlinology" to a more diversified and sophisticated approach. This alteration in course was due to a variety of reasons. Kremlinology was a product of the cold war and was focused on the urgent necessity to determine what made the Kremlin tick: Who were the most important personalities, what factors influenced policy, how were decisions made, what was the predictability of future policies? During the 1930s and 1940s research in related disciplines of Soviet studies, such as economics, education, or culture, were often prejudiced by ideological biases; they either sought to justify Sovietization or to prove the diabolical nature of the system. During the 1950s it became increasingly important to determine who was "winning" the cold war and to predict Soviet moves. Work in related disciplines was gradually oriented toward these requirements. The combined efforts added to the general body of knowledge but not to profundity. Between 1965 and 1967, for example, a wide majority of the scholars in the field characterized the party leadership as "fumbling and mumbling," following haphazardly a policy of "outward expansion of an inwardly declining society."[1] Yet it had already taken the painful decision to alter defense priorities from minimum to maximum deterrence by attempting to secure strategic parity, and was sufficiently confident and self-assured to participate in the detente process. It had become apparent that new direction and techniques would be necessary to match the degree of change that was occurring in the Soviet system itself.

A second reason for the present transition in Soviet studies was the atmospheric changes that took place roughly between 1968 and 1972. These included the erosion of bipolarity and the acceleration of multipolarity; the attainment of strategic parity and the emergence of the detente process; the reestablishment of Soviet tolerance levels during the Prague crisis and its unexpected military involvement in Egypt; domestic unrest and challenges to institutions and values in the United States; the dramatic change in Soviet foreign policy from dealing with one issue at a time to conducting multiple-issue diplomacy; and the challenges of modernity to both great powers. These developments introduced new dimensions into great power relations and particularly into Soviet foreign policy. They added another phase in the Kremlin's interpretation of the international system and its preferred role in that system. This apparent turning point in the evolution of Kremlin policy underscored the need to probe even deeper into societal composition and interests.

A third general reason for the transition in Soviet studies has been the expansion, refinement, and elaboration of the nomothetic tools necessary to conduct more systematic investigation of social phenomena. At the same time, members of the Soviet system have gradually opened certain components of their respective societies to less restricted investigation. Both developments have intensified and increased the relevance of social scientific studies of the Soviet system.

A final factor has been the rise and persistence of polycentrism or the credibility of national communism. It is no longer adequate to concentrate attention on Kremlin decisions. It is now clear that all communist states have attained a high degree of autonomy, if not unfettered independence, as in the case of China. As such, members of the socialist commonwealth exercise a wide range of constraints on Soviet policy, both external and internal. Indeed, a form of coalition politics, with mutual respect for individual national interests, is now practiced among the Warsaw Pact countries. The motive force behind polycentrism is the persistence of societal differences that necessitate variation on the Soviet model for social progress. The asymmetrics in these differences and variations have been the subject of intense investigation by both Western scholars and ruling communist elites. The level of dissimilarities has proliferated Soviet studies into that of comparative communism and nurtured the growing debate over the utility of comparative politics versus modernization in studying the Soviet system.[2]

One of the first victims of this transition in Soviet studies was the former methodological framework. Totalitarianism had been extended a ubiquity that dominated Western research almost to an extent it was presumed it reflected dominance within the Soviet system. This concept presumed omnipresent political control, unquestioned political discipline and unresisting societal mobilization. Inquiries into the functions, structures, communications, social organization, and public interests were less important than the examination of decision making at the top of the monolithic apparatus.

Most scholars presently agree that the Soviet system is not now totalitarian and probably never was, if one applies Hans Bucheim's definition that totalitarianism is the demand for unlimited control over the world and hence social life which is translated into political action.[3] Benjamin Barber aptly stated the majority position when he concluded, "Totalitarianism is to modern science what reason was to Luther; a conceptual harlot of uncertain parentage, belonging to no one but at the service of all."[4]

It is now widely held that the Soviet form of government is a slightly less onerous "authoritarian" brand, in which a strong one-party system exercises the functions of legitimation of political interests, recruitment of political leadership, and social interest aggregation in policy making.[5] But its inability to exercise all the instruments of totalitarianism denies it absolute monopoly over these functions at all times. The party's authority is subject to continuous competition both politically, over legitimacy and succession, and socially, from modernity and urbanization. To preserve its monopoly of decision making, the party attempts to control the pace of modernization through repression and slowing down social change. The Soviet party has successfully imposed a model for social mobilization that transformed the old order into new institutions. It is now moving through a consolidation stage to a more adaptive phase. Ideology as a legitimizing and motivating factor has lost its luster, indicating not decay, but growing stability. The former exaltation of the leader over the party has been reversed, with the party enjoying greater prestige and influence. Patronage is likely to remain the hallmark of political success, but as the party moves from mobilization it must become more adaptive to the legal-rational challenges to its authority.

As modernity goals have been gradually achieved, despite the repeated damage inflicted by successive revolutions from above, the Soviet government has been transformed into a conservative bureaucracy. The net result is that as the party moves to the adaptive stage its authority is likely to be challenged more, not less, from competing demands for more authentic political participation, wider latitude for national preferences, accelerated economic productivity, and product diversification. These claims may rise increasingly from continuing reservations about legitimacy, alienation, and the influence of pluralizing elites.[6] In facing these challenges, the party must cope with both the increasing complexity of decision making in the modernization process and the difficulty of aggregating interests in a system where all organization has been subordinated to a single apparatus. Instead of a general staff, Soviet leaders now require a coordinating staff that can accurately measure and interpret influence and interests. In a model where there is more potential than actual influence and which has no systematic means for aggregating interest, innovative technocrats and critical intellectuals assume a disproportionate weight of influence over informally organized groups.[7] Despite the "pluralism of elites" in the Soviet Union, there remains almost no reliable empirical means by which to ascertain the impact of their decisions.[8] And only in East Germany, a nation with a radically different social composition from that of the USSR has a "counterelite" of technocrats been identified as an entrenched, influential faction within the party.[9]

Thus, as Richard Lowenthal has sagely observed in the early 1960s, the USSR has at last entered the postrevolutionary stage.[10] The party no longer seeks to legitimize its rule by imposing forcibly transformations on society, as under Stalin, or even reforming its structure in less violent ways, as under Khrushchev. It simply presents itself as the indispensable guardian of continuing growth in Russian power and prosperity. Yet for the first time since the October Revolution, the initiative for political and social change is largely passing especially from the party and state into the hands of an increasingly modern and mature society. The party now finds itself occasionally in a defensive role, both at home and in the bloc. It has rejected both experiments in liberalism and Stalinism, and has reverted to older policy-state methods of harrassment and persecution. These methods have penalized intellectual independence and cultural development; but they have assured steady yet unspectacular technological progress and expansion of power.

Thus, there appears to be insufficient evidence to support the often heard contention that Soviet leadership is fumbling and the party edifice is crumbling. True, the party and state hierarchy are more stable than any other modern state—there have been fewer changes in leading personalities and institutions than in any other European society since 1939.[11] But there are signs of modernization within the society proper that have given rise to the new demands and claims. These changes were not anticipated by the entrenched hierarchy of Marxist authorities, but they have effectively coped with these contingencies. However unimaginative their innovations may appear, it would be unwise to accept the predictions of the Soviet dissidents about the corrosion and collapse of the system. The very exposure to protest resulting from timid modernizing changes is likely to be sufficiently alarming to keep the Kremlin sensitive to the realistic elements in public opinion.

Such cautious generalizations about the future development of Soviet society are, of course, conjectural. Zbigniew Brzezinski has speculated about five feasible courses of change and evolution: oligarchic petrification, involving the maintenance of the dominant role of the party and the retention of the essentially dogmatic character of the ideology; pluralist evolution, prescribing the transformation of the party into a more pluralistic body somewhat like that of Yugoslavia, and the ideological erosion of its dogmatic tradition; technological adaption, involving a transformation of the bureaucratic-dogmatic party into a technologically expert party, emphasizing expertise and efficiency rather than political loyalty and party discipline; militant fundamentalism, nurturing a revivalist effort to rekindle ideological fervor and revolutionary idealism; and political disintegration, resulting in internal paralysis in the ruling elite, the rising self-assertiveness of various key groups within it, splits in the armed forces, restiveness among the youth and intellectuals, and open disaffection among the nationalities.[12]

While there is abundant evidence supporting arguments that the USSR could evolve along each of these courses, Brzezinski concludes that barring an upheaval resulting from internal paralysis—and causing either the dramatic appearance of social democracy, or, more likely, the seizure of power by a revivalist dictator—the probable pattern for the 1980s is that of a marginal shift toward the combination of the pluralist evolution and technological adaptation variants: limited economic and political pluralism, intense emphasis on technological competence, within the context of a still authoritarian government representing a coalition of the upper echelons of the principal interest groups. This could be the beginning of the return to the Western Marxist tradition, but, at most, only a slow and cautious beginning. Thus, the most accurate picture of Soviet leadership for the next decade would be that of conservative, brutally realistic men, with guarded and cautious attitudes toward the masses, attuned to opportunities by which to enhance Soviet prestige and authority abroad. The conservativism and constraint of the past ten years are likely to persist in the foreseeable future.

Thus, the eclipse of the totalitarian model was the consequence of a growing awareness of the process of change that was occurring within the Soviet system. The two basic alternative approaches were pioneered by H. Gordon Skilling applying group organization and interests theory,[13] and John H. Kautsky employing development and modernization principles.[14] While the two approaches would appear to be complementary, Kautsky has recently advanced the argument that there is nothing unique in communism that makes societies within the Soviet system dissimilar from noncommunist societies at similar levels of development. In other words, the overriding demand of all societies at similar levels of development is the imperative of modernization peculiar to that stage. Thus, techniques of comparative politics should be applied vertically and horizontally between levels of modernity not across ideological boundaries.[15]

This rather extreme view discounts the importance of the value that Communists profess and which Western academics cannot singlehandedly disavow. As long as Communists maintain as their highest value faith in the ultimate conversion of the entire world to communism, they will insist upon preserving the present division between Communists and noncommunists, a distinction that cannot be dismissed by noncommunists however hard they persist. But this should not discredit the importance of modernization theory in the study of the Soviet system; indeed it tends to accentuate the asymmetries between the members of the Soviet system and the noncommunist societies they hope to overtake.

The modernization process has been defined in many ways. Cyril Black acknowledges that it is composed of many social aspirations and needs, but holds that the highest single component is societal integration.[16] But David Apter argues that the chief dilemmas in the integrative process are the consequences of industrialization.[17] Modern states have attached the highest priorities to achieving a high degree of economic prosperity, confronting them with the problems associated with industrialization or the transition to the postindustrial state. The closer a society comes to advanced industrialization the greater is the political problem of controlling and integrating the entire process. Thus, the transition to and through industrialization requires an exceptionally well organized political system, able to excise a high degree of regimentation. But postindustrial societies place increasing emphasis on the generation and application of knowledge at an ever accelerating rate, necessitating the decentralization of political controls. The specific dilemma for Communists is how to ensure that the various sectors of society can develop the necessary self-regulating mechanism that will allow the party to assume a noncoercive, mediating and coordinating role, and yet generate a high information environment.

It is at this juncture that Skilling's pluralizing elites and group interests approach assumes relevance. The pioneering work of Peter C. Ludz on party elites indicated the avenue out of the dilemma chosen by East Germany, probably the most industrialized communist state.[18] The specialist elites that had become indispensible to the party during the advance toward industrialization became even further entrenched as the process continued. Over time, their expertise was first sought by the political authorities. Later the specialists began seeking greater participation in the decision-making apparatus in all sectors of society. They have not sought control of the apparatus for political purposes, but merely participation in decision making in order to shape the nature of social changes.[19] How such groups and elites function in the process of change has been the subject of extensive debate among Western scholars (see below).

But change under modernization impulses was not the only period of transition interesting to students of Soviet studies. Communist parties came to power with the explicitly stated task of introducing the most radical societal changes prescribed in modern history. The severity of the undertaking required comprehensive political control which necessarily compartmentalized and restricted access to information. Samuel Huntington has pointed out the importance of conducting empirical studies of change over both the revolutionary and modernizing periods in each sector of society.[20] Paul Godwin argues further that case studies of social changes have now been advanced to the point where a more complicated frame of analysis is both warranted and necessary. The comparative analysis of change should also include the variables in the relationships themselves among the sectors. Investigations should now be conducted to determine whether patterned relationships occur among the changes within and between the sectors, that is, the extent to which changes in relationships themselves influence changes in other sectors or the system as a whole.[21] This recommendation is indeed ambitious, but it indicates the advanced state of the art in comparative communism studies, certainly a methodological progression that is at least abreast of the efforts of the socialists themselves to solve the problems associated with modernization.

THE STATE OF COMMUNISM

The Soviets and their supporters now claim that a socialist commonwealth exists based upon the principles of socialist unity of purpose and separate roads to socialism and the legal corpus embodied in the international proletarianism or, more currently, socialist internationalism. The commonwealth is a concept, not an institution, that represents the transition of communism away from a movement and into a viable political entity, which embraces a calculated measure of national communism within the constraints prescribed by socialist objectives. But in studying communist evolution over time, it is necessary first to depict it in its formative stages.

George Lichtheim has refined Marxism down to its simplest terms.[22] Marxism, like other humanistic philosophies, holds that there is a human essence that reaches fulfillment through participation in historic progressions. These progressions are propelled forward by dialectical antagonisms identified as class struggles. The prime mover in the transitions between the last three phases of development—bourgeois, socialist, and communist—is the proletarian class through its efforts first to develop class consciousness; then to overcome "alienation" by reversing the property ownership relationship; and finally to secure social integration by satisfying all individual needs and thereby removing the sources of class conflict. Marx's views on these basic tenets changed substantially during his life, partly because of his own maturation and partly as a result of social changes in the industrializing countries.

During the 1960s it was fashionable to follow the lead of Western Communists and noncommunists such as Sidney Hook in reexamining the distinctions between the writings of the young and the old Marx. The young Marx was viewed as a more compassionate man dedicated to the humanization of mankind by the removal of oppression, and the older Marx was pictured as an entrenched intriguer, fighting for the universal acceptance of his ideas and domination of the workers' movement. However colored, important differences occurred in his outlook toward the movement between the publication of the *Communist Manifesto* in 1848 and *Capital* in 1867. In 1848 the industrialization of key European countries was still developing and the accompanying bourgeois revolution was incomplete. The proletariat, at that point, was to aid in the urgent task of bringing the bourgeois to power, to act as the pace setters for bourgeois radicalism. By the 1860s this task had been completed and the bourgeois and capitalism were in full authority. Class distinctions had sharpened and the proletariat was more mature, posing as the main antagonist to a fully developed bourgeois society. Thus, two separate rules for the proletariat were envisioned depending upon the level of development in the target society. Marx, then, was a dialectician concerned with the unique internal structure of a social organism and the forces of opposition that existed within the organism, a distinction later overlooked by Engels, who was a mechanistic materialist. Engels was a determinist and was more concerned with technological positivism or the manner in which technology propelled society along a unilinear path. Marx, on the other hand, saw history as a multilinear process in which each society moved in accordance with the opposites of which it was composed.[23] The emergence of different levels of analysis by Marx himself and Engels' own variations led inevitably to conflicting interpretations by his followers seeking to ensure their own political interests.

A key issue in Lenin's struggle for power within the Russian Social Democratic Party was the level of societal development in Russia and the class awareness of the proletariat. Faced with Marx's two models, even the most radical elements concluded that the acceleration of the bourgeois revolution was the only feasible alternative for backward Russia. After April and especially August 1917, however, Lenin shifted to the later model, representing his coup d'etat as a "dictatorship of the proletariat." These decisions required ingenious innovations on both Marx's models. The bourgeois revolution was still embryonic and capitalism was not fully developed. As a result the working class remained small and too weak to survive in a democratic movement. Thus, without the germinating influence of ripening capitalism, the issue of class consciousness became increasingly important in the revolutionary movement.

Socialist theory, to that point, has been relatively consistent on the issue of class consciousness. According to early Marxists, the purpose of socialist theory was not to impose its own aims upon the movement, but to illuminate and clarify the movement's own goals—the process of self-awareness. It was not to tell the workers what the theorists prescribed, but what the workers themselves sought. It was this process of self-awareness that was to afford the proletariat the advantage of the vanguard position among masses, defining the goals for the entire society. But the Russian working class and Social Democratic Party were too badly split between trade-union reformists and revolutionaries to have any hopes of projecting class consciousness on a viable nation-wide basis.

In response, Lenin first abandoned the fiction of democracy and spontaneity as the grounds for legitimizing political rule and then formulated the concept of elitist leadership. He sought an intellectual leadership that could compensate for the lack of wide-scale self-awareness by imposing the guidelines for the proletarian dictatorship from above. To preserve discipline within the elite, he insisted that its members be recruited largely from proletarian ranks, rather than, as the Mensheviks argued, from the bourgeois intelligentsia. The self-regulating rigidity of this concept soon led to contradictions and frustrations. Under Lenin, emphasis shifted among the elite from the class to the party, which was the instrument of the proletarian dictatorship. When the exigencies for preserving the revolution required consolidation of political power, people like Rosa Luxemburg feared it signaled the imposition of party authority over not just the opposition, but over the working class as well. To compensate for the abrogation of democracy and spontaneity, and to offset the onerous aspects of elitist rule, Lenin devised two key respirators: ideology and universal materialism. Ideology, based on faith in the future and rising expectations, was to be the legitimizing device for minority rule, the bridge between the tiny party and the toiling masses. It was to be both a source of inspiration and guidance, and a means for confirming the efficacy of party decisions and the scientific authenticity of socialism. Universal materialism was to provide the economic base to assuage individual needs and complaints and later to serve as groundwork for modernization. To achieve these ends, however, Lenin reverted to bourgeois principles and values, while "consolidating socialism in one country."[24]

Stalin produced little theoretical ingenuity and his pragmatic intensification of Lenin's norms resulted in aberrations of gargantuan scale. Yet the Stalinist contributions to the practice of communism under the Soviet model are likely to have a lasting effect. Indeed, it was the revolt against Stalinism, first by the Yugoslavs and then by other societies, that produced the main post-Lenin modifications of theoretical Marxism. The revolt was a consequence of Stalin's singular shift of party attention from social justice and societal needs to the accretion and preservation of physical power based upon acceptance of mandatory ideological norms. The attainment of power for its own sake became the highest permitted value.

The last two decades of communist development have witnessed the emergence of two main trends: a resurrection of interest in elevating the values of social justice, and the practical problems of adopting the Soviet development model to the unique features of other nations. The former demands resurfaced pragmatic questions about the future course of socialism: the appropriate relationship of the workers to the leadership; the responsiveness of bureaucracies to societal needs; the re-allocation of power; the redefinition of socialist morality and its utility as a motive force; preferred resource allocations for desired growth rates; the replacement of class conflict with criteria for income distribution; problems of incentives, productivity, alienation and engagement; and the correlation between individual freedom and societal progress. During two decades, nearly every ruling communist party challenged the conventional Soviet interpretation of these issues, punctuating graphically the new relevance of issues to values in socialist thinking. It is now appropriate to summarize briefly the problems encountered as changes occurred on such issues and values.

MULTIPLIER EFFECTS OF CRISES
ON THE PROBLEM OF CHANGE

Economic Reforms

One of the first crises to develop in the post-Stalin era occurred in the economic sector. By the late 1950s and early 1960s an unconcealable decline had been registered in economic growth rates, particularly in Eastern Europe. The immediate effect was that the capital output ratio rose sharply, that is, larger increments of capital investments were required to produce the planned quantity of production. The Soviet command economy had responded to the centralized requirements for accelerated quantitative output, but it had failed to meet the market demand for shifting to qualitative criteria and huge inventories of unsold products had accumulated. Industrial development under the Soviet model had resulted in a specific structural orientation strongly favoring extensive development within the total economic system. And the central question then facing Soviet planners was whether structural changes could be made to rectify production deficiencies without drastically overhauling the system. More puzzling, could structural development be shifted to the point that both the structure and the system could return to a mutually reinforcing balance? Could the shift from extensive to intensive development, or from heavy to light industry, be achieved efficiently and without losses that could destabilize the existing system? Finally, could the appropriate reforms be accomplished without political decentralization and the introduction of organized pressure groups? (It should be noted that reforms of the scale necessary could only be directed from the top, or induced laterally from supply and demand pressures.)

On the question, "What is to be done?" parties, bureaucracies and economists split into two rival factions. The conservatives advocated retaining party and state institutions intact and preserving the concept of the plan. They acknowledged, however, the necessity for nationalizing the use of economic levers and criteria for efficiency. They argued for adoption of realistic prices without altering the method for their derivation. They sought the introduction of incentives for efficiency, such as capital charges, rents, interests, and so on. Production criteria were to be altered from stressing gross output to socially useful products, commodities for which there was a demand. These minimal reforms were to be implemented by improving the supply of sophisticated information through cybernetics and other technology-intensive means. Finally, they argued that the minimal reforms would generate decontrol, since they required that a larger number of decisions would have to be made locally.

The progressive faction advocated adoption of a guided market economy which would include those bureaucratic changes necessary to reduce the degree of state interference or the introduction of noneconomic factors into production. This would require altering economic structures as well and should be accompanied by accelerating decontrol proportionally to the rise in the complexity of the economy. Several revisions of the plan were required, whereby it would provide only nonbinding guidelines primarily for the sake of coordination. The prime indicator of success was to be profitability. The use of economic levers was to be increased and banking transactions were to be conducted on a strictly commercial rather than political basis. Finally, a more open pricing system would have to be introduced to ensure efficiency, profitability and technological intensification.

Discussions of implementing the reforms centered on these key problems. Under the command economy, pricing is designed to clear markets and produce revenues.[25] This is difficult to do without supply and demand pressures that can determine appropriate prices. The improvised Soviet technique is to calculate prices based on average cost of fuel, labor, capital, and so on. But the complexity of determining real costs of all components results in months and years of delay. Consequently, final prices have to incorporate estimated increases. Furthermore, because of the extensive use of barter rather than trade, no lateral pressures can influence estimated prices. When contemplating the reforms, the problem is compounded. How can a badly structured economy, using obsolete machinery and producing out-dated goods accurately forecast prices and profits for reformed production and thereby determine the economic feasibility of introducing the necessary changes.

Yugoslavia and Hungary introduced a three-tiered pricing schema, whereby prices would be fixed on raw materials and essential producer goods, allowed to float and be determined by market pressures between fixed limits on semi-finished and finished products, and freed of all restrictions on most consumer goods. It was expected that by partially opening pricing to market influences, under the concept known as guided market, the profit incentive would induce greater efficiency and increase labor productivity. Both would foster greater investment in advanced technology and would gradually intensify industry. (Most socialist economists express faith that technology will be the panacea for increased labor productivity. This is because of the continuing backwardness of the agricultural sector and its failure to provide new labor reserves and the rapid growth of the services sectors, which combined threaten long-term industrial labor shortages.) In both experiments it was expected that pricing reforms would result in structural change without impairing system stability. But the entire Hungarian economic reform program was terminated as counter-productive and the Yugoslav proposal was aided by simultaneous cuts in the unprofitable extensive-oriented plants and the heavy infusion of foreign exchange that permitted the purchase of technology abroad.

Equally fundamental in socialist thinking is the problem of reordering the concept and content of centralized planning. Conventionally the plan is a detailed specification of all aspects of the social product. It is a legally binding document that prescribes the contributions or outputs of all social organizations. The central plan is subdivided into component parts, reaching down to the smallest units. The requirements of the plan are determined by submitting initial inquiries to all components, attempting to determine actual and future capabilities. Since efficiency and rewards are based on meeting the plan's provisions, responses from the components at all levels are inaccurate; each must hedge against contingencies. Thus, central authorities have no precise data on the actual capabilities of the economy. Contributing to this inaccuracy is the heavy emphasis placed during the mobilization phase on the expansion of production facilities with little concern paid to marketability or the final disposition of the products ("The USSR produces the heaviest teapots in the world"). Finally, the plan has built in preferences and priorities favoring heavy industry and defense industries that tend to perpetuate the skewed structure of the economy.

Reforms would require a genuine decontrol that would assure managers an active role in planning. This can only be achieved by changing the indicators for success to those that would stimulate the quality of production and the saleability of end products. Managers should no longer be jeopardized by revealing true potentialities of their facilities and should be encouraged to improve efficiency through the introduction of some form of profitability as the main indicator of success. But the formula for profitability must include a wide range of contributing factors, such as prices, wage policy, investment funds, social benefits, and government fiscal and monetary policies and practices.

In the Soviet system a distinction has developed between government monetary policy and practice. Two separate systems of money circulation exist: one budgetary, including tax revenues and budgetary outlays, and the other consumer, consisting of wages and consumer outlays. In a depressed socialist market, the consumer bought what was offered. As wages increased ahead of improvement in product quality and diversification, the consumer could either spend or save. The sharp rise in inventories indicated that consumers were saving in increasing amounts. Savings are undesirable because they represent unbought goods and thereby planning efficiency and because they demonstrate the gap between the two systems of money circulation. The vast bulk of government revenues come from turnover taxes included in the price of all commodities. Unbought goods therefore also denied the government planned income, dislocated monetary and fiscal policies and forced contingency remedies. (During 1970 in Poland the value of unsold inventories increased at twice the rate of retail sales and finally rose to 500 billion zlotys or half the total GNP!)

Reform would require improvisations that could bring the two circuits back into closer symmetry where the consumer system could reinforce the budgetary one. Savings have to be brought into the market and thereby be made available for reinvestment. Credits and incentives for improved quality plus greater sensitivities to market demands are imperative if the dislocations are to be remedied.

The final crucial factor is the dilemma over extensive versus intensive development. Up to the late 1950s strict centralized planning and rigid controls had been adequate for restoring war-ravaged economies. But by then readily available resources of labor and raw materials were consumed. Political priorities required increased emphasis on industrialization and therefore greater investment for expansion of production along existing preferences. This resulted in the extension of existing facilities or the construction of new ones in the same industries, without regard to technological improvements or overall efficiency. As stocks of unsold products gradually increased, demands for intensive investments, rather than extensive investment, became urgent. Intensive investment funds were needed for plant modernization, advance technology, improved labor skills, and more effective management. But funds were not readily available because of rising inventories. The danger was first recognized by the most industrialized East European countries, East Germany and Czechoslovakia. (In 1963, the Czechoslovakian economic growth rate declined to zero.)

In devising reforms, the main problem is how to find additional funds. Should they be attracted from savings, diverted from other sectors, or recouped by closing inefficient enterprises. Movement in any direction will require a reassesment of existing priorities and will necessitate political decisions. Hedging in all directions will perpetuate the dilemma and result in falling technologically further behind the West without solving the basic issues.

Partial reforms were introduced or tested, but usually only piecemeal and in single areas of economic policy. In 1966 the USSR cautiously introduced a modified form of the profitability indicator in planning. But over time the impact was steadily reduced by constant governmental intervention at all levels of planning and production. As early as 1963 East Germany institutionalized many of the reformist arguments raised by Soviet academician Evsei Liberman and others. There was no question of introducing market influences or of abolishing central planning but merely of perfecting the system. The plan expressed basic objectives and several parameters for final output. Initiative and achievement were left to the individual enterprise and a newly established regional coordinating administration (VVB). The stimulant for efficiency was to be exercised through the use of economic levers and material incentives. Price reforms did not eliminate administrative pricing, they merely introduced more realistic figures. Within these controls, general efficiency was to be perfected by the use of improved information flow and the self-regulating concepts, derived general system theory, and cybernetics, as expounded by Professors George Klaus and Uwe Heuer.

In 1968 Hungary introduced its New Economic Mechanism (NEM) in two stages. It was not conceived as a new conceptual framework for reform, but merely a refinement of mechanisms of central steerage that would stimulate modernization. Macroeconomic decisions were to remain centralized and prescribed in the plan. Micro-decisions were to become the prerogatives of local management, and profit was to become the main indicator of success. Several braking features, called indirect regulators, were to be retained by central authorities that could ensure plan fulfillment by directing how local funds were to be allocated, that is, profit-sharing, reserves, social benefits, wages, and so on.

Thus, virtually all aspects of plant activities from raw material purchases to the size of the labor force could be directly influenced by the indirect regulators. To consolidate the industrial base, enterprises were merged into conglomerates that became industry-wide monopolies, creating the highest degree of industrial concentration in Eastern Europe. A three-tiered price structure was introduced, with fixed prices only on raw materials, and minimum and maximum levels were established for other industrial products.

The pressure for modernization had become acute in Hungary because 40 percent of its national income comes from foreign trade. Quality improvements had become imperative to compete successfully, even in Eastern Europe where it conducted 70 percent of its trade at an annual deficit in 1967 of 2.8 billion florints. State subsidies for unprofitable plants had reached 35 billion florints by 1968.

But the NEM produced less than satisfactory results. The forced mergers did not eliminate unproductive plants, they merely allowed them to ride piggyback on the profitable ones. Accordingly, state subsidies increased by 1971 to 53 billion to support inefficiency. The monopolies tried to compensate for the legacy of unprofitable operations by exploiting the new price structure. They demanded and gained the maximum allowable prices for their products and the lowest possible for their inputs. This created sharp inflationary pressures that were ultimately passed on to the consumer. To increase profitability, managers held wages down by curtailing bonuses and, with the available supply of relatively cheap labor, there was little incentive to invest heavily in technology-intensive improvements. But the severe inflation created labor instability with workers constantly seeking higher paying jobs. (In 1969-70 the labor turnover equalled 80 percent of the entire industrial work force.) The result was a sharp decline in skill levels and in the quality of end products. Consequently, vital trade continued to drop; the deficit reached 4.4 billion by 1971, nearly double that in 1968, and represented 15 percent of the total exports. In a rescue effort, investment went out of control. In 1971 106 billion florints were invested, and by year's end 80 percent remained tied up in unfinished projects.

By 1973 the end result was only a slight increase in national income over 1968, drastic economic dislocations, repeated state intervention, and growing alarm among Hungary's trading partners, particularly the USSR. After Brezhnev's visit to Budapest in November 1972 retrenchment measures were announced. Prices were adjusted and the margins reduced, wages in the lower brackets were raised, trade with the West was curtailed, investments were frozen at 1971 level, additional credits were banned, heavy income taxes were imposed on higher salaries, and an increased number of centralized controls were reintroduced. But these measures were unable to offset further a decline in trade and increases in inflation. The dismissal of NEM supporters from the Hungarian Cabinet in March 1974 signaled the demise of the Hungarian experiment in economic reforms.

Societal Change—Aspirations and Constraints

The task of measuring or depicting the nature of social change presently taking place in the Soviet system is complicated by the variety of characterizations of the previous and existing societies. For example, Allen Kassof has labeled Soviet society an "administered society," which he defines as "one in which an entrenched and extraordinarily powerful ruling group lays claim to ultimate and exclusive scientific knowledge of social and historical laws and is impelled by a belief not only in the practical desirability, but the moral necessity of planning, direction and coordination from above in the name of human welfare and progress."[26] Convinced that there should be complete order and predictability in human affairs, the elite is not only interested with the commanding heights, but also in the detailed regulation of the entire range of social life. The elite rejects the possibility of uncoordinated social integration and development. The only social good is one that is administered as prescribed by the overall social plan. Thus, experts are servants rather than independent masters or practitioners of reform and development. Their potential for independent influence is decisively cut short by the elite's insistence that all decision making is political and therefore beyond the purview of any other group.

A less strident model has been presented by T. H. Rigby in his notion of "organizational societies."[27] In the command society he depicts, one party (the ruling elite) is active and the other party (the governed) is passive in determining policy and societal development. This requires a high degree of obedience to centralized direction. As a result Stalin's career was characterized by two main features: his attempts to control the state apparatus and his efforts to expand the functions of the apparatus into all aspects of life.

Such paradigms differ fundamentally with those offered by such proponents of groups and pluralizing elites as Milovan Djilas in his *New Class* and Peter

Ludz in his *A Party Elite in Transformation*. Djilas perceived the emergence of a new group of managers in Yugoslavia with traditional middle class aspirations and wielding political power within the state apparatus that was potentially beyond the party's control. Ludz identified with precision a group of technicians and specialists within the East German party whose authority was based on their expertise which had become indispensable to the traditionally trained party cadre.

Donald Treadgold and Richard Pipes have pointed out that Russia has a long record of established groups with articulated interests that were products of the nature of czarist society that have not basically changed.[28] Since there were and still are no guaranteed civil rights, the individual had no security under the law. Justice was predicated upon power and was arbitrarily administered. Personal security therefore was sought through economic materialism and political favors. The government ruled by privilege and required service and obedience in return for favors. Accordingly, individuals organized into groups and classes to compete for favors and privileges or to defend those already granted. The groups seldom challenged the source of privilege and security, the czar and church. Competition was lateral or with the next higher echelon; it was never completely vertical. These attributes appear to be as applicable to contemporary Soviet society as to czarist society.

Thus, there appears to be little doubt that interest groups exist in some form in the Soviet system. The task is to identify them correctly, determine their structure, scope, and composition, and to ascertain their methods of interest formulation and articulation.

Gordon Skilling launched this undertaking when he convincingly argued that pluralism of elites had taken place in Soviet society that had created an imperfect monism in which the party remained more equal than other groups, who, however, were not denied influence.[29] These are not interest groups in the Western sense with shared characteristics, but rather they are identifiable through common attitudes and claims. These associations are not formal organizations but loose informal clusterings that articulate distinctive interests. Skilling calls them "demand groups." The strength of their influence depends upon their proximity to strategic positions in the state and party apparatus. For example, the military or secret police would have more influence than schools and cultural organizations. (This formulation does not take into account ethnic dissidence.)

Franklyn Griffiths refined this paradigm by referring back to Bentley's original notion that the purpose of group formulation is merely to articulate interests, not make demands.[30] The vehicles for articulation are often informal: at work, private correspondence, letters to newspaper editors, etc. Thus, they are not groups as such, but merely instruments for the articulation of social tendencies. These tendencies usually remain general and vague and therefore act as signals rather than claims or demands. The claimant knows that direct contact made for specific requests are more likely to be honored, but most often uses signals as the preferred means to influence change. The party recognizes this function as an important public safety valve and informally encourages its implementation. In line with Pipes' argument, this type of organization allows the state to exercise a high degree of control over the claims raised and in granting only those favors it regards appropriate.

Philip Stewart has pointed out that there are significant differences between actual and potential influence of these groups or articulated tendencies because of the local party secretary at all levels retains a monopoly on decision making.[31] While the party maintains ultimate control of policy, it has become the arbiter of influence, an interest aggregating and meditating function. As modernization has progressed, decision making has become more complex and local leaders have been compelled increasingly to consult with experts or their counterparts to avoid disastrous decisions. Such multiplex facets of contemporary decision making impose group-like constraints on the party. The power of recommendation reinforced by cross-group communication and fertilization is the key to the relationship between the group and the central authority.

The reasons for group formation also vary. Gordon Skilling maintains that groups developed for two main reasons: the lack of opportunity for the citizenry to participate in political expression and decision making, and the state's intentional encouragement of group formation as a means of personal identification and engagement with the state, and of ultimate physical control. Chalmers Johnson holds that change stems largely from frustration. Mobilization from above to achieve utopia has been successful in some sectors at the expense of others. Such uneven development engenders frustration and alienation. When the mobilization process is successful and fully mature, it produces a crisis that requires either fundamental reform or internal unrest.

Controls necessary at the mobilization stage become dysfunctional in the modernization phase and obvious remedies, such as the introduction of a market economy, threaten leaders and institutions necessary to apply reforms compounding the revitalizing process with redundancy.

Jeremy Azrael challenges the modernization thesis as a replacement for totalitarianism and mobilization.[32] He maintains that in the post-Stalinist period there have actually been increased attempts to mobilize in the USSR, China, and Yugoslavia, but by different means. Consequently, he argues, it is the idea of elites that is more important than group dynamics in societal transformations. T. H. Rigby has added his criticism of the group dynamics thesis.[33] He does not attack the concept of group interests but the notion that all political action can and must ultimately be reduced to group interests. He also questioned the arbitrary definition of groups. In formulating a valid hypothesis about group dynamics, Rigby argues that the following questions must be asked:

1. What is the common interest or property that defines the group as a distinct subsystem?

2. What are the pertinent contradictions with interests or properties of other groups?

3. What is the mechanism for forming and articulating group opinion?

4. What is the nature of the bond between the group and the political leadership; and to what extent is the political elite itself a distinctive group?

Rigby points out that under Stalin particular attention was paid to dissociate his lieutenants from any group or power base. He allocated assignments of jurisdictions to personal rivals and frequently changed appointments or responsibilities. As a result, group characteristics remained ambigious and the bonds between groups and the political elite, or the instruments of rule, were subject to constant change. In the period 1953-59, however, the political environment began to stabilize because of the decline in the use of terror, improved communications between the rulers and the ruled, and the growing rivalry over the instruments of power. Competition for power was most noticeable between the party and the police during March-June 1953, the party and the government during 1954-57, and between the party and the army during 1957-59.

Actions and alignments during these periods seemed to depend not on the respective leader's past career patterns as much as on current responsibilities and jurisdictions. Furthermore, competing groups were not always identical with particular instruments of rule. Some divided along department or regional lines, that is, the June 1957 decentralization crisis produced clear conflicts of interests between central and regional officials. Finally, other factors than group interests figured prominently in actions during this period, such as the personality of Khrushchev. Thus, the most reliable grouping during this period (which can also be readily identified in the Brezhnev era) seems to be the personal following or patronage of given members of the elite. This patronage does not seem to be confined to specific institutional structures or instruments of rule. Patronage bonds apparently stem from close relationships at some time in the past and are not unlike the "old boy" system prevalent in the British bureaucracy.

But even if one argues that political elites based on patronage are the most plausible groups in the Soviet system, Rigby observes that distinct reservations persist about their organization and operation. For example, it is reasonably clear what the leader can do for the client, but what can the client do for the patron? Is the bond of loyality or fidelity reminiscent of feudal times compatible with the mobility required for modernization? Is the tenacity and longevity of the bonds based solely on presumed personal effectiveness of both partners and can this be realistically assumed to hold over time? Do such bonds exist at all levels, and with what intensity? What is the nature of patronage in the informal groupings so common in the Soviet system? Must actions be analyzed in terms only of patronage, or are local rivalries and conflicts equally important?

Does this competition, Rigby asks, demonstrate autonomy and latitude for action? Do patronage groupings have not only identifiable interests and goals, but the capabilities to achieve them at other groupings' expense? And can this capability be exercised independently from the patronage system? Finally, is patronage a method of subordination and control that perpetuates insecurity and systemic instability, or a viable means for aggregating group interests?

Rigby's questions about the viability of ruling elites indicate the difficulty in verifying the organization and operation of groups in the Soviet system. While it may be widely accepted that various types of groups exist, there is not reliable evidence about how they function and the nature of their impact or degree of influence in the decision-making process.

The Role of Class Structures in a Centralized Society

Marxists of all stripes attach less importance to group development and elite pluralization than do Western sociologists. Only in the past several years have scholars in the Soviet system demonstrated interest in this area.[34] The main reason for this apparent indifference or apathy about group dynamics is that the class struggle is regarded by Marxists as the key to social progression. Their attention is riveted to the nature of class antagonisms. By definition, advancement toward ideological goals is measured by the decline in class structure and societal conflicts. The revolutionary process destroyed the class structure of czarist society, but the policies of both Lenin and Stalin created new social divisions that are properly regarded as striations within the persisting class alignments. Striations were the consequences of the demands for mobilization. But as the Soviet system moves toward modernization, it has become increasingly aware of the problem of assimilating Western nomothetic principles of group dynamics and of preserving the axioms of class struggle.

Talcott Parsons defines social striations as "The differential ranking of the individuals who compose a given social system and their treatment as superior and inferior relative to one another in certain socially important aspects."[35] David Lane defines the same term as, "the division of society into a heirarchy of strata, each having an unequal share of society's power, wealth, property or income and each enjoying an unequal evaluation in terms of prestige, honor or social esteem."[36] In actuality class striations within the Soviet system do not follow horizontal lines, but rather vertical delineations determined by functional not goal orientations.

Marx took a more simplistic view of class structure than the refinement implied in the striation approach.[37] Society in the industrialized states of the late nineteenth century was for the first time in history reduced to only two classes: exploiters and the exploited toiling masses. All class identifications were related to the means of production. Even intellectuals could be categorized by the degree of their associations with either extreme in a polarized society. Each new ruling class in history has grown from its opposition to the oppression of the previous ruling classes. The dialectic would spawn the rise of socialists as the new ruling class which, because of its enlightenment and understanding of the correlation between human dignity and justice and the means of production, would relieve society of its tensions. Marx insisted that the reduction in class tensions could best be achieved by the process of liberation from below, a function and manifestation of class awareness. Class awareness was the instrument for the destruction of all societal barriers and the institutionalization of individual equality. While Marx saw egalitarianism as the cardinal property of a classless society, he was keenly concerned about the premature introduction of such demands. He regarded calls for equality before class barriers were eliminated as manifestations of trade unionist reformism that retarded or impeded the vital revolutionary transformations necessary to create a classless society.

After the revolution, Lenin was faced with the difficult task of devising the pragmatic guidelines for achieving a seamless society and determining when progress was being made in its attainment. Egalitarianism became a crucial issue for the various factions within the party for both ideological and economic reasons. Lenin insisted that until the revolution was consolidated, the practice of unequal privileges must be maintained. During the consolidation phase, it would be necessary to pay foreign and bourgeois experts excessive wages for their skills because of the technological backwardness of Russia. For Lenin, the lack of culture among the peasantry was the main reason for the persisting need for inequality. Therefore his solution was to civilize the peasants and upgrade their consciousness and expertise to that of the specialists. This rationale was the justification for his plan for electrification and education of the countryside.

Stalin recognized that after the comparative liberalism of the New Economic Program in the mid-1920s the imperatives necessary to restart social mobilization would meet better resistance. Forced industrialization and collectivization would trigger violence and would require counterviolence to succeed. Stalin maintained that both political coercion and material incentives were essential to ensure mobilization and progress toward the erosion of class barriers. This imposition of the class struggle from above was deemed vital for the consolidation of the dictatorship of the proletariat and was to be maintained for the duration of the consolidation phase. It was a deliberate policy of personal distinctions and privileges, an intentional attempt to generate striations.

In 1929 Stalin abolished all ceilings on salaries to top party members. In 1931 sweeping wage differentials were introduced in industry. By 1934 the final victory of socialism was proclaimed by the elimination of all capitalism bourgeois experts and the remnants of capitalism from all phases of society. And by 1936, the complete victory of socialism was evidenced by the eradication of all class antagonisms. Only the three classes of the toiling masses remained—the workers, peasants, and intellectuals. At the same time, material incentives reached the highest differentiation.

Fundamentalist Marxists condemned the policy of incentives as the source of antagonism among previous societies that would provide a corrupting influence among socialists. Defenders of the practice argued that incentives were vital to maximize the mobilization process, but that no danger of moral corruption existed because money could be accumulated but no longer used for the exploitation of other members of the society.

Khrushchev told the 21st Soviet Party Congress that despite the excesses of Stalin the proletarian dictatorship was consolidated and socialism was now irreversible. The new task was to construct the economic base for the development of communism. He argued that communism could be achieved only if the socialists surpassed the level of production in the developed capitalist countries and raised labor productivity to a level above that of the West. In this speech he called for "catching and surpassing the United States in the production of meat, milk and eggs." He warned, however, that to pass prematurely to the stage of distribution according to one's needs when the economic conditions for this have not yet been created would impair the development of communism. "Egalitarian Communism" would only eat up accumulated funds and make impossible the further expansion of production. Rather than egalitarian communism that would eliminate incentives and class striations, he advocated achieving the intermediate target of "goulash Communism."

During the post-Stalinist decade, incentives leading to social striations began to expand. They were no longer mainly material benefits and physical security. With side benefits, ratio in income distribution between the highest and lowest was probably 300:1. Yet the categories of wage differential were reduced in 1958 from 12 to seven. But excessive wages no longer increased personal motivation because of the limited purchasing capability in a depressed consumer market. Greater emphasis was gradually placed on the attainment of influence. The attributes of influence most frequently sought were higher education, social mobility as an avenue to prestige, and party membership. Khrushchev repeatedly used sweeping reforms as additional means of personal motivation.

Brezhnev, on the other hand, has stressed stability rather than reform. Both contemporary Soviet authorities and citizens agree that remarkable progress has been made in social development since World War II, their most frequent point of reference. Moreover, the family unit remains strong and social values are widely shared. Differences exist about tactics but less so about broad goals. Increasingly conspicuous consumption confirms that material differentiation persists. The emphasis placed on personal achievement by both the state and individual, however, tends to ensure the continuing efficacy of the incentive system in providing social mobility and personal performance. Thus, the degree of shared values and goals, coupled with the outlets of mobility, provide a level of stability, even rigidity, to the present striations that the political elite is anxious to perpetuate.

The correlation between material incentives and class striations within the Soviet system can also be illustrated by comparisons with East European cases. One of the sharpest contrasts with the USSR has occurred in Czechoslovakia. Differences in the wage spread generally decreased during the 1950s and the socialization of industry; they increased during the severe slumps of the 1960s, and again decreased in the post-Dubcek era. Average wages in 1971 continued to reflect partiality for those engaged in direct production. Coal miners earned 2,827 kronas per month, project planners 2,699, teachers 1,821, retail trade workers 1,694. Differences also occurred between economic sectors. The wage earning ratio of engineers/technicians to blue collar workers varied from 142:100 in 1967, to 131:100 in 1971, largely because of the return to preferential wage differentials for direct production. The earnings ratio between white collar and blue collar workers also reflects this trend. In 1965 it was 86:100, in 1967 90:100, and in 1970 85:100. The persisting strength of blue collar workers through the periods of slump, reform, and restitution is unique in the experience of East Europe and among industrialized nations. (Modernization in other nations has been achieved by shifting the bulk of the labor force from the blue to the white collar sectors through the use of increased incentives.)

The USSR's continued preferential treatment for the blue collar sector partially explains its nagging economic stagnation and the limited worker support for the Dubcek Action Plan—the reforms would have cut labor incentives and eliminated unprofitable enterprises. There were several reasons for this preference; some were structural factors based on an industrialized economy and others were unique to Czechoslovakia. There was no need for the Communists to construct a heavy industry which already existed and the continued availability of most consumer goods precluded serious dislocations. More than in other East European countries, economic recovery and expansion required increases in labor productivity rather than structural changes. A more fundamental reason for the emphasis on direct production, however, was the idealism attached to physical labor. Czechoslovak sociologists acknowledged that the peculiar wage differentials create class striations, but argue that this has provided a proletarian base. Pavel Machonin holds that the composition of strata is based on five factors: the complexity of work, participation in management, class position (worker or intellectual), cultural level of leisure, and level of education.[38] By these criteria, Czechoslovakia is probably the most socialist and most egalitarian society in the Soviet system. Yet the level of industrialization produced by this reduction in social stratification is unacceptable to those socialists who argue that a classless society cannot be envisioned without an economic base comparable to that of the capitalist antagonists. Czechoslovakia has become highly integrated but remains economically stagnant.

Yugoslavia provides another interesting comparison. The conventional three classes exist in Yugoslavia, but striations are complicated by antagonism among the eight major ethnic groups and among the three main churches, ideological differences over how to advance socialism, and the continuing strength of family and clan ties that restricts mobility and trans-strata identification. Furthermore, because of the private ownership of land, many peasants live on their farms and work in nearby factories, blurring the distinctions between sectors of the labor force. Finally, because of the early break with Stalinism and favorable economic developments, elites became entrenched in the bureaucracies, industries, and party.

In October 1971 a nation-wide conference was convened of Yugoslav sociologists to examine the question of "why the greatest social power and wealth are in the hands of the upper strata and the least are in the hands of workers and peasants."39 The conference concluded that the reasons for the creation of such rigid striations were as follows:

1. overemphasis on economic determinism, which condemned the market as the responsible factor for persisting social ills;
2. this in turn stifled initiative and insured the reapplication of tried but worn-out solutions for continuing problems;
3. social immobility contributed to the lack of creativity and was due to educational deficiencies, not the inability physically to move (Yugoslavia has over one million workers employed abroad); and
4. the lack of new blood has engendered insecurity among members of the top echelons who seek perpetuation of the status quo through increased systemic rigidity.

In reaching these conclusions, the conference acknowledged that the main dilemma before Yugoslavia was how to make material rewards and social prestige both personally desirable and ideologically acceptable. Contending schools of thought registered widely differing viewpoints. Professor Milan Kangraga defended the rightists' position by arguing that the expanding middle class was becoming indispensable for national economic development. This new authority was due to persisting bourgeois elements within the society, the growth of parliamentarianism, and the political nature of self-management. Consequently, the party is now relegated to the role of merely arbitrating between contending groups with declining powers to intervene for the sake of societal welfare. He insisted that corrective measures were indispensable to preclude the onset of complete paralysis and to restore party authority.

The left was represented by Professor Mihailo Márkovic. He argued that the chief problem in the postcapitalist society (he dropped the term socialist) was the acquisition and manipulation of power. In the present state of development, the techno-burocratic stratum exercises control over the means of production. Its usurpation of the surplus value of labor (profit) in the form of privileges is the reason for this stratum's political power and influence in societal orientation. The lack of conflict between the technocrats and politicos is due to a mutual appreciation of the indispensability of each other's roles. With this type of special arrangement, politicians can still act arbitrarily and deci-sions are often based on balance of power principles rather than rationale. Self-management has now been relegated to the bureaucracy and technicians whose main task is to maintain law, order, and conformity. Thus, according to Mar-kovic, the system now "permits blackmail, ultimatums, mistreatment of the majority by the minority, and intolerable slowness in the resolution of vital issues."

These have become the standard criticisms of the new left in Eastern Europe, and the saga of self-management is its bitterest disappointment. Self-management was envisaged as an instrument for promoting classlessness. By institutionalizing egalitarianism in decision making about economic production, the lower strata could challenge at will the privileges and influence of the upper striations and ensure that barriers could not be erected. But the workers have become increasingly disillusioned with the management apparatus. This lack of participation has been due to the growing complexity of industry, dif-ferentiations in educational levels, ethnic antagonisms, and the highly personal-ized incentive systems which reduced interests in mutual cooperation. But probably the most unexpected reason has been the spin-off of the party's efforts to provide greater personal security. By attempting to guarantee civil rights and reduce the arbitrary exercise of power, it has introduced a new sense of legalism that has complicated simplistic management practices. As manage-ment has become increasingly concerned with legal provisions and constraints, the worker has accordingly become further mystified and alienated from the decision-making process. Self-management is now more symbolic than substan-tive.

The number two man in the party, Edward Kardelj, tried to bridge this gap between the conferring sociologists. He called for the restitution of the value of private property and private work. Enhancement of the importance of private work would necessarily result in the accumulation of private property which, in turn, would reinforce the stratification of the society. But the provision that private capital could not be used for exploitive purposes would prevent any abuses. Furthermore, the admissibility of the fruits of private work would enhance the individual's identification with societal welfare and well-being and, in turn, should increase his interest in active participation in self-management at all levels of social engagement. Finally, Kardelj maintained that strengthening social participation was the most reliable means of eliminating those factors that bolstered stratification barriers.

Thus, even in Yugoslavia the problems associated with incentives for social motivation and formation of social stratifications with their inherent antagonism remain largely open questions. Do the inducements mentioned above tend to perpetuate or increase the competitive and aggressive nature of the recipients? At what point are they likely to induce docility, passivity, and indifference? Since inducements are based on productivity and education or other socially transferable skills, are they both ideological compromises and manifestations of failure? If the society works only for bread alone, is this an admission that the party has failed to inculcate a sufficient degree of socialist morality? If the party has failed to induce sufficient motivation to ensure individual participation for idealistic reasons or for the promotion of prescribed societal goals, has it achieved alternatively the degree of social integration envisioned in the reduction of the classes to only three? Has the socialization of industry and a portion of agriculture resulted in the extent of classlessness envisioned as commensurate with this degree of change in the property relationship? If not, what is the level of social integration or lack of social conflict?

There are several useful criteria for measuring social integration within the Soviet system. They include the extent to which these standards have been met:

1. elimination of legal and institutional discrimination and offensive demonstrations of personal prejudices;
2. acceptance of the individual's right to personal preferences;
3. social mobility based on merit exclusively;
4. acceptance at all levels of social organization of minority views;
5. recognition by ruling elites of the legitimacy of group interests—especially those of new or emerging groups; and
6. reduction of barriers and constraints to intermarriage among ethnic groups.

Conversely, several rough criteria for identifying social antagonism can also be outlined. They would include the following:

1. level and nature of exploitation felt by a repressed group or individuals;
2. nature and competitiveness of material and social aspirations of the various striations;
3. perception of commonality of interests and shared values;
4. nature and degree of personal security and how it is achieved;
5. degree of individual frustration and alienation and the presumed source; and
6. the type of social organization and its ability to amplify or respond to personal alienation and dissatisfaction.

The Party—Its Nature and Role

Marx's concepts of political organization and the functions of parties were subject to change and refinement during his life. Yet his commitment to party democracy and mass participation remained constant throughout his writings. The vagueness of some of his notions reflected the general state of the art and level of insight into political structures common to the mid-nineteenth century. It is difficult, for example, to determine whether Marx believed that Communists had unique political functions to perform and should be organized accordingly or whether they should merely participate in existing conventional parties. Because of the lack of a concise definition of the nature and role of political organizations, it is necessary to reconstruct his views, in part, from statements about what parties should not do, as well as positive assertions about political behavior.[40]

In discussing the initial draft of the Communist Manifesto known as the Principles of Communism, Engels answered question 16, about whether private property could be abolished by peaceful means, by stating that Communists know only too well that all conspiracies are not only futile but harmful.[41] Revolutions are not made deliberately and arbitrarily, but are the result of circumstances independent of the particular parties and classes involved. By forcefully suppressing the proletariat, the capitalists were promoting a revolution and the Communists will join the fight. To this end the Communists would work with other socialist organizations that are fully aware of the conditions of their emancipation. In other words, a party was to be a mass organization and existing organizational concepts were probably adequate.

The Manifesto was the first formally adopted platform of the Communist League. Section 1 describes the necessity for organizing the proletariat into a class and subsequently into a party reflecting its class structure. Section 2 outlines the relationship of Communists to the proletarian class. Communists are distinguished from the rest of the class because "they are the most advanced and resolute section of the class, pushing forward all the others through their clear understanding of the line of march and ultimate general conditions. They can be identified by their continual emphasis on common class interests, regardless of nationalities, and by their constant association with the movement as a whole, rather than with a particular segment.

At that time, the term class was regarded as being ultimately synonymous with party. The appropriate means of organizing the class was through stimulating self-awareness about the workers' strengths and their exploitation. This class consciousness would generate its own leadership through genuinely democratic procedures. In 1850 Marx emphasized this point in a reprimand of the German members of the league for their secretive activities. At that time the German Communists were under severe governmental pressure and were attempting to survive by going underground. But Marx insisted that those who attempted to turn a communist society into a conspiracy must be dismissed from the league. Engels later emphasized that until the proletariat was fully united into an organized class, political action would simply be premature.

Thus the purpose of the Communist League was more social than political. (Sir Karl Popper argues that since Marx contended that economics and class relations were the fundamental determinants in social conditions, this entailed

acceptance of the "impotence of politics.") The league was merely a loose affili-
ation of local workers' societies which eventually sent representatives to London
in 1848 to elect a central committee and adopt a general statement of aspirations in the form of the Manifesto. The central committee served only as a communication center for proselyting activities. It had no authority and was able to
provide only marginal moral support. Under increasing governmental pressure
against leftist organizations, it quickly became an anachronism. At no time did
it function as a party or serve an important political purpose.

In 1864, the International Working Men's Association (later known as the
First Socialist International) met in London to formally succeed the defunct
league. The general purpose of the association was to gain wider recognition of
the workers problems and aspirations. In the inaugural address Marx stated his
desire that the association be able to recruit vast numbers of workers through its
growing awareness of their mutual problems. But again, the rules adopted by the
association prescribed its activities to serving merely as a "clearing house for proletarian affairs." Participation in the association was open to any working men's
societies that advocated emancipation. Individual membership, activities, and
responsibilities remained exclusively within the authority of the local societies.
The intentional lack of politicization of the association was reminiscent of the
league and its utility to local societies was equally marginal.

The experience of the 1871 Paris Commune demonstrated the ineffectiveness of the association and convinced Marx that a new era had emerged in which
capitalism was so firmly entrenched that more energetic political activities would
be required. Marx was also quick to recognize, in an address entitled "On the
Civil War in France," that the commune signaled the danger that both the
example and the leadership of the international movement was shifting toward
France and radicalism. Marx attempted to regain the initiative at the 1872 Hague
Congress of the association by introducing an amendment to Artical 7 of the
rules: "The Proletariate can act as a class only by constituting itself as a distinct
political party."

This represented an important shift in emphasis. Formerly, Marx advocated the organization of a distinct workers' class from which would emerge a
political structure. At the Hague he accepted the necessity of politicizing the
movement and organizing it into a party which could then be instrumental in
promoting class awareness and expanding the social base of the movement. Marx
defended this reversal by arguing that the former socialist sects were no longer
relevant to the maturity of the socialist movement and that a more viable political organization was now vital for the achievement of the movement's aims. But
even at the end of his life, Marx insisted that the movement, organized as a
party, should be only a loose democratic assembly of local societies, without
strict central authority or discipline. It was to be mainly a rallying point for
socialist sentiments and aspirations. His insistence on decentralization was a
direct consequence of his conviction that each capitalist society would follow its

own developmental laws toward its inevitable demise. The only transnational political function that an international party could and should perform was to encourage the intensification of class consciousness. Conversely, the one activity the movement could not undertake was the promotion of local or international conspiracies. All clandestine operations remained an anathema for Marx and counterproductive to the development of class awareness.

The Franco-Prussian War in 1871 signaled the collapse of the First International. The war was not a rallying point for socialists or a means for consolidating internationalism, but was a source of renewed nationalism that intensified existing differences. The British socialists were horrified by the violence of the commune; the Germans were exhilarated by the new horizons of a unified German state; the French and smaller national parties became increasingly committed to anarchism and syndicalism; and Bakunin became the archrevolutionary of the period. These divergent forces were viewed by Marx as serious challenges to the sanctity of his philosophy. While professing no concise concept of political organization, he was not apolitical by instinct or in practice. As Bakunin characterized him, "As a German and a Jew he is an authoritarian from head to heels."[42] He first attempted to dominate the international movement by ousting the Proudhonists and Baluninists, and then to subordinate it by perpetuating its ineffectiveness. At the 1869 Basel Congress the Marxist-dominated central council lost its preeminent authority over the international and the remainder of Marx's life was consumed with political in-fighting, characterized by hatred and vindictive actions against his socialist opponents that outweighed his domination of the capitalists.

When the international collapsed as a political tool, Marx was also disgusted with the passivity of British socialism, as espoused by Hyndman, and demonstrated his abiding hatred for French individualism as represented by Pierre-Joseph Proudhon, Jules Guesde and Jean Jaures.[43] In these circumstances he devoted his energies to the formation of a viable national party that could advance his ideas. The German socialist party was the largest leftist party at that time and potentially the most powerful. After first splitting the party, leaving the majority to the moderate Lassallist faction, he sought a reconciliation in 1875 under the leadership of his disciple Karl Liebknecht. In his *Critique of the Gotha Program* he attacked the agreement as capitulationist and clearly indicated his apprehension that the German was prepared to seek evolution rather than reform through political participation in a country where parliamentarianism was more symbolic than substantive. His growing frustration led Marx, during his latter years, to seek more positive action and a more comprehensive political program. Searching for new approach with the desperation of an old man, Marx even went so far as to tell the Russian radical, Vera Zasulich, that agrarian Russia with its tradition of populism and social organization around the village *mir* could conceivably become the fountainhead of the world revolution.

But to his death Marx was unable to organize a political action plan that would ensure the advancement of his ideas—the nature and role of the party remained unclear.

After his death the factionalism that had contributed to the demise of the First International was intensified. The German Social Democratic Party was the largest, most influential, and probably the most moderate of the leftist organizations (it won 493,000 votes in 1877, 550,000 in 1887 and 1,427,000 in 1890). The Erfurt Program adopted by the 1891 Party Congress consecrated the dominance of Lassallian ideas of state socialism over those of a Marxist international revolution. Even though the program was adopted with Engels' approval and endorsed by the Second International founded in 1889, the call to violence was formally emitted. Karl Kautsky and Eduard Bernstein became the spokesmen for the revisionist Marxists who called for conventional political organizations that would accelerate worker awareness and ensure responsible participation in the social change.[44] This has remained the dominant strain among West European socialists and the source of severe contradictions within the Second International.

As a Russian, Lenin's ideas of political organization were strongly influenced by populism and the Narodnikis of the late nineteenth century, though he renounced this heritage, as he called it, early in his career. It was not the romanticism of the movement but the organization, actions and demands for reform that impressed young Lenin so profoundly that his ideas of political activities gradually became antithetical to those of both Marx and the German revisionists. The first Russian Marxist political body was organized in Geneva in 1883 by Plekhanov, Axelrod, and Zasulich. Lenin was identified with the socialist movement within Russia while still in his teens and helped found in 1895 "The Union of the Struggle for the Emancipation of the Working Class" in St. Petersburg, for which he received a four-year prison term. During this period he wrote two treatises on party organization: *The Draft and Explanation of a Program for the Social Democratic Party* defines the party's primary function merely as assisting the worker's struggle—it was not expected to lead the struggle. The party would embrace all strata and classes of society who opposed the existing absolute rule and were prepared to organize worker awareness of exploitation. In the 1899 *Draft Program for Our Party* he reiterated these orthodox Marxist lines but placed new un-Marxian emphasis on the role of the peasant. He explicitly refused to discuss tactics or specific actions, arguing that the party congresses and newspapers were the appropriate vehicles for such debates.

The orthodoxy of these views probably stem from Lenin's parochialism at that time and the general backwardness of Russian intellectualism. Only when he arrived in Geneva did he grasp the profundity of the revisionist challenge and the necessity of choosing sides between the evolutionists and revolutionists. In 1902, Lenin felt compelled to write a personal response to the Erfurt Program and the Bernstein opportunists in *What is to be Done*. Lenin condemned the revisionist contention that trade unionism was the most appropriate organization for increasing worker awareness and countered with the most definitive statement yet proposed for the distinctive functions of a Marxist political party. First, he stressed that a revolutionary party could not be a reformist party and therefore must have different characteristics from the conventional socialist parties. In itemizing these unique features he pointed out that in the revolutionary party there must be absolute unity between theory and practice, giving political activism a new sanctity and implying that the intellectual leadership must come from the workers' ranks. His condemnation of revisionism confirmed that the party should be alert to two threats, the ruling classes and the heretical socialists. For the first time he referred to the party as a vanguard, strengthening the trend toward elitism and activism. The party was to preserve its vanguard position by ensuring its theoretical purity, to be maintained by constant vigilance. He argued that class consciousness would not automatically emerge from economic evolution; it must be inculcated by action. The party must be constantly aware of the dangers of mass spontaneity, which seeks immediate solutions and is susceptible to compromise and modernization. Since political action was a dominant force over economic determinism, the party must be composed of professional revolutionaries, not trade unionists. Both their intentions and their activities placed them beyond the pale of established governmental authority and would force the revolutionaries to be as secretive as possible.

This logic led to the concept of the vanguard composed of elite, disciplined, intellectual theorists dedicated to societal conspiracy. The immediate implication was that for reasons of survival the elite party would become aloof or removed from the masses, as Marx warned the German comrades in 1850. Lenin responded to this criticism by using the dialectic. The needs of the masses had become so urgent, because of desperation and the oppression of the ruling classes, that the masses would spawn leaders ready to take radical steps and prepared to ensure the success of revolutionary measures. This cause and effect linkage would provide the fraternal bondage that would produce a unified classless society.

The questions of elitism and conspiracy underscored the focal position Marx had attached to democracy and mass participation in social progression. Lenin's program for revolutionary success required centralism to a degree at least commensurate to that of the oppressing authorities. Rosa Luxemburg, a leading figure in the German socialist movement, challenged the correctness of this conceptualization.[45] She argued that Lenin's requirement for centralization would make the party's decision-making body, the Central Committee, its only thinking element and thus would deny Marx's entire social analysis by condemning his faith in the worker. Even as a temporary measure, she insisted, it would be disastrous to substitute the workers' control over the party for the party's control over the workers. The fact is that social democracy is not joined to the organization of the proletariat, she argued; it is itself a function of the proletariat.

These were damning charges for any orthodox Marxist and Lenin replied in *One Step Forward, Two Steps Backward.* His main defense was the outright denunciation of the principle of democracy. He insisted that it was an onerous remnant of bourgeois values; it merely served the function of establishing and then siding with the majority; it raised the question of minority rights that were compromising to revolutionary discipline, and therefore it might be discarded as a concept and a value. After the revolution the issue of legitimization compounded the question of democracy. How could a tiny conspiratorial party with only minimal support even from the Russian workers, who numbered only 4 million in a land of 100 million peasants, establish the credibility of its authority? The question of legitimacy was exacerbated by the dual facts that the masses were gradually accepting the importance and validity of Western democratic traditions, and that there were no historic precedents that could prescribe appropriate substitutes for these principles in a revolutionary environment. Thus Lenin's chief task in political matters was to devise an original concept that would ensure the authority of his regime by providing tangible evidence of a fraternal bond between the vanguard party and masses.

In *The Immediate Tasks of the Soviet Government*, written after the catastrophic concessions granted to the Germans in the Treaty of Brest-Litovsk which ignited the Civil War, Lenin experimented with conceptual innovations that would both expand the public attractiveness of the party and improve the management of a rapidly expanding political organization. (Party membership had mushroomed from 115,000 in 1918 to 576,000 in January 1921, reflecting both a sense of opportunism by fellow-traveling leftists and the sudden bureaucratic needs of an opposition party that had acquired administrative responsibilities at a national level.) Lenin introduced the concept of democratic-centralism in a crude and unrefined form as a contrast to his only conceivable alternative— Proudhonist anarchism. The concept of democratic-centralism was envisioned as a guarantee of the fullest personal freedom possible through ensuring that every citizen could participate in the legislative process by organizing discussion of laws decisions, and in choosing and replacing representatives at appropriate levels of administration. But the concept was unclear, since all representatives were expected to accept the principle of obedience and were required to transmit the rationale for party decisions, not articulate constituency interests. Thus, the principles of both recall and representation were soon negated in practice.

The final refutation of Western concepts of democracy was administered in the October 1919 publication of *Economics and Politics in the Era of the Dictatorship of the Proletariat.* In this work Lenin argued that democratic practices were characteristic of the class structure and property relationships of bourgeois societies. They necessarily reflected and reinforced the instruments of oppression inherent in this form of society. Freedom from such onerous oppression necessitated the eradication of all forms of former dominance, especially the artifice of representative government.

It is difficult to determine whether Lenin's final public condemnation of democratic principles and espousal of centralism was the consequence of the exigencies of the Civil War or an opportunistic exploitation of the war for consolidation of the Bolsheviks' position. It was probably a combination of both. While the Bolsheviks were fighting for survival during the Civil War, the issue of centralism seemed imperative. Yet centralism was challenged by growing resistance labeled "workers opposition," dissident groups in the countryside and the opposing political parties, mainly the Mensheviks and the Social Revolutionaries.

By 1921 the issue of political legitimization and the role of the party had reached a critical point unassociated with wartime requirements. Domestic policies aggregated under the rubric of war communism had largely proved either inadequate or disastrous and the economy and the state of life were in shambles. The Kronstadt Mutiny in February over the sailors' demands for a return to pure Bolshevik principles revealed that cleavages persisted, despite the victorious outcome of the Civil War and intervention by 14 foreign states. Thus, at the Tenth Party Congress in March 1921 the issue of legitimacy and the role of the party had become the uppermost question for the consolidation of the revolution. Radical changes would be required to provide the moral authority for government and to deal with the existing and anticipated opposition to further measures toward centralization.

At the Eighth Party Congress, Lenin had succeeded in gaining approval for the condemnation of any opposition to party decisions. At the Ninth Congress he secured recognition of the necessity to identify the opposition. The Tenth Congress adopted the principle of the party's right and obligation to identify, discipline, and ultimately purge oppositional elements. To soften the harsh formula for elitist discipline, Lenin refined his notion of democratic centralism. Full participation by citizens and party members would be expected at all levels of societal engagement before specific decisions were taken. After decisions were made, however, no dissent would be tolerated. This obvious compromise between participation and subordination negated the onerous right of minority expression, fundamental to democratic principles. Lenin's innovation permitted continued drive toward centralization, necessary for the consolidation of the revolution, and exhibited the facade of public participation to improve the change for legitimization.

He also increased party attention to ideology as a bridging mechanism between the vanguard and masses. Faith in the future was to be the mutual bond of confidence between the leaders and the led. Class awareness coupled with historic determinism was to replace the concept of constituency representation and public accountability. Ideology was to be more than a mere stimulant or source of inspiration; it was to insure the credibility of communist rule against all forms of challenge or opposition. And to guarantee the proper utilization of ideology, its employment was to remain exclusively in the hands of the party.

Thus, Lenin must be credited with the genius for perceiving that drastic departures in political organization were required if the social transformations the Bolsheviks envisioned were to succeed. He recognized that radicalization of conventional political parties was inadequate and that a different form and composition of organization was essential to the successful engineering of the revolutionary process. Lenin's insistence that the communist undertaking was unique resulted in the pioneering of new and unprecedented forms of political organization that have had a lasting impact on the evolution of the Soviet system.

Leon Trotsky sharply criticized these innovations when he belatedly endorsed Rosa Luxemburg's denunciation of centralism.[46] He pointed out that the dictatorship of the proletariat was not really a Marxian concept but was largely an invention of Lenin. If this dictatorship means anything at all, according to Trotsky, it is that the vanguard of the class is armed with the resources of the state in order to repel all dangers, including those emanating from the backward layers of the proletariat itself. He later argued that the concept of centralism Lenin regarded as vital for consolidation had led to the bureaucratization of the revolution, with the Central Committee replacing the party, the Politburo replacing the Central Committee and finally the chairman replacing the Politburo. Such criticisms of the Leninist party were exaggerated and inaccurate, especially during the NEP period. Lenin's inability to establish the degree of centralization and control necessary to advance the revolution were recognized by Stalin as major shortcomings that must be overcome before the revolution could be returned to its true course. Lenin's death in 1924 and his reluctance or inability to sponsor an heir apparent pointed up another grave weakness of the Bolshevik party system—the succession issue. Theoretically, the chairman of the Politburo, the executive organ of the party, is elected by the full membership of the Central Committee, the party's main decision-making body. This office is retained at the discretion of the committee. But since the chairman nominates members for the Politburo and the Politburo determines the membership of the Central Committee, over time the chairman can control the composition of both bodies. Furthermore, political power and the attainment of high office in the Soviet system are dependent on patronage and favoritism. In practice, then, accretion of political power is as much a function of infighting and manipulation of irregularities as it is of intellect and moral character. Stalin's pursuit of power underscored the dangers of this weakness.

Stalin justified his quest for power in two volumes published shortly after Lenin's death, *The Fundamental of Leninism* and *The Problems of Leninism*, in which he asserted that certain tenets of the Marxist concept of the state had been inadequately defined. Many comrades, he argued, had overlooked the danger of the capitalist encirclement of the Soviet Union and had underestimated the vitality of the bourgeois societies. In other words, he maintained that the threat to the revolution was as grave then as before, which would require both increased vigilance and a reordering of the party. Centralization became an even greater concern for Stalin than it had been for Lenin. To achieve the political controls necessary to reintroduce the vigors of the revolution after the NEP with its inherent compromises with bourgeois values, Stalin felt compelled to annihilate the Leninist party apparatus and its functions. He sought the erection of a party structure with its affiliates in the state administration that would be totally subservient and unquestionably reliable. Stalin was apparently convinced that he was correctly interpreting the zig-zag policies Lenin had proclaimed and accelerated the process of purging and party renewal started as early as 1919. Major partywide purges occurred in 1919, 1921, 1924, and virtually every year thereafter until the Second World War.

But the renovation could not be completed until the leading personalities were eliminated from power. Trotsky was removed from the Ministry of War in January 1925 and gradually isolated. At the 14th Party Congress in March 1925, Stalin introduced his reiteration of the Leninist term of "socialism in one country" as an attack on "the left opportunists," Zinoviev and Kamenev, who advocated an immediate abandonment of the NEP. The offending leaders were demoted and a year later ousted from the party for their continued opposition. The opposition argued that the revolution had been a success under Lenin but was going astray under the existing leadership. They could not openly advocate leadership changes, however, without challenging the principle of democratic centralism and thereby subjecting themselves to disciplinary actions. At the party congress in December 1927 Stalin was able to eliminate the leftist opposition en masse and then turned on his former right-wing allies, Bukharin, Rykov, and Tomsky, who refused to accept his sudden judgment that the economy had been restored to a level at which it could withstand a return to Bolshevik tenents.[47] By 1930 all potential opponents had been reduced to ineffectuality and the party leadership was reconstituted with Stalin's proteges. Stalin's confidence in the subordination and loyalty of the renewed party justified the introduction of his own revolution—the Bolshevization of first agriculture and then industry. But widespread resistance persisted, resulting in fundamental compromises in agriculture on the value of private property and severe dislocations in industry. The consequence was an even greater centralization and subordination through the arbitrary use of terror.[48]

Under Stalin the party was transformed into a manipulative organ to ensure social control. It was no longer able to function as a vanguard for public enlightenment. Moreover, because of its heritage as the cradle for ideological dogma, it retained a potential threat for Stalin throughout his career and remained subordinated to the state-police apparatus. The mortification of such a transformation was acknowledged in the political succession struggle following Stalin's death in 1953, in which Beria, the head of the police state within a state, was the first victim.

By decapitating the terror machine, the surviving leaders agreed to refrain from the future use of such practices among themselves. This was the beginning of de-Stalinization, formally inaugurated by Khrushchev in 1956. The provision of greater personal security gradually allowed the party to regain a portion of its dignity and confidence, but not all of its former functions. Indeed its recuperated strength led to resentment against Khrushchev's continued manipulation of the apparatus to ensure the promotion of his ideas. While assuming as many as nine key party and state posts, he purged his opponents in 1957 and engineered repeated party reorganizations that tended to perpetuate the sense of dislocation and insecurity. Eventually the party became sufficiently disenchanted to force Khrushchev's retirement.

Under Brezhnev's chairmanship the party has recovered even more of its prestige and independent influence. But both society and the party have changed dramatically since the 1920s. The revolution is secure and its legitimacy within the USSR is no longer seriously challenged, decision making is shared with non-political experts, and ideology has lost its former inspirational luster. The party's leading role within the society is still important, but its main function now is to aggregate interests and arbitrate disputes, a manifestation of the progress of the modernization process within the Soviet system.

How does the renewed party operate internally? At every level of organization the party serves as a means of establishing immediate priorities for social needs and identifying problems related to the implementation of the state-planned program and the party's own guidelines for social development. It also serves as a vehicle for personal involvement in the political process and for group participation in decision making. Membership is determined at the local level where first secretaries accept candidates for a probational period of several years upon the recommendation of at least two local members. Full membership is a decision of the entire cell made upon the recommendation of the first secretaries and with the consent of the central party administration. Approximately every four years a general review of the state of the party is initiated. During the first stage, a report and election procedure is conducted over a four-to-six-month period at the local level. The cell reviews the reports of its various committees and boards to appraise past progress, future trends, continuing problems. It then formulates an overall report and recommendations for future action, and elects new local officials to serve the cell during the next period and to represent it at the next highest level. The procedures of reporting and elections are then conducted at the district, regional, and finally the national levels. After the national party congress has provided the guidelines governing party policy for the next four years the delegates disseminate the information back to the various levels of activities. Before electing officials, all party membership within the cell are considered, and the performance and attitude of each cell member and new candidates are reviewed by the cell executive committee. This process of party renewal eliminates members who do not meet prescribed standards.

The election rules for both party and state officials vary within the Soviet system. In the USSR there are only single candidacies for each post. All candidates are screened and nominated by the local first secretary. Opposition is expressed by the failure to cast a valid ballot. In practice, however, refusal to vote is regarded as censure of the party in general and not of an individual slate of candidates.

In Poland multiple candidacies are required. Fifteen percent more nominations are made than the number of positions. All names are listed alphabetically and the voter selects the number of candidates equal to the offices. Those candidates with the highest number of votes over 50 percent are elected. To guarantee that party standards are preserved, all nominations are also made by the first secretaries. This partial modification in representational procedures was designed to improve the identification of the party with the masses by providing some means of ensuring the popularity and accountability of elected officials. And the procedures work as intended within prescribed constraints: In 1972 only 48 percent of the party officials in Krakow were reelected, only 56 percent were reelected throughout the country, and only 64 percent of the first secretaries were returned to office.[49]

Yugoslavia has been experimenting with election laws since the inception of its concept of workers' self-management. The interest in greater local participation in decision making, however, was compounded by the exigencies of the nationalities question. Given the number of local councils and the continuing ethnic rivalries, Yugoslavia has constructed the most elaborate party and state organizations in the world. As a result of this intricate system of checks and balances, elections have become a complicated maze of procedures that provoked voter dismay. In principle, elections are open, and any citizen or party member who has been active in social affairs may apply to the local secretaries of either the Socialist Alliance or the party for nomination in state or party elections. The secretaries perform a screening function by verifying the applicant's credentials, and in practice are able to eliminate undesirable elements. Multiple candidacies are now commonplace. The effective use of the principle of recall has preserved the party's control over individual behavior of elected officials.

There have been both positive and negative consequences for these liberalized election procedures. By reducing the level of party intervention and control over the screening and nominating functions, candidates are increasingly elected, based on their popularity. And popularity is frequently a product of appeals to nationalism and ethnic emotions. Thus, in freeing the election procedures, Yugoslavia has inadvertently intensified the most dangerous single social problem—the nationalities question. On the positive side, however, the latest rules have contributed to the withering away of the party rather than the state. They parallel recent decisions to reduce the extent and frequency of party intervention in the routine administration of state affairs. The Yugoslavs maintain that their party has now progressed through the full cycle of leading and organizing revolutionary society. They claim that it has finally become a truly Marxist, not Leninist, party, which emphasizes enlightenment and moral guidance not coercion and control. The true test for such assertions will come, as in the case of Lenin, over the issue of succession after Tito's death. Edvard Kardelj has been appointed his successor, but if the transition is not orderly, probable political rivalries will exacerbate existing ethnic tensions. Tito has repeatedly warned that a deterioration in ethnic relations could endanger the entire fabric of the society and the position of the Communist Party. To prevent such a breakdown, a return to centralism and the Leninist model of control could become an inevitable choice.

The Role of Law in Socialist Development

In Western Europe, law has become a codex of rules that order social behavior and regulate governmental policy. But the Marxists have been compelled by the nature of their general philosophy to adopt an entirely different understanding of the role of law in societal development. According to Marx, it must not be forgotten that law has just as little independent history as religion. So law had a similar function as an opiate of the masses. It was a tool employed by the ruling classes to exploit and oppress the equally legitimate rights of the other classes. Law then, for Marx, was an expression of class will, a weapon in the struggle, and an instrument of coercion.

It follows in socialist logic that the content and form of law is a product of the economic character of any given state. The primacy of economics over politics and other societal features dictates that the superstructure of every state be determined by its systemic economic base. Law, like culture and other attributes, forms the matrix of socialist reality, but cannot adversely affect the state. Law is merely one of many instruments of policy, it is not the mandate for policy. Only revolution can produce basic organic changes. And in a revolutionary society where the proletariat has gained the preponderant position, it will determine the appropriate economic characteristics of the state as well as the values upon which other social attributes must be based, such as rules and legal norms.

After the revolution Lenin's actions rather than his pronouncements were the most convincing evidence of his conceptualization of law and jurisprudence in the socialist society. The urgent demands for consolidating the revolution and defeating external and internal enemies reinforced the Marxian dictum that law follows policy in a socialist state. Only after the more critical political and military needs were met did Soviet theorists tackle the task of analyzing the nature of socialist law. If the Soviet state was now different from other states by virtue of the revolutionary change in the economic base, how did it differ in terms of legal norms? Were there legal principles and concepts that were universally applicable, such as the theory of consent? Or could a state claiming unique attributes be eclectic about selecting those norms that suited its purposes and reject without penalties other norms. If law is a class tool and international law is an extension of internal law, would there not be variants in the norms for legal intercourse between states at different levels of development? Finally, if the party because of its leading role is responsible for goals and guidelines for social behavior, is the role of law then purely negative and punitive?

Early Soviet theorists such as P. I. Stuchka and Eugene A. Korovin addressed such questions and concluded that the socialist state was unique in requiring an unusual set of legal norms.[50] They disclaimed the Western contention that a single codex existed and insisted that several distinct legal systems were discernible. This diffused pattern was the result of the marginal level of cooperation and shared interests among states in dissimilar stages of progress. Korovin then argued that universalism was plausible but only after the final victory of communism and the general endorsement of the Marxist values. In the interim the rise of socialism had created a new "transitional" form of law which integrated some traditional legal practices with goals of socialist justice. The transitional form was therefore superior to earlier systems and should be emulated by other societies.

The rejection of these contentions by nonsocialist legal scholars led to continuing controversy among Soviet theorists. The question of the uniqueness of the USSR and therefore the degree of separateness it should be entitled to became a central debate during the massive purges in the 1930s. The Stalinist faction was finally able to force general acceptance of a narrow interpretation that viewed the USSR as being so distinctive that it must reject all bourgeois legal tenets or risk the dangers of contamination.[51] In the postwar era when greater collaboration with nonsocialist states was practiced, the hardline position was partially revised but not to the permissive selectivity accepted by Lenin.[52]

Under Khrushchev several innovations were made in the legal system. The concept of peaceful coexistence was devised to govern legal intercourse between socialist and nonsocialist states. It called for the mutual respect for the principles espoused by the two sides and for the abandonment of attempts to impose rival values. To govern relations among the states within the Soviet system, the concept of international socialism was expanded beyond the former idea of international proletarianism, which related only to fraternal parties. The new concept was essentially an extension of class law from the Soviet Union into East European countries to provide a common legal framework for relations among socialist states. Finally, Khrushchev proposed in 1959 to revise Stalin's 1936 constitution and eliminate existing anachronisms. The key motive for writing a new document appears to have been the same reason for Stalin's revising Lenin's constitution, that is to produce one's own legitimizing instrument which would certify that a new level of development had been achieved.

The Soviet constitutional documents upon which legal norms are predicated have an aspirational rather than a prescriptive quality. They register both the state of social progression and the broad goals to be achieved. Definition of specific guidance for their attainment is left to the party. Khrushchev had publicly announced in 1956 that the socialist revolution was irreversibly established. The need for mobilization had been superseded by the requirement for surpassing the United States through modernization, which could be facilitated by providing a new constitutional framework for development.

But did the new social conditions alter the basic tenets of the society? Did they change the purpose of early constitutions? Was the new purpose to provide a binding contract between the ruled and the rulers; or a prescription of governmental responsibilities and prohibitions, or a definition of citizens' rights and duties in terms that were not expectations but actual guarantees? A constitution committee was organized within the Central Committee in 1960 to deliberate the implications of such questions but apparently no serious actions were undertaken. Brezhnev resurfaced the idea of constitutional reform in 1966 and eight years later the proposal was still in the committee. The problems related to constitutional reform are so fundamental to the legitimization process that the Soviets have apparently opted to pursue two alternative courses: to strengthen the practice of law through the expansion of its administrative applications such as arbitration courts, without tampering, for the time being, with theoretical innovations, and to permit other members of the system to initiate their own constitutional reforms.53

The constitutional reforms in both Yugoslavia and Hungary are those most reflective of these changes in the Soviet system. Yugoslavia has had four separate constitutions under communist rule (1946, 1953, 1963, and 1974). Each document represented major conceptual changes, such as the introduction of worker's self-management in 1953 and the separation of powers in 1963. The nature of the documents also changed perceptively. The 1946 constitution was a victory statement with the itemization of the means for consolidation of communist rule. Succeeding ones have become increasingly definitive about the organization and responsibilities of government. This trend has been accelerated by the frequent use of amendments (the 1963 constitution was amended 36 times and the last contained 21 separate chapters).

The pace of change is a reflection of the rapid shift of Yugoslavia from mobilization to modernization. But probably more important, it is a direct consequence of the growing ethnic tensions. Each document has been more elaborate in defining those structures (their composition and responsibilities) that can act as checks and balances against the possible political and economic domination of one ethnic group over the others. Mandatory rotation of offices, intricate weighted voting schemes at different levels and on various issues, presidential succession procedures, structural balances, and reserved powers for specified levels of administration are outlined precisely in the constitution. Thus, the Yugoslav constitutions have become the most prescriptive legal documents for the conduct of government actions in the Soviet system, if not the world.

But is explicit institutionalization of political power a manifestation of the incorporation of pluralism, as the party supporters argue, or is it evidence of the inability of socialism to cope with traditional ethnic problems, as the critics charge? There is evidence that "constitutionalism and legality," as the Yugoslavs call the process, is taking root and may prove sufficient to ease Yugoslavia through the political succession crisis and into more placid waters. The best evidence of this durability has been the effective functioning of an independent judiciary modeled after the American system. The Supreme Court is endowed with both appellate and original jurisdiction and has acted repeatedly to curb governmental powers. Its prerogatives appear to be sufficiently well respected so that it will be able to exercise restraint against abuses of power in all but the most tumultuous circumstances.

OBSERVATIONS

This blend of five main substantive issue areas is intended to provide a topographical overview of the important problems and a framework in which other policy areas such as agriculture, education, and culture may be examined. A survey of the other areas reinforces many of the observations derived from the above selections.

In no other social system has the function of change held such a prominent position among both rulers and the ruled. Other revolutionary societies have sought a transfer in the disposition of political and economic power, but then have immediately attempted to consolidate and preserve the new order. Only Lenin's revolution set a deliberate course of continuing progressions that would ultimately eliminate the entire political structure of state and world societies. As interpreted by Stalin through his successors, however, the imperatives of class struggle and industrialization dictated the centralization of state authority and the superimposition of political mandates over all other aspects of societal behavior. The result has been a political experience unique in modern history. The ideological justification for the party's minority rule is predicated upon its pledge to promote continuously progressive changes, yet its survival to ensure these progressions depends upon its ability to guarantee stability, security, and legitimacy—a triad of concepts so intertwined that a challenge to one jeopardizes the stable state of the others, binding them into a mutual reinforcement of the status quo at the political level.

The Soviet state is thus a paradox in the Leninist sense. It has introduced less change or reform in the political sphere in either elites or institutions than any society since World War II (Andrei Gromyko, for example, has been either deputy or full foreign minister for 30 years). Changes have been introduced, but at lower rungs of social order such as industry, agriculture, and education. Indeed, it may be hypothesized that the degree of radicalization, or proximity of reforms to Leninist norms, depends upon their perceived impact of political authority. Youth education poses a relatively intangible direct threat to the party's role and has been one of the best examples of Leninization. Reforms in the economic sector appeared initially to rationalize the means of production and thereby ultimately introduce an era of universal materialism necessary for the advancement of socialism. The contradiction between mobilizing a society using Stalinist inducements and modernizing ones requiring decentralization of authority, massive amounts of information, and greater latitude for local decision making became apparent in the economic reforms. The Soviet resolution has been to avoid the conventional standards for modernization and the sources of the continuing stagnating economic growth by linking increased industrial production with a greater flow of information, without curtailing the state's right of intervention or direction.

The failure of the early economic reforms and the reversion to economic stagnation is, in part, a reflection of unofficial or unauthorized changes in the social order. The proliferation of group and personal interests is due largely to disillusionment with the amount of change authorized by the party, the continuing austere quality of life, and to the degree of authoritarianism necessary in order to preclude any change in institutions that could relieve these problems. (Cyril Black has pointed out that since 1900 the relative standard of living of the Russians has not changed. They have ranked nineteenth or twentieth in all quality of life indexes for the third quarter of the century, and several smaller Asian nations have surpassed their standards.)[54] Paradoxically the formation and articulation of group and individual interests is not due to a lack of confidence in the party. Individuals accept the function of the state and even the need for authority. They seek to augment their lives by pursuing interests and activities not explicitly prescribed by law or adequately enforced by the bureaucracy. The consequence has been increased self-consciousness, self-confidence, and self-identification—the opposite of collective integration. These subtle and unauthorized social changes are not the harbingers of vocal protest or massive unrest; they are not synchronized with the sentiments of the few intellectual dissenters. They do represent, however, a lack of identification of the masses with the avowed objectives of the party and its claims to guide them to socialism.

Ideology has successfully legitimized the party's minority rule; but it has failed to provide a new opium for the masses, a faith in the future that will assuage present and expected hardships. Either a return to ideological fundamentalism or the formal introduction of genuine social reforms with a corresponding decline of state authority are the most apparent alternative courses for converting the Soviet system of societies with stable political structures into viable progressive societies.

NOTES

1. Richard Lowenthal, "Soviet-American Relations and World Order: The Two and the Many," Adelphi Papers, no. 66, International Institute of Strategic Studies (IISS), (March 1970), p. 11.

2. For the utility of studying dissimilarities, see Oran R. Young, *Systems of Political Science* (Princeton: Princeton University Press, 1968); and "Political Discontinuities in the International System," *World Politics,* April 1968.

3. Hans Bucheim, *Totalitarian Rule: Its Nature and Characteristics* (Ontario: Burns and MacEachem, 1968).

4. Carl J. Friedrich, Michael Curtis, and Benjamin R. Barber, *Totalitarianism in Perspective: Three Views,* 1969, p. 19.

5. Samuel Huntington and Clement Moore, *Authoritarian Politics in Modern Society,* 1971.

6. Gordon H. Skilling and Franklyn Griffiths, *Interest Groups in Soviet Politics* (Princeton: Princeton University Press, 1970).

7. Phillip D. Steward, *Political Power in the Soviet Union: A Study of Decision Making in Stalingrad,* 1968.

8. Frederic J. Fleron, Jr., *Communist Studies and the Soviet Sciences* (Chicago: Rand McNally, 1971).

9. Peter C. Ludz, *A Party Elite in Transformation,* 1970.

10. Richard Lowenthal, "Continuity and Change in Soviet Foreign Policy," *Survival,* January-February 1972.

11. Tiber Szamuelz, "Five Years After Khrushchev," *Survey,* Summer 1969.

12. Zbigniew Brzezinski, "The Soviet Past and Present," *Encounter,* March 1969; also ibid., "Transformation of Degeneration," *Problems of Communism,* January-February 1966; *Dilemmas of Change in Soviet Politics,* (New York: Columbia University Press, 1969); and *Between Two Ages: America's Role in the Technotronic Age,* 1971. John S. Reshetar Jr. has added a slightly different analysis in *The Soviet Polity: Government and Politics in the USSR* (New York: Dodd, Mead & Co., 1971); as has Brian Crozier, *The Future of Communist Power,* 1970; and Jerry Hough, "The Soviet System: Petrifaction or Pluralism?," *Problems of Communism,* March-April 1972.

13. Gordon H. Skilling, "Interest Groups and Communist Politics," *World Politics,* April 1966; and Skilling and Franklyn Griffiths, op. cit.

14. John H. Kautsky, *Political Change in Underdeveloped Countries: National and Communism* (New York: Wiley & Sons, 1962); "Communism and the Comparative Study of Development," *Slavic Review,* March 1967; *Communism and the Politics of Development,* 1967, and *The Political Consequences of Modernization* (New York: Wiley & Sons, 1972).

15. John H. Kautsky, "Comparative Communism versus Comparative Politics," *Studies in Comparative Communism,* Spring/Summer 1973.

16. Cyril E. Black, *The Dynamics of Modernization,* 1966.

17. David Apter, "Political Systems and Developmental Change," in David T. Holt and John E. Turner, eds., *The Methodology of Comparative Research,* 1970, p. 158; also *The Politics of Modernization,* 1965.

18. Peter C. Ludz, ed., *Changing Party Elite in East Germany* (Cambridge: MIT Press, 1972).

19. Carl Beck and James M. Malloy, *Political Elites: A Mode of Analysis,* 1971; Roger E. Kanet., ed., *The Behavioral Revolution and Communist Studies* (New York: Free Press, 1971); Milton C. Lodge, *Soviet Elite Attitude Since Stalin* (Columbus: Merrill,

CHANGE IN THE SOVIET SYSTEM

1969); and R. Barry Farrell, *Political Leadership in Eastern Europe and the Soviet Union* (Chicago: Aldine, 1970). The best overall discussion is the compilation edited by Chalmars Johnson, *Change in the Communist Systems* (Stanford, Cal.: Stanford University Press, 1970).

20. Samuel P. Huntington, "The Change to Change: Modernization, Development, and Politics," *Comparative Politics*, April 1971.

21. Paul H. B. Godwin, "Communist Systems and Modernization: Sources of Political Crisis," *Studies in Comparative Communism*, Spring/Summer 1973.

22. George Lichtheim, "Marxism and Marxology," *Problems of Communism*, July/ August 1966, p. 15.

23. Norman Levine, "Anthropology in the Thought of Marx and Engels," *Studies in Comparative Communism*, Spring/Summer 1973.

24. For a neorevisionist criticism of Lenin's role in derailing Marxism, see Frederic and Lou Jean Fleron, "Administration Theory as Repressive Theory," *Newsletter on Comparative Studies of Communism*, November 1972, and the subsequent discussion in the August 1973 issue.

25. According to Marxist theory, price is not a value; labor is the value and remains constant. A given amount of labor can equal a fixed quantity of consumer goods (bread, shoes, and so on). It cannot be equated, however, with a fixed quantity of machines, since machines participate in the production cycle. Prices become indispensable in establishing the relationship between the value of labor and the value of machines. There is an abundance of Western literature cited in the bibliography, but for a brief introduction into the issues and problems of reform, see L. A. D. Dellin and Herman Gross, *Reforms in Soviet and East European Economics*, 1972.

26. Allen Kassof, "The Old Administered Society," *World Politics*, July 1964, pp. 153-54.

27. In ibid., see T. H. Rigby, "Traditional Market and Organizational Societies."

28. Donald W. Treadgold, *Twentieth Century Russia*, 1964; and Richard Pipes, "Russia's Exigent Intellectuals," *Encounter*, January 1964, pp. 79-84.

29. See op. cit., footnote 13.

30. Ibid.

31. Steward, op. cit. See also, Joel J. Schwartz and William R. Keech, "Group Influence and the Policy Process in the Soviet Union," *American Political Science Review*, September 1968.

32. Jeremy Azrael, "Varieties of De-Stalinization," in Chalmers Johnson, *Change in Communist Systems*, op. cit., 1970.

33. T. H. Rigby, "Crypto-Politics," *Survey*, January 1964. He was attacking particularly Roger Pethybridge, *A Key to Soviet Politics*, 1962.

34. S. M. Lipset and Richard R. Dobson, "Social Stratification and Sociology in the Soviet Union," *Survey* 19, no. 3 (Summer 1973); Murray Yanowitch and Wesley A. Fischer, *Social Stratification and Mobility in the USSR* (White Plains: International Arts & Sciences Press, 1973). See also, John S. Shippee, "Empirical Sociology in the Eastern European Communist Party-States," in Jan F. Triska, ed., *Communist Party-States* (Indianapolis: Bobbs, Merrill Co., 1969).

35. Talcott Parsons, *Essays in Sociological Theory, Pure and Applied* (New York: Free Press, 1954), p. 166.

36. David Lane, *Politics and Society in the USSR* (New York: Random House, 1970), p. 382.

37. Sir Karl Popper, *The Open Society and its Enemies* (Princeton: Princeton University Press, 1952).

38. Pavel Machonin, "Social Striation in Contemporary Czechoslovakia," *American Journal of Sociology* 75, (1969).

39. Radio Free Europe, research memo #1314, "Yugoslav Sociologists Discuss Country's Internal Conflict," June 3, 1972.

40. For a traditionalist interpretation see Robert C. Tucker, *The Marxist Revolutionary Idea* (New York: Norton, 1969), which contains a bibliography of Marxist literature; and Adam B. Ulam, *The Unfinished Revolution*, 1960; and Max Eastman, *Reflections on the Failure of Socialism* (Greenwich, Conn.: Devin Aldair, 1955).

41. Karl Marx and Frederick Engels, *Selected Works*, Vol. 1 (New York: International, 1968); *Selected Correspondence of Marx and Engels*, 1934; and Sidney Hook, *From Hegel to Marx: Studies in the Intellectual Development of Karl Marx* (Ann

42. Hampden J. Jackson, *Marx, Proudhon and European Socialism*, 1962, p. 129.

43. See particularly, Pierre-Joseph Proudhon, *La Guerre et la Paix* (New York, Garland), *Philosophie de la Misere* (New York: Arnd Press, 1972), *Philosophie du Progres*, 1853, *La Revolution Sociale*, 1851.

44. See especially, Eduard Bernstein, *Evolutionary Socialism* (New York: Schoken, 1961); see also Karl Kautsky, *The Class Struggle–The Erfurt Program* (New York: Norton, 1971); and *The Dictatorship of the Proletariat* (Ann Arbor: University of Michigan Press, 1964).

45. Rosa Luxemburg, *The Russian Revolution* (Ann Arbor: University of Michigan Press, 1971); and ibid, *Collected Works*, 1922.

46. Leon Trotsky, *The History of the Russian Revolution* (Ann Arbor: University of Michigan Press, 1957); and ibid, *The Revolution Betrayed* (New York: Pathfinder Press, 1973).

47. N. Bukharin, *Historical Materialism*, 1924; and ibid, *ABC's of Communism*, 1966.

48. For documentary evidence of the degree of resistance in the province, see Merle Fainsod, *Smolensk Under Soviet Rule*, 1958.

49. Karl Marx and Frederick Engels, *The German Ideology*, 1965, p. 79; also Hans Kelson, *The Communism Theory of Law*, 1955.

50. P. I. Stueka, "A General Doctrine of Law," in *Soviet Legal Philosophy*, 1951; and Eugene A. Korovin, *International Law of the Transitional Period*, 1924; and *Contemporary International Public Law*, 1926.

51. See, for contrast, Eugene B. Pashukanis, *Encyclopedia of the State and of Law*, 1929; and *Essays in International Law*, 1935; and John N. Hazard, "Cleansing of Soviet International Law of Anti-Marxist Theories," *American Journal of International Law*, January 1939; and "Pashukanis is no Traitor," ibid., April 1957.

52. Compare, for example, Sergey Krilov, "The Principle Notions of the Rights of Man," *Recueil des Cours de l'Academie de Droit International* 1, 70, 1947; and A. Y. Vinshinsky, *Questions of International Law and International Politics*, 1949.

53. On the de facto extension of administrative legalism see, for example, Peter Feuerle, "State Arbitration in Communist Countries: The Differentiation of Functions," *Studies in Comparative Communism* 4, nos. 3 and 4 (July-October 1971).

54. See Black, op. cit; also see Robert G. Wesson, "Viability of the Leninist Synthesis," *Orbis*, Winter 1974.

SELECTED BIBLIOGRAPHY
OF CONTEMPORARY MATERIALS
IN COMPARATIVE COMMUNISM

With few exceptions, this bibliography consists of only English titles of articles, monographs, and books published between January 1965 and December 1975. The following journals were included in the survey. (Occasional articles which were cited in other sources are included in the bibliography, but not in this list.)

Primary	*Occasional Contributions*
American Political Science Review	*British Journal of Sociology*
Canadian Slavic Studies	*Government and Opposition*
Current History	*Polish Round Table*
East European Quarterly	*Journal of Politics*
Foreign Affairs	*Modern World*
International Affairs	*Science and Society*
International Political Science Abstracts	*Australian Quarterly*
International Social Science Journal	*Columbia Law Review*
UNESCO-PARIS	*Journal of Contemporary History*
Midwest Journal of Political Science	*Polish Sociological Bulletin*
Newsletter on Comparative Studies of	*International Labor Review*
Communism	*Czech Papers*
Problems of Communism	*Comparative Politics*
RAND Publications (selected 70-72)	*Journal of Economic Abstracts*
Russian Review (RR)	*East Europe*
Slavic Review	*American Economic Journal*
Social Compass: International Review	*Swiss Review of World*
of Social Religious Studies	*Affairs*
Soviet Studies	*Socialist International*
Studies in Comparative Communism	*Information*
Studies in Soviet Thought (SST)	
Studies on the Soviet Union	
Survey	
The Western Political Quarterly	
World Politics	
World Marxist Review	
Orbis	
Political Science Quarterly	

The entries have been confined exclusively to domestic-policy areas of the East European countries and the Soviet Union, minus Albania. The bibliography is organized, for convenience's sake, along the same lines of inquiry outlined in the methodology section, but which will be repeated here:

To facilitate the use of the bibliography, a simple set of guidelines has been used as a substitute for full annotations. The Roman numeral indicates the level of audience and the letter designates roughly the substantive nature of the article or book.

I—Undergraduate and general public
II—Graduate students
III—Postdoctoral—specialized
C—Conceptual
G—General subject
S—Statistical
T—Technical or specialized

The bibliography does include a number of general bibliographies dealing with these and related topics:

Hammond, Thomas T., comp. *Soviet Foreign Relations and World Communism: A Selected, Annotated Bibliography of 7,000 Books in 30 Languages.* Princeton, N.J.: Princeton University Press, 1965. 1240 pp. (Coverage principally through 1962)

Pundeff, Marin. *Recent Publication on Communism: A Bibliography on Non-periodical Literature, 1957-1962.* U.S.C. 1962.

World Communism. A Selected Annotated Bibliography. Prepared by the Legislative Reference Service of the Library of Congress for the Senate Committee on the Judiciary. Washington, GPO, 1964. 394 pp. Document no. 69. Coverage through September 1963. See also Supplements 1964-69, published in 1972.

Horecky, Paul L. *Basic Russian Publications: An Annotated Bibliography on Russia and the Soviet Union.* Chicago: University of Chicago Press, 1962.

Horecky, Paul L. *Southeastern Europe: A Guide to Basic Publications.* Chicago: University of Chicago Press, 1969. 755 pp. Covers the Balkans, including Hungary and Romania.

USSR: Strategic Survey: A Bibliography. 1971 edition. Department of the Army.

Soviet Intelligence and Security Services 1964-1970: A Selected Bibliography of Soviet Publications with Additional Titles from Other Sources. Congressional Research Service, Library of Congress, 1972.

Communist Eastern Europe: Analytical Survey of Literature. Department of the Army, 1971.

Prpic, George J. *Eastern Europe and World Communism: A Selective Annotated Bibliography in English.* Cleveland: John Carrol University, 1966. 148 pp.

Bibliography of Social Science Periodicals and Monograph Series: Rumania, 1947-1960. Washington, Department of Commerce, 1961. See also, others in this series of foreign social science bibliographies, such as *Poland, 1945-1962* (1964); *Eastern Zone of Germany, 1948-1963* (1965); *Mainland China, 1949-1960* (1961), and so on.

Monthly List of Russian Accessions. Library of Congress, GPO, 1948–. See also, *Monthly List of East European Accessions.*

The American Bibliography of Russian and East European Studies for 1957 (   ). American Association for the Advancement of Slavic Studies, annual. Books and articles. No annotations.

Kraus, David H., and Anita R. Navon, eds. *The American Bibliography of Slavic and East European Studies for 1973.* Washington, Library of Congress, 1975.

The USSR and Eastern Europe: Periodicals in Western Languages, 1967, Library of Congress. 89 pp.

Laziteh, Branko, in collaboration with Milorad M. Drachkovitch, *Biographical Dictionary of the Comintern.* Stanford, Calif.: The Hoover Institution Press, 1973. 458 pp.

Czechoslovakia: A Bibliographic Guide. 1967, 157 pp. L.C.

Bulgaria: A Bibliographic Guide. 1965, 98 pp. L.C.

Rumania: A Bibliographic Guide. 1963, 75 pp. L.C.

East Germany: A Selected Bibliography. 1967, 133 pp. L.C.

Bako, Elemer. *Guide to Hungarian Studies,* Vols. 1, 2. Hoover Institution Bibliographical Series 52. Stanford, Calif.: Hoover Institution Press, Stanford University, 1974. 1218 pp.

Spector, Sherman D., and Lyman Legters, comps. *Checklist of Paperbound Books on Russia and East Europe.* Albany: University of the State of New York, 1966. 79. pp.

Birkos, Alexander S., and Lewis A. Tumbs, comps. and eds. *Academic Writers Guide to Periodicals: II East European and Slavic Studies.* Kent, Ohio: Kent State University Press, 1973.

Harris, C. D. *Guide to Geographical Bibliographies and Reference Works in Russian or on the Soviet Union.* Chicago: University of Chicago, Department of Geography, 1975. 478 pp.

Hoskins, Janina, comp. *Polish Books in English 1945-1971.* Washington, D.C.: Library of Congress, 1974. 163 pp.

Treml, Vladimir. *Input-output Analysis and the Soviet Economy: an Annotated Bibliography.* New York: Praeger, 1975. 180 pp.

Zalewski, Wojciech. *Russian Materials in the Main Library of Stanford University: A Collection Survey.* Stanford, Calif.: Stanford University Libraries, 1974. 19 pp.

Foreign Affairs Bibliography published by the Council on Foreign Relations in New York. Volume 1 covers 1919-32; subsequent volumes cover 1932-42; 1942-52 and 1952-62. See also, a selected bibliography for 50 years published in 1972.

1. ECONOMIC DEVELOPMENT AND POLITICAL CHANGE: PARTIAL REVOLUTION AND ECONOMIC GROWTH

Economic Planning

Aboucher, Alan. *Soviet Planning and Spatial Efficiency: The Pre-War*   III T
Cement Industry. Bloomington: Indiana University Press, 1971.

Arnold, Karl-Heinz. *The New Economic System*. Dresden, Verlag Zeit   III T
im Bild, 1967.

Balinky, Alexander, et al. *Planning and the Market in the USSR: The*   II T
Sixties. New Brunswick, N.J.: Rutgers University Press, 1967.

Bandera, V.N. and Z.L. Melnyk. *The Soviet Economy in Regional*   II T
Perspective. New York: Praeger, 1973.

Bauman, Zygmunt. "Twenty Years After: The Crisis of Soviet-Type   I G
Systems." *Problems of Communism* 20, no. 6 (November-
December 1971).

Benjamin, Roger W. and John H. Kautsky. "Communism and Eco-   II T
nomic Development." *American Political Science Review* 62
(March 1968).

Bergson, Abram. *Planning and Productivity Under Soviet Socialism*.   III T
Pittsburgh: Carnegie Press, Carnegie-Mellon University, 1968.

——. "Soviet Economic Perspectives: Towards a New Growth Model."   III C
Problems of Communism (March/April 1973), p. 3.

——. "Toward a New Growth Model." *Problems of Communism* 22   III G
(March-April 1973).

Berend, Ivan T. and Gvörgv Ránki. *Economic Development in East-*   II T
Central Europe in the 19th and 20th Centuries. New York:
Columbia University Press, 1974.

Berend, Ivan T. and G. Ránki. *Hungary: A Century of Economic*   II T
Development. New York: Barnes and Noble Books, 1974.

Bernard, Phillipe J. *Planning in the Soviet Union*. New York: II G
Pergamon, 1966.

Bicanic, Rudolf. *Economic Policy in Socialist Yugoslavia*. London: II G
Cambridge University Press, 1973.

Bornstein, Morris, ed. *Comparative Economic Systems*. Homewood,   II G
Ill.: Irwin, 1965.

Bornstein, Morris. *Plan and Market, Economic Reform in Eastern Europe*.   III G
New Haven: Yale University Press, 1973.

Bornstein, Morris and Daniel Fusfeld, eds. *The Soviet Economy: A Book*   II G
of Readings. Homewood, Ill.: Irwin, 1966.

van Brabant, Jozef. *Essays on Planning, Trade and Integration in Eastern*   II T
Europe. Rotterdam: Rotterdam University Press, 1974.

Bros, Wlazdzimierz. *The Market in a Socialist Economy.* London: Routledge II T
and Kegan Paul, 1972.

Brown, A.A. and E. Neuberger, eds. *International Trade and Central*   III T
Planning. Berkeley: University of California Press, 1968.

Brubaker, Earl R. "A Sectional Analysis of Efficiency Under Market and   III S
Plan." *Soviet Studies* (January 1972).

Bryson, Phillip J. and Erich Klinkmuller. "Eastern European Integration—   II G
Constraints and Prospects," *Survey* 21, no. 1 (Winter-Spring 1975):
101-27.

Brzeski, A. "Inflation in Poland." Ph.D. dissertation, Berkeley, University   I T
of California, 1964.

Buky, Barnabas. "Hungary's KEM on a Treadmill." *Problems of Com-*   II G
munism 21, no. 5 (September-October 1972).

Bush, Keith. "Soviet Capital Investment Since Khruschchev: A Note."   II S
Soviet Studies (July 1972).

———. "The New Five-Year Plan." *Problems of Communism*   III T
(July-August 1966).

———. "The Progress Made in Industry." *Bulletin for the Study of the*   I G
USSR (October 1966).

Campbell, Robert. "Economic Reform in the USSR." *American Review*   II G
(May 1968).

Campbell, Robert. *Some Issues in Soviet Energy Policy for the Seventies.*   II T
Joint Economic Committee "Soviet Economic Prospects for the
Seventies." Washington, D.C.: Congress of the United States (17 June
1973).

Campbell, Robert W. "Economics: Roads and Inroads." *Problems of*   I G
Communism 14 (December-November 1965).

———. *Soviet Economic Power.* 2d ed. Boston: Houghton-Mifflin, 1966.   II

———. *Soviet-type Economics: Performance and Evolution.* New York:
Houghton-Mifflin, 1974.

Carr, E.H. and R.W. Davies. *Foundations of a Planned Economy, 1926-1929.* I G
New York: Macmillan, 1971.

Chandra, N. "Kantorovitch's Macro-Economic Model and Soviet Methods of
Balance." *Journal of Economic Abstracts* (June 1967).   III T/S

Chawluk, Antoni. "Economic Policy and Economic Reform." *Soviet*   I G
Studies 26, no. 1 (January 1974): 98-119.

Cicplak, Tadeusz N. *Poland Since 1956.* New York: Twayne, 1972.   I G

Clark, Roger A. *Soviet Economic Facts, 1917-1970.* London: III S
Macmillan, 1972.

Cobeljic, Nikola and Radmila Stojanovie. *The Theory of Investment*   III C
in a Socialist Economy. White Plains, N.Y.: International Arts
and Sciences Press, 1969.

Cohn, Stanley H. *Economic Development in the Soviet Union*.   III G
Lexington, Mass.: D.C. Heath, 1970.

"Communism and the Comparative Study of Development."   II C
Slavic Review 26, no. 1 (March 1967): 14.

Conklin, D.W. "Barriers to Technological Change in the USSR: II T
A Study of Chemical Fertilizers." *Soviet Studies* (January 1969).

Conolly, Violet. *Siberia Today and Tomorrow: A Study of Economic*   II G
Resources, Problems and Achievements. London: Collins, 1975.

Conquest, Robert, ed. *Industrial Workers in the USSR*. New York: III T
Praeger, 1967.

Conyngham, William J. *Communist Party in Soviet Industrial Admin-*   II G
istration: The Khrushchev Years. Stanford, Calif.: Hoover Institute
Press, 1972.

Day, Richard B. *Leon Trotsky and the Politics of Economic Isolation*.   II T
London: Cambridge University Press, 1975.

Degras, Jan, ed. *Soviet Planning*. New York: Praeger, 1965.   II G

Dellen, Brant and Jan Ake. *Reformists and Traditionalists, A Study of*   II T
Soviet Discussions about Economic Reform, 1960-1965. Stockholm:
Raren and Sjogren, 1972.

Dmitriev, V.K. *Economic Essays on Value, Competition and Utility*.   II T
London: Cambridge University Press, 1974.

Dobb, Maurice. *Socialist Planning: Some Problems*. London: II G
Lawrence and Wishart, 1970.

———. *Soviet Economic Development, 1917*. New York: International   II G
Publishers, 1966.

———. *Welfare Economics and the Economics of Socialism*. London: II C
Cambridge University Press, 1973.

Dodge, Norton T., ed. *Analysis of the USSR's 24th Party Congress*   III T
and 9th Five-Year Plan. Mechanicsville, Md.: Cremona Foundation,
1971.

———. *Women in the Soviet Economy: Their Role in Economic,*   III S
Scientific and Technical Development. Baltimore: Johns Hopkins
University Press, 1966.

Elliot, Iain F. *The Soviet Energy Balance: Natural Gas, Other Fossil*   II T
Fuels and Alternative Power Sources. New York: Praeger, 1974.

Ellman, Michael. *Planning Problems in the USSR: The Contribution of*   III T
Mathematical Economics to their Solution, 1960-1971. London:
Cambridge University Press, 1973.

———. *Soviet Planning Today*. London: Cambridge University Press, 1971.   II G

Fischer-Galati, Stephen. *Twentieth Century Romania*. New York: I G
Columbia University Press, 1970.
Fitzlyon, K. "Plan and Prediction." *Soviet Studies* (October 1969).   II T
Flakierski, H. "Polish Postwar Economic Growth." (A Comment on   I G
Prof. Whalley's Article). *Soviet Studies* 27, no. 3 (July 1975).
Gado, Otto, ed. *Reform of the Economic Mechanism in Hungary:*   II T
Development 1968-1971. Budapest: Akademiaia Kiado, 1972.
Gamarnikow, M. "Comecon Today." *East Europe* 13 (3 March 1964).   II G
———. "A New Economic Approach." *Problems of Communism* (Septem-   I G
ber-October 1972): 21.
Gill, Richard Rockingham. "USSR Exploited by Comecon." *RFE*   II C
Research: Communist Area (June 2, 1966).
Gillette, Philip S. "Recent Trends in Soviet Trade." *Current History*   I G
67, no. 398 (October 1974): 169-72.
Goldman, Marshall I. "Soviet Economic Reform: Does It Still Have a   II C
Future?" *Current History* (November 1968).
———. "The Soviet Economy in a World of Shortages." *Current History*   I T
67, no. 398 (October 1974): 164-68.
———. "The Soviet Economy: New Era or Old Error?" *Current History*   II G
(October 1973): 168.
———. "The Soviet Dual Economy." *Current History* (October 1970).   II G
———. *The Spoils of Progress: Environmental Pollution in the Soviet*   II T
Union. Cambridge, Mass.: The M.I.T. Press, 1972.
Goldmann, Josef and Karel Kouba. *Economic Growth in Czechoslovakia*.   II S
White Plains, N.Y.: International Arts and Sciences Press, 1969.
———. *Economic Growth Under Socialism, Including an Experimental*   III S
Application of Klecki's Model to Czechoslovak Statistical Data.
Prague: 1969.
Gottheil, Fred M. *Marx's Economic Predictions*. Evanston, Ill.: North-   II C
western University Press, 1966.
Greenslade, Rush V. "The Soviet Economy in Transition." In *Joint*   II C
Economic Committee, New Directions in the Soviet Economy.
Washington, D.C.: U.S. Government Printing Office, 1966.
Greer, Thomas. *Marketing in the Soviet Union*. New York: Praeger, 1973.   I G
Gregory, Paul R. and Robert C. Stuart. *Soviet Economic Structure and*   II T
Performance. New York: Harper & Row, 1974.
Grossman, Gregory. "Economic Reform: A Balance Sheet." *Problems of*   I G
Communism 15, no. 6 (November-December 1966).
———. *Economic Systems*. Englewood Cliffs, N.J.: Prentice-Hall, 1967.
Guelfat, Issac. *Economic Thought in the Soviet Union—Concepts and*   II C
Aspects—A Comparative Outline. Liege: Martinus Alijhoff, 1969.
Hamiliton, F. E. Ian. *Yugoslavia: Patterns of Economic Activity*. New   II S
York: Praeger, 1968.

Hanson, Philip. *Advertising and Socialism. The Nature and Extent of*   II G
Consumer Advertising in the Soviet Union. London: Macmillan,
1974.

Hanson, Philip, Dr. "External Influences on the Soviet Economy Since   II T
the Mid-1950's Import of Western Technology." CRESS Discussion
Paper No. 7.

Hardt, John. "West Siberia: The Quest for Energy." *Problems of Com-*   I T
munism 22. Washington, D.C. (May/June 1973).

Hardt, John P.; Stanley H. Cohn; Dimitri M. Gallik; and Vladimir G.   III S
Theml. *Recent Soviet Economic Performance: Selected*
Aspects (Strategic Studies, Dept. Paper RAC-P-38). McLean, Va.:
Research Analysis Corp., 1968.

Hegedus, Andros and Maria Markus. "The Role of Values in the Long-   II T
range Planning of Distribution and Consumption." The Sociological
Review Monograph: Hungarian Sociological Studies. University of
Keele, 1972.

Held, Joseph. "Hungary: Iron Out of Wood." *Problems of Communism*   I G
15, no. 6 (November-December 1966).

Hoffman, George W. *Regional Development Strategy in Southeast Europe*.   II C
New York: Praeger, 1972.

Holesovsky, Vaclav. "Problems and Prospects." *Problems of Communism*   II G
14 (September-October).

Holt, Robert T. and John E. Turner. *The Political Basis of Economic*   II G
Development. Princeton, N.J.: Van Nostrand Reinhold, 1966.

Holzman, Franklyn D. "Some Notes on Over-Full Employment Planning,   III T
Short-run Balance and the Soviet Economic Reforms." *Soviet*
Studies (October 1970).

Horvat, Branco. *Business Cycles in Yugoslavia*. White Plains, N.Y.:   II T
International Arts and Sciences Press, 1971.

Hutchings, Raymond. *Soviet Economic Development*. New York: Oxford   II G
University Press, 1971.

Ingram, David. *The Communist Economic Challenge*. New York: Praeger,   II G
1965.

Janossey, Ferenc. *The End of Economic Miracles, Appearance and Reality*   II G
in Economic Development. Translated by Hedy Jellinek. White
Plains, N.Y.: International Arts and Sciences Press, 1972.

Jowitt, Kenneth. *Development: The Case of Romania 1944-1965*.   II G
Berkeley: University of California Press, 1971.

Kahrs, Karl H. "East Germany's New Economic System from the Point   II T
of View of Cybernetics." *East European Quarterly* (September
1972).

Kaser, Michael. *COMECON: Integration Problems of the Planned*   III T
Economics, 2d ed. London: Oxford University Press, 1967.

Kaser, Michael. *Soviet Economics*. New York: McGraw-Hill, 1970.   II G
Katz, Abraham. *The Politics of Economic Reform in the Soviet Union*   I G
New York: Praeger, 1972.
Kirschen, E.S., ed. *Economic Policies Compared: West and East*. Vol. 1:   II T
General Theory. New York: American Elsevier, 1974.
Kish, George. *Economic Atlas of the Soviet Union*. 2d rev. ed. Ann Arbor: II G
University of Michigan Press, 1971.
Korbonski, Andrzey. "Comecon." *International Cancellation* no. 549   II G
(September 1964).
Kramer, John M. "The Energy Gap in Eastern Europe." *Survey* 21, no. 1   I G
(Winter-Spring 1975): 65-78.
Krejci, Jaroslav. "Measurement of Aggregate Efficiency in the Czechoslovak II T
Economy." *Soviet Studies* 26, no. 4 (October 1974).
Lamberg, Robert. "The Comecon: Twenty Years Old and in Its Third   III G
Crisis." *Swiss Review of World Affairs* (March 1968).
Lange, Oskar and Fred M. Taylor. *On the Economic Theory of Socialism*.   II C
New York: McGraw-Hill, 1966.
Laulan, Yves, ed. *Exploitation of Siberia's Natural Resources*. Brussels: II G
NATO, Directorate of Economic Affairs, 1974.
———. *Prospects for Soviet Economic Growth in the 1970's*. Brussels: II S
NATO, 1971.
Levy, Marion J., Jr. *Mechanization: Latecomers and Survivors*. New   I G
York: Basic Books, 1972.
Lewih, Moshe. *Political Undercurrents in Soviet Economic Debates:*   II G
From Bukharin to the Modern Reformers. Princeton: Princeton
University Press, 1975.
Liberman, Evsey G. *Economic Methods and the Effectiveness of Pro-*   II T
duction. White Plains, N.Y.: International Arts and Sciences
Press, 1971.
———. "Plan-Profit-Premium." *Current Digest of the Soviet Press*   II G
(October 14, 1962).
Liberman, Yevsei. "The Soviet Economic Reform." *Foreign Affairs*   I G
(October 1967).
Lowenthal, Richard. "Development Versus Utopia in Communist Policy."   II G
Survey nos. 74/75 (Winter-Spring 1970).
Lyons, Eugene. *Workers Paradise Lost*. New York: Funk and Wagnalls,   II C
1967.
Mazour, Anatole G. *Soviet Economic Development, Operation Outstrip*   II T
1921-1965. Princeton, N.J..: Van Nostrand, 1967.
McMillan, Carl H. "Some Recent Developments in Soviet Foreign Trade."   I G
Canadian Slovanic Papers 12 (Fall 1970): 243-54.
McNally, Patrick. "Marxist Ideology and the Soviet Economy." *Studies in*   II C
Soviet Thought (SST) (September 1972).

Mellor, Roy E.H. *Eastern Europe: A Geography of the COMECON*   I G
   Countries. New York: Columbia University Press, 1975.
Mihailovic, Kosta. *Regional Development, Experiences and Prospects in*   II G
   Eastern Europe. U.N. Research Institute for Social Development,
   Geneva, vol. 4. The Hague: Mouton, 1972.
Mikoyan, S. "Economic Forum in Geneva." *International Affairs* no. 5   I G
   (May 1964).
Milenkovitch, Deborah D. *Plan and Market in Yugoslav Economic*   II G
   Thought. New Haven: Yale University Press, 1971.
Montias, J. Michael. *Economic Development in Communist Rumania*.   II G
   Cambridge: MIT Press, 1967.
Murgescu, Costin. *Romania's Socialist Economy*. Translated by Leon   II T
   Jaeger. Bucharest: Meridiane Publishing House, 1974.
Neal, Fred Warner and Winston M. Fish. "Yugoslavia: Towards a   I G
   Market Socialism." *Problems of Communism* 15, no. 6 (November-
   December 1966).
Neuberger, E. *Central Planning and its Legacies*. RAND P-3492, 1966.   III G
——. *The Legacies of Central Planning*. RAND RM-5530-PR, 1968.   III G
New Directions in the Soviet Economy. Five volumes. Washington: III T
   Joint Economic Committee of the U.S. Congress.
Nove, Alec. *An Economic History of the USSR*. Allan Lane Press, 1969.   I G
——. "Market Socialism and its Critics." *Soviet Studies* 24 (July 1,   II G
   1972).
——. *The Soviet Economy: An Introduction*. New York: Praeger, 1969.   I G
Novozhilov, V.V. *Problems of Cost-Benefit Analysis in Optimal Planning*.   III S
   White Plains, N.Y.: International Arts and Sciences Press, 1970.
Ofer, Gur. *The Service Sector in Soviet Economic Growth: A Com-*   II G
   parative Study. Cambridge: Harvard University Press, 1973.
Paul, Gregory. *Socialist and Non-Socialist Industrialization Patterns:*   III S
   A Comparative Appraisal. New York: Praeger, 1970.
Pejovich, Svetozar. *The Market-Planned Economy of Yugoslavia*. Minne-   II G
   apolis: University of Minnesota Press, 1966.
Polach, Jaroslav. "The Development of Energy in Eastern Europe." In   II T
   Joint Economic Committee, *Economic Developments in the
   Countries of Eastern Europe*. Washington, D.C.: Congress of the
   U.S.
——. "The Energy Gap in the Communist World." *East Europe* (April   I G
   18, 1969).
——. "Nuclear Power in East Europe." *East Europe* (May 1968): 3-12.   I T
Portes, Richard D. "The Tactics and Strategy of Economic Decentrali-   II C
   zation." *Soviet Studies*. April 1972.
Powell, Raymond P. "Economic Growth in the USSR." *Scientific*   II G
   American (December 1969).

Prybyia, Jan S. "The Soviet Economy." *Current History* (October 1972) I G
Pryde, Philip R. *Conservation in the Soviet Union*. London: Cambridge I T
University Press, 1972.
Pryor, Frederick L. "Barriers to Market Socialism in Eastern Europe in the II G
Mid-1960s." *Studies in Comparative Communism* 3, no. 2 (April
1970).
———. *Property and Industrial Organization in Communist and Capitalist* II T
Nations. Bloomington: Indiana University Press, 1974.
Raupach, Hans. "The Impact of the Great Depression in Eastern Europe." I G
Journal of Contemporary History (October 1969).
Roosa, Ruthe Amende. "United Russian Industry." *Soviet Studies* II G
(January 1973).
Rosen, Steven J. and James R. Kurth. *Testing Theories of Economic* I G
Imperialism. Farmborough, Mass.: Lexington Books, D.C. Heath,
1974.
Schaefer, Henry Wilcox. *Comecon and the Politics of Integration*. New I G
York: Praeger, 1972.
Selucky, Radoslav. *Economic Reforms in Eastern Europe: Political Back-* II G
ground and Economic Significance (Praeger Special Studies in
International Economics and Development). New York: Praeger,
1972.
Shabalin, A. "The Comprehensive Programme of Integration." *Inter-* I G
national Affairs no. 4 (April 1975): 14-20.
Shaffer, Harry G. "An Economic Model in Eclipse." *Problems of Com-* I G
munism (November-December 1968).
Sharlet, Robert S. *Building a Communist System: The Soviet Union as a* II G
Developing Country. New York: Pegasus, 1970.
Sharpe, Myron E., ed. *Planning, Profit and Incentives in the USSR*. II G
2 vols. White Plains, N.Y.: International Arts and Sciences Press,
1966.
Sherman, Howard J. "The Economics of Pure Communism." *Soviet Studies* II C
(July 1970).
———. *The Soviet Economy*. Boston: Little Brown & Co., 1969.
Sik, Ota. *Plan and Market Under Socialism*. White Plains, N.Y.: Inter- II G
national Arts and Sciences Press, 1967.
Simmons, Michael. "Western Technology and the Soviet Economy." *The* II G
World Today 31, no. 4 (April 1975): 166-72.
Simon, B. "The Economic Policy of the Communist Party of Czecho- III G
slovakia in Industry." *World Market Review* (July 1967).
Sirc, Ljubo. *Economic Devolution in Eastern Europe*. New York: Praeger, III G
1969.
Smelser, Neil J. "Notes on the Methodology of Comparative Analysis of II C
Economic Activity." *Social Science Information* (UNESCO) 6:
2-3 (April-June 1967).

Smolinski, Leon. "Towards a Socialist Corporation: Soviet Industrial   II T
Reorganization of 1973." *Survey* 20, no. 1 (Winter 1974): 24-35.

Sosnovy, Timothy. "The New Soviet Plan: Guns Still Before Butter."   I G
Foreign Affairs (1966).

Soviet National Income and Product 1958-1962. RAND RM-4394-PR   III S
part 1, 1965, RM-4881-PR part 2, 1966.

Spigler, Iancu. *Economic Reforms in Rumanian Industry*. London: Oxford   II T
University Press, 1973.

Spulber, Nicholas, ed. *Foundations of Soviet Strategy for Economic*   II T
Growth. Bloomington: University of Indiana Press, 1964.

———. *Soviet Strategy for Economic Growth*. Bloomington: University of   II C
Indiana Press, 1969.

———. "The Soviet Economy in the 1970's." *Current History* (October 1969)   I G

Sutton, Anthony C. *Western Technology and Soviet Economic Develop-*   II T
ment, 1945-1965. Volume 3 in a 3-volume series. Stanford, Calif.:
Hoover Institution Press, 1973.

———. *Western Technology and Soviet Economic Development 1945-1965*.   II T
Stanford, Calif.: Hoover Institution Press, 1975.

Timar, Janos. *Planning the Labor Force in Hungary*. White Plains, N.Y.:   II S
International Arts and Sciences Press, 1966.

Tlusty, Z. "Aggregate Growth Model: Projection of the Conditions for the   III T
Long-Term Growth of the Czechoslovak Economy." *Czechoslovak*
Papers (November 1968).

Treml, Vladimir G., ed. *The Development of the Soviet Economy: Plan*   II S
and Performance. New York: Praeger, 1968.

Treml, Vladimir G. and John P. Hardt, eds. *Soviet Economic Statistics*.   II S
Durham, N.C.: Duke University Press, 1972.

Treml, Vladimir; Dimitri M. Gallik; Barry L. Kostinsky; and Kurt W.   II G
Krager. *The Structure of the Soviet Economy*. New York:
Praeger, 1972.

Turek, O. "Czechoslovakia Economists on Planning and the Market Mech-   II G
anism Under Socialism." *World Marxist Review* (April 1968).

Soviet Economic Performance 1966-1967. Joint Economic Committee.
Washington: U.S. Congress, 1968.

Turner, Carl B. *An Analysis of Soviet Views of John Maynard Keynes*.   III C
Durham, N.C.: Duke University Press, 1969.

Ward, Benjamin. "Political Power and Economic Change in Yugoslavia."   II C
American Economic Review 58, no. 2 (May 1968).

Weissman, Benjamin M. *Herbert Hoover and Famine Relief to Soviet Russia,*   I T
1921-1923. Stanford, Calif.: Hoover Institution Press, 1974.

Weitzman, Phillip. "Soviet Long-term Consumption Planning: Distribu-   I G
tion According to Rational Need." *Soviet Studies* 26, no. 3 (July 1974):
305-21.

White, James D. "Moscow, Petersburg and the Russian Industrialists in   II G
Reply to Ruth Amende Rossa." *Soviet Studies* (January 1973).

Wilczynski, Josef. "Atomic Energy for Peaceful Purposes in the Warsaw   II T
Pact Countries." *Soviet Studies* 26 (October 1974) 386-90.

_____. *Socialist Economic Development and Reforms From Extensive to*   III T
Intensive Growth Under Central Planning in the USSR, Eastern
Europe and Yugoslavia. London: Macmillan, 1972.

_____. *Technology in COMECON: Acceleration of Technological Progress*   II T
through Economic Planning and the Market. New York:
Praeger, 1974.

Wolfson, Murray. *A Reappraisal of Marxian Economics.* New York: II C
Columbia University Press, 1966.

Wright, Arthur W. "The Soviet Economy." *Current History* 51, 302   II G
(October 1966).

Yanowitch, Murray. *Contemporary Soviet Economics, A Collection of*   III T
Readings from Soviet Sources. In two volumes. White Plains,
N. Y.: International Arts and Sciences Press, 1969.

"Yugoslavia: Democratic Centralism and Market Socialism." *The World*   II T
Today (April 1973).

Zaleski, Eugene. *Planning Reforms in the Soviet Union, 1962-1966: An*   III T
Analysis of Recent Trends in Economic Organization and
Management. Chapel Hill: University of North Carolina
Press, 1967.

Zielinski, Janusz G. *Economic Reforms in Polish Industry.* London: I T
Oxford University Press for the Institute of Soviet and East
European Studies, University of Glasgow, 1973.

– *On the Theory of Socialist Planning.* London: Oxford University   III C
Press, 1968.

Zinam, Oleg. "Soviet Regional Problems: Specialization versus Autarky."   III G
Russian Review (RR) (April 1972).

Price Structure

Anderson, S. *Soviet National Income, 1964-1966 in Established Prices.*   III S
RAND RM-5705-PR (1968).

Becker, Abrahm S. "The Price Level of Soviet Machinery in the 1960s."   I S
Soviet Studies 26, no. 3 (July 1974): 363-79.

Csirosnagy, Bela. *Pricing in Hungary.* Occasional Paper 19, Institute of   III T
Economic Affairs. London, 1968.

_____. *Socialist Price Theory and Price Policy.* Budapest: Akademiaki   I T
Kiado, 1975.

Hewett, Edward A. *Foreign Trade Prices in the Council for Mutual*   II T
Economic Assistance. London: Cambridge University
Press, 1974.

Kramer, John M. " Prices and the Conservation of Natural Resources   III S
in the Soviet Union." *Soviet Studies* (January 1973).

Lavelle, Michael J. "The Soviet 'New Method' Pricing Formulae."   II T
Soviet Studies 26, no. 1 (January 1974).

Marczewski, Jean. "The Role of Prices in a Planned Economy."   II S
Soviet Studies (July 1971).

Marer, P. *Postwar Pricing and Price Patterns in Socialist Foreign*   III S
Trade, (1946-1971). Bloomington: Indiana University
Press, 1972.

"Prices in Czechoslovakia's Trade with the EEC." *Foreign Press*   III G
Digest. Washington, D.C. (28 September 1967).

Schaefer, Henry. "A Note on Over-Full Employment Planning,   II G
Priorities and Prices." *Soviet Studies* (July 1971).

Schroeder, Gertrude. "The 1966-67 Soviet Industrial Price Reform: II S
A Study in Complications." *Soviet Studies* (April 1969).

Spechler, Martin C. "Decentralizing the Soviet Economy: Legal   II T
Regulation of Price and Quality." *Soviet Studies*
(October 1970).

Macroeconomic Levels (taxes, interest rates, and so on)

Abouchar, Alan. "The New Soviet Standard Methodology for Invest-   III T
ment Allocation." *Soviet Studies* (January 1973).

Adam, Jan. "Taxation of the Population in Czechoslovakia." *Soviet*   I T
Studies 26, no. 1 (January 1974).

Amacher, Ryan. *Yugoslavia's Foreign Trade.* New York: III S
Praeger, 1972.

Athay, Robert E. *The Economics of Soviet Merchant Shipping Policy.*   III T
Chapel Hill: University of North Carolina Press, 1971.

Banera, V. N. "Market Orientation of State Enterprises During NEP."   III T
Soviet Studies (July 1970).

Becker, A. S. *National Income Accounting in the USSR.* RAND P   III T
4223-Series P-4223-1969-72.

Bergson, Abram. "The Comparative National Income of the USSR and   III T
the United States." In Conference on Research in Income and
Wealth, National Bureau of Economic Research, *Interna-*   III S
tional Comparisons of Prices and Output. New York:
Columbia University Press, 1972.

Brown, Emily Clark. *Soviet Trade Unions and Labor Relations.*   III T
    Cambridge: Harvard University Press, 1966.

Brown, J. F. "Reforms in Bulgaria." *Problems of Communism*   II G
    15 (May-June 1965).

Brubaker, Earl R. "The Age of Capital and Growth in the Soviet   III T
    Non-agricultural Non-residential Sector." *Soviet*
    Studies (January 1970).

Bush, Keith. 'Environmental Disruption: The Soviet Response."   II G
    Radio Liberty Research Paper #48, New York, 1972.

_____. "Environmental Problems in the USSR." *Problems of*   I G
    Communism 21, no. 4 (July-August 1972).

_____. "The Returns: A Balance Sheet." *Problems of Communism*   IIG
    (July-August 1967).

Campbell, Robert W. *The Economics of Soviet Oil and Gas.*   III T
    Baltimore: Johns Hopkins Press, 1968.

Carter, James Richard. *The Net Cost of Soviet Foreign Aid.*   II S
    New York: Praeger, 1973.

The Soviet Military Technological Challenge. Washington, Center for   II T
    Strategic Studies, Georgetown University, 1967, (Special
    Report Series no. 6).

Chapman, Janet. *Wage Variation in Soviet Industry*. Santa Monica,   III S
    California: Rand Corporation Memorandum, RM-6076-PR,
    1970.

"Comprehensive Program." Adopted by 25th Session of Council for   II S
    Mutual Economic Assistance at Bucharest in July 1971
    (translation). *Soviet and East European Foreign Trade.*
    White Plains, N. Y. (Fall-Winter 1971-72).

Conolly, Violet. *Beyond the Urals: Economic Developments in*   III T
    Soviet Asia. London: Oxford University Press, 1967.

"The Crisis in the Soviet Raw Materials Base." *The Many Crises*   II T
    of the Soviet Economy. U. S. Congress, Senate, Committee
    on the Judiciary, 88th Congress, 2d Session (1964).

Davies, R. W. *The Development of the Soviet Budgetary System.*   II G
    London: Cambridge University Press, 1973.

Dellin, L. A. D. "Bulgarian Economic Reform—Advance and   II G
    Retreat." *Problems of Communism* 19, no. 5 (September-
    October 1970).

Dienes, Leslie. "Issues in Soviet Energy Policy and Conflicts Over   III T
    Fuel Costs in Regional Development." *Soviet Studies*
    (July 1971).

    Dimitrijcvic, Dimitrijc and George Moresich, eds. *Money and*
    Finance in Contemporary Yugoslavia. New York: Praeger, 1973.

Economic Performance and the Military Burden on the Soviet Union.   II S
    Washington, D.C.: Joint Economic Committee, U. S. Congress,
    U. S. Government Printing Office, 1970.

Ellman, Michael. *Economic Reform in the Soviet Union.* REP Press   III S
    vol. 35. Brandstreet 509 Planning (1969).

Ernst, Maurice. "Postwar Economic Growth in Eastern Europe." In   II T
    U. S. Congress, Joint Economic Committee. *New Directions
    in the Soviet Economy.* Washington, D. C., 1966, pp.
    875-916.

Fallenbuchl, Z. M. "Comecon Integration." *Problems of Communism*   II G
    22 (March-April 1973).

_____ "Investment Policy for Economic Development: Some Lessons   II T
    of the Communist Experience." *The Canadian Journal of
    Economics and Political Science* 1 (1963).

_____ "Some Structural Aspects of the Soviet-type Investment   II T
    Policy." *Soviet Studies* (Glasgow) (April 1965).

Farrell, John P. "Bank Control of the Wage Fund in Poland."   I T
    Soviet Studies 27, no. 2 (April 1975): 265-87.

Feiwel, George R. *New Currents in Soviet-type Economies.*   II G
    Scranton, Pa: International Textbook Company, 1968.

_____ *New Economic Patterns in Czechoslovakia.* New York: II G
    Praeger, 1968.

_____ *The Soviet Quest for Economic Efficiency, Issues,*   III G
    Controversies and Reforms. New York: Praeger 1972.

Felker, Jere. *Soviet Economic Controversies: The Emerging Marketing*   III S
    Concept and Changes in Planning. 1960-1965, MIT.

Frankel, Theodore. "Economic Reform: A Tentative Appraisal."   I G
    Problems of Communism (May-June 1967).

Friedmann, Wolfgang, "Freedom and Planning in Yugoslavia's Economic   II C
    System." *Slavic Review* 25, no. 4 (December 1966).

Friss, I. *Reform of the Economic Mechanism in Hungary.* Budapest: II T
    Akademia Kiado, 1969.

Furubotn, Eirik G. "Bank Credit and the Labor-managed Firm: The   I T
    Yugoslav Case." *Canadian (American) Slavic Studies* 8, no. 1
    (Spring): 89-105.

Garmarnikow, Michael. *Economic Reforms in Eastern Europe.*   II T
    Detroit, Michigan: Wayne State University Press, 1968.

_____ "Industrial Cooperation: East Europe Looks West."   I G
    Problems of Communism 20, no. 3 (May-June 1971).

_____ "A New Economic Approach." *Problems of Communism*   I G
    21, no. 5 (September-October 1972).

_____ "Poland Returns to Economic Reform." *East Europe.*   I T
    New York (November-December 1969).

———. "The Polish Economy in Transition." *Problems of Communism*   I G
19, no. 1 (January-February 1970).
———. "Political Pattern and Economic Reforms." *Problems of Communism* II C
18, no. 2 (March-April 1969).
Garibit, Jerzy. "The Polish Economy: Models and Muddles." *Survey*   II T
17, no. 3 (Summer 1971).
Garvy, George. *Money, Banking and Credit in Eastern Europe.* New York: III S
Federal Reserve Bank of New York.
Giffen, James Henry. *The Legal and Practical Aspects of Trade with the*   I G
Soviet Union. New York: Praeger, 1969.
Goldman, Marshall. "Economic Revolution in the Soviet Union." *Foreign*   III G
Affairs 45, no. 2 (January 1967): 319-32.
———. "Externalities and the Race for Economic Growth in the USSR: II G
Will the Environment Ever Win?" *ASTE Bulletin.* Washington,
D. C. (Spring 1971).
———. "The Reluctant Consumer and Economic Fluctuations in the   III S
Soviet Union." *Journal of Political Economy* 73, no. 4
(August 1965): 366-80.
———. "Soviet Economic Growth Since the Revolution." *Current*   II S
History (October 1967).
———. *Soviet Foreign Aid.* New York: Praeger, 1967.   I G
———. *The Spoils of Progress.* Cambridge : M. I. T. Press, 1972.   II G
Grdjic, G. "Comparative Computations of Yugoslav National Income   III S
According to Material and Comprehensive Concepts of Produc-
tion." *Journal of Economic Abstracts* (June 1967).
Gregory, Paul R. "Some Indirect Estimates of Eastern European Capital   II T
Stocks and Factor Productivity." *Soviet Studies* 27, no. 1
(January 1975).
Hanson, Philip. *The Consumer in the Soviet Economy.* London: II T
Macmillan, 1968.
Hardt, John P. and V. G. Treml, eds. *Soviet Economic Statistics.*   III S
Durham, N. C.: Duke University Press, 1972.
———. "West Siberia: The Quest for Energy." *Problems of Communism*   I G
(May-June 1973).
Heldman, Dan. C. "The Need for Controls." *Problems of Communism*   I G
16, no. 1 (January-February 1967).
Hoeffding, O. *Recent Structural Changes and Balance of Payments*   III S
Adjustments in Soviet Foreign Trade (Euro Trade). RAND-P-
3601 (1967).
Hoffman, George W. *Regional Development Strategy in Southeast*   II G
*Europe: A Comparative Analysis of Albania, Bulgaria, Greece,
Romania and Yugoslavia.* New York: Praeger, 1972.

Holesovsky, Vaclav. "Labor and the Economic Reforms in   III G
   Czechoslovakia." University of Massachusetts Labor
   Relations and Research Center (April 1968): 2-6.
Holland, W. B. , ed. *Soviet Cybernetic Review*, "Soviet R & D   III T
   Redirected: Academy of Science Annual Meeting
   Reports." RAND RM 6200/*-PR (September 1970).
———. *Soviet Cybernetics Review*. RAND Series RM 6000 PR.   III T
   1967-1969 RM 6200 PR (1970).
Hooson, David. "The Outlook for Regional Development in the Soviet   III G
   Union." *Slavic Review* 31, no. 3 (September 1972).
Horvat, Branko. *Business Cycles in Yugoslavia.* Translated by Helen   II S
   M. Kramer. White Plains, N. Y.: International Arts and
   Sciences Press, 1971.
Horvath, Janos. "Economic Aid Flow from the USSR: A Recount of   II G
   the First Fifteen Years." *Slavic Review* (December 1970).
Hunter, Holland. *Soviet Transport Experience: Its Lessons for*   III T
   Other Countries. Washington, D. C.: The Brookings
   Institution, 1968.
Hutchings. Raymond. "Periodic Fluctuation in Soviet Industrial   IIIS
   Growth Rates." *Soviet Studies* (January 1969).
———. "Soviet Defence Spending and Soviet External Relations."   II G
   International Affairs 47, no. 3 (July 1971).
Jasny, Naum. *Soviet Economists of the Twenties: Names to be*   II G
   Remembered. London: Cambridge University Press, 1972.
Jaster, R. S. "CEMA's Influence on Soviet Policies in Eastern   II G
   Europe." *World Politics* 14, no. 3 (April 1962).
Johnson, Arthur J. "Rumania-Soviet Polemics: An Escalation of   I G
   Pressures on Bucharest?" Radio Free Europe Research
   report (April 22, 1970).
"Joint Investments by Yugoslav and Foreign Economic Organi-   II S
   zations." *Yugoslav News Bulletin.* New York, no. 438
   (December 1972): 7.
Jordan, Lloyd. "R & D in Bucharest." *Survey* no. 76   III T
   (Summer 1970).
Jowitt, Kenneth. *Revolutionary Breakthrough and National*   II G
   Development, The Case of Romania, 1944-65. Berkeley:
   University of California Press, 1971.
Judy, Richard W. "The Case of Computer Technology." In Stanislaw   III T
   Wasowski, ed., *East-West Trade and the Technology Gap:*
   A Political and Economic Appraisal. New York, 1970, pp.
   43-72.
Kaplan, N. "The Retardation in Soviet Growth." *The Journal of*   II G
   Economic Abstracts 6, no. 4 (1968).

Kaplan, N. M. *Earnings Distributions in the USSR*. RAND RM   III S
6170 (November 1969).

———. *The Record of Soviet Economic Growth*. Santa Monica,   II S
RAND Corporation, RM-6169 (November 1969).

Kaser, Michael. "COMECON: Organization, Function."   II G
World Today (April 1972).

Katz, Abraham. *The Politics of Economic Reform in the Soviet*   II G
Union. New York: Praeger, 1972.

Kautsky, John. *Communism and the Politics of Development*.   II G
New York: Wiley & Sons, 1968.

———. "Communism and the Comparative Study of Development."   II C
Slavic Review 26, no. 1 (March 1967).

Kelzer, Williem. *The Soviet Quest for Economic Nationality:*   III G
The Conflict of Economic and Political Aims in the
Soviet Economy, 1953-1968. Rotterdam: UP, 1971.

Kerschner, Lee. "Cybernetics: Key to the Future." *Problems*   I T
of Communism 14 (November-December 1965).

Kirsch, Leonard Joel. *Soviet Badges*. Cambridge: The MIT   II S
Press, 1972.

Klatt, Werner. "The Politics of Economic Reforms." *Survey*   II G
70-71 (Winter-Spring 1969).

Kish, George. *Economic Atlas of the Soviet Union*. Ann Arbor: I G
University of Michigan Press, 1971.

Koral, Alexander. *Soviet Research and Development: Its*   III S
Organization, Personnel and Funds. Cambridge, Mass.:
MIT, 1965.

Kohler, Heinz. *Economic Integration in the Soviet Bloc: With*   II T
an East German Case Study. New York: Praeger, 1965.

Kouba, Karel. *Economic Growth in Czechoslovakia: An Introduc-*   II C
tion to the Theory of Economic Growth under
Socialism. Prague: 1965.

Kretschmar, Robert S., Jr. and Robin Foor. *The Potential for*   III T
Joint Ventures in Eastern Europe. New York:
Praeger, 1972.

Marek, Antoni. "The Draft for a New Wage System in Poland."   II T
Radio Free Europe Research Report, April 1, 1970.

McAuley, Mary. *Labor Disputes in Soviet Russia 1957-1965*.   III T
Oxford: Clarendon Press, 1969.

McMillan, C. H. "Soviet Specialization and Trade in Manufactures."   II G
Soviet Studies (April 1973).

Mieczkowski, Bogdan. "Estimates of Changes in Real Wages in   II S
Poland During the 1960's." *Slavic Review* 31, no. 3
(September 1972).

Miller, Dorothy and H. G. Trend. "Economic Reforms in East   II G
    Germany." *Problems of Communism* 15, no. 2 (March-
    April 1966): 29-36.

Montias, John Michael. "Background and Origins of the Rumanian   II G
    Dispute with Comecon." *Soviet Studies* 16, no. 2
    (October 1964).

_____. "Obstacles to the Economic Integration of Eastern Europe."   II G
    Studies in Comparative Communism 3, no. 4 (July-October
    1969): 38-60.

Mueller, G. and H. Singer. "Hungary: Can the New Crane Survive?"   II G
    Problems of Communism 14 (January-February 1965).

Nagy, Karoly. "Hungary's Alienated Workers." *Problems of*   I G
    Communism (July-August 1966).

Newth, J. A. "The 1970 Soviet Census." *Soviet Studies*   II S
    (October 1972).

North, Robert N. "Soviet Northern Development: The Case of NW   II G
    Siberia." *Soviet Studies* (October 1972).

Nove, Alec. *Economic Rationality and Soviet Politics.*   II C
    New York: 1964.

Pearton, Maurice. *Oil and the Romanian State.* Oxford: II T
    Clarendon Press, 1971.

Pervushin, S. P., et. al. *Production Accumulation and Consumption.*   III T
    White Plains, New York: International Arts and Sciences
    Press, 1967.

Podolski, T. M. *Socialist Banking and Monetary Control: The*   II T
    Experience of Poland. London: Cambridge University
    Press, 1973.

Polack, J. "Nuclear Energy in Czechoslovakia: A Study in   II T
    Frustration." *Orbis* (Fall 1968).

Pommer, H. J. "Reforms in Eastern Europe: Report on a Confer-   I G
    ence." *Problems of Communism* 15 (September-October 1966).

Projection of the Population of the USSR by Age and Sex 1969 to   III S
    1970. U. S. Department of Commerce, Washington, D. C.
    Series P-91, December 1969.

Rausch, Howard. "Soviet Technology." *The Atlantic* 223, no. 2   I G
    (February 1969): 29-35.

Pryde, Philip R. *Conservation in the Soviet Union.* London: Cambridge   II G
    University Press, 1972.

Riabchikov, Evgeny. *Russians in Space.* Garden City: Doubleday, 1971.   II G

Sandor, E. "Hope and Caution." *Problems of Communism*   I G
    19 no. 1 (January-February 1970).

Schaefer, Henry. "Rumania's Economic Turn to the East." Rumanian   II G
    Background Report no. 7. Radio Free Europe Research (EERA),
    March 4, 1971.

Schroeder, Gertrude E. "Soviet Economic Reform at an Impasse."   II G
      Problems of Communism (July-August 1971).
_____ "Soviet Technology: System vs. Progress." *Problems of*   II G
      Communism 19, no. 5 (September-October 1970).
Schwarz, Harry. "Comecon Clouds Hint at a Storm." New York   I G
      Times (August 7, 1966).
_____ "Soviet Asks East Bloc Members to Pay for the Use of   I G
      Technology." New York *Times* (November 17, 1966).
Selucky, Radoslav. *Economic Reforms in Eastern Europe.*   III T
      Translated by Zdeneh Elihs. New York: Praeger, 1972.
Shabad, Theodore. *Basic Industrial Resources of the USSR.*   II G
      New York: Columbia University Press, 1969.
Shaffer, Harry G. and Jan S. Pryby, eds. *From Underdevelopment*   III G
      to Affluence: Western Soviet and Chinese Views.
      Appleton-Century-Crofts, 1963.
Shaffer, Harry G. "Out of Stalinism." And V. Holesovsky. "Problems   II G
      and Prospects." In "Czechoslovakia's New Economic Model."
      Problems of Communism 14, no. 5 (September-October 1965).
_____ "Progress in Hungary." *Problems of Communism* 19
      (January-February 1970).
Shalton, William. *Soviet Space Exploration: The First Decade.*   II G
      New York: Washington Square Press, 1968.
Shechy, Anne. "Population Changes in the Baltic States."   III S
      East Europe, no. 4 (1965).
_____ "Some Aspects of Regional Development in Soviet Central   II T
      Asia." *Slavic Review* 31, no. 3, (September 1972).
Sik, Ota. "The Economic Impact of Stalinism." *Problems of*   II G
      Communism 20, no. 3 (May-June 1971).
Skurski, Roger. "The Factor Proportions Problem in Soviet Internal   II T
      Trade." *Soviet Studies* (January 1972).
Smith, Canfield F. "The Rocky Road to Communist Unity."   I G
      East Europe 18, no. 2 (February 1969): 3-10.
Spulber, Nicholas, ed. *Foundations of Soviet Strategy for Economic*   III T
      Growth: Selected Soviet Essays 1924-30. Bloomington:
      Indiana University Press, 1969.
Sukijasovic, Miodrag. *Foreign Investment in Yugoslavia.* Dobbs   II G
      Ferry, N. Y.: Oceana Publications, Inc., 1970.
_____ *Yugoslav Foreign Investment Legislation at Work:*   III T
      Experiences So Far. Dobbs Ferry, N. Y.: Oceana Publi-
      cations, 1970.
Sutton, Anthony C. *Western Technology and Soviet Economic*   II G
      Development 1917-1930. Stanford, Calif.: Hoover
      Institution, 1968.

Swainiewicz, S. *Forced Labour and Economic Development.*   II G
London: Oxford University Press (for the Royal Institute of International Affairs), 1965.

Taagepera, Reini. "National Differences within Soviet Demographic   II S
Trends." *Soviet Studies* (April 1969).

Treml, Vladimir G. "A Note on Soviet Input-output Tables."   II S
Soviet Studies (July 1969).

Treml, Vladimir G. and John P. Hardt, eds. *Soviet Economic*   III S
Statistics. Durham, N. C.: Duke University Press 1972.

Uren, Philip E. "Economic Relations Among the Communist States."   II C
*The Communist States at the Crossroads: Between Moscow
and Peking.* New York: 1965.

Wasowoski, Stanislaw, ed. *East-West Trade and the Technology Gap:*   II G
A Political and Economic Appraisal. New York: Praeger, 1970.

Weinstein, E. K. *The Soviets Try, Try Again: The Soviet Economy*   II G
and the New Return. RAND P-3399, 1966.

Wieczinski, Joseph L. *Economic Consequences of Disarmament:*   III G
The Soviet View. RR (July 1968).

Willver, Charles K. "A Non-monetary Index of Economic Develop-   III S
ment." *Soviet Studies* 17 (April 1966).

Wiles, P. J. D. *Communist International Economics.* New York: I G
Praeger, 1969.

Wiles, P. J. D., ed. *The Prediction of Communist Economic*   II G
Performance. New York: Cambridge University Press, 1971.

Zaleski, E., et al. *Science Policy in the USSR.* Paris: Organization   II G
for Economic Cooperation and Development, 1969.

Zwass, Adam. *Monetary Cooperation Between East and West.* White   II T
Plains, New York: International Arts and Sciences Press, 1975.

Management Principles

Broekmeyer, M. J., ed. *Yugoslav Workers' Self Management.* Boston: I G
Dordrecht D. Reidel Publishing Co., 1970.

Campbell, Robert W. "Management Spillovers from Soviet Space   III T
and Military Programmes." *Soviet Studies* (April 1972).

Conyngham, William J. *Industrial Management in the Soviet Union.*   II T
Stanford, Calif.: Hoover Institution, 1973.

Dolquchits, L. A. "Pre-service and In-service Managerial Training for   III T
Industry and Building in the Byelorussian SSR." *International
Social Service Journal* 20, no. 1 (1968).

Dragicevic, Adolf. "Self-management and the Market Economy."   II C
Socialist Thought and Practice 30 (1968).

Feshbach, Murray. "Soviet Society in Manpower Management." II T
  Problems of Communism (November-December 1974): 25-33.
Geza, Peter Lauter. *Manager and Economic Reform in Hungary.* II T
  New York: Praeger, 1972.
Grossman, Gregory. "Innovation and Information in the Soviet III T
  Economy." *American Economic Review* 56, no. 2
  (May 1966).
_____."Invitation and Information in the Soviet Economy." II G
  American Economic Review (May 1966).
Guroff, Gregory. *The Legacy of the Pre-revolutionary Economic* II G
  Education: The St. Petersburg Polytechnic Institute.
  (*Russian Review*) July 1972.
Hardt, John P., et al. *mathematics and Computers in Soviet Economic* III T
  Planning. New Haven: Yale University Press, 1967.
Hutchings, Raymond. *Seasonal Influences in Soviet Industry.* London: III S
  Oxford University Press, 1971.
Jackson, Marvin R. "Information and Incentives in Planning Soviet III T
  Investment Projects." *Soviet Studies* (July 1971).
Jendrychowski, S. "The New System of Planning and Management in III T
  Poland." *World Marxist Review* (December 1967).
Kaser, Michael and Janusz G. Zielinski. *Planning in East Europe:* III T
  Industrial Management by the State. London: The Bodley
  Head, 1970.
Manerich, Efim. "The Management of Soviet Manpower." *Foreign* I G
  Affairs (October 1968).
Osipov, G. V. *Industry and Labor in the USSR.* London: Tavistock I T
  Publications, 1966.
Richman, Bairym. *Soviet Management.* Englewood Cliffs, N. J.: II G
  Prentice-Hall, 1965.
Ryavec, Karl W. "Soviet Industrial Management: Challenge and Res- II G
  ponse, 1965-1970." *Canadian Slavic Studies* 5, no. 2
  (Summer 1971).
_____ "Soviet Industrial Management, the Communist Party, and II G
  the Economic Reform: The First Two Years." *The Western*
  Political Quarterly (September 1970).
_____ "Soviet Industrial Managers, Their Superiors and the Eco- II G
  nomic Reform." *Soviet Studies* (October 1969).
Sanardziga, Milos and George Klein. "A Perspective View of Self- III G
  management in a Socialist Context." *Studies in Comparative*
  Communism 4, nos. 3 and 4 (July-October 1971): 105-10.
"The Science of Management: Three Levels." *CDSP* 25, no. 16 III T
  (6 June 1973).

Sharp, Samuel L. "The Yugoslav Experiment in Self-Management: II G
   Soviet Criticism." *Studies in Comparative Communism* 4, nos.
   3 and 4 (July-October 1971): 169-78.
Spulber, Nicolas. *Socialist Management and Planning.* Bloomington: II G
   Indiana University Press, 1971.
Staller, George. "Czechoslovakia: The New Model of Planning and   III T
   Management." *American Economic Review* (May 1968).
Vasilev, S. "Operating the New Economic System in Sovia." *World*   II S
   Marxist Review (December 1967).

Organization

Adizer, Ichak. *Industrial Democracy: Yugoslav Style: The Effect*   III T
   of Decentralization on Organizational Behavior. New York:
   The Free Press, 1971.
Banks, J. A. *Marxist Sociology in Action: A Sociological Critique*   III S
   of the Marxist Approach to Industrial Relations. Harrisburg,
   Pa.: Stackpole Books, 1970.
Bartol, M. "Soviet Computer Centres: Network or Tangle?" *Soviet*   III T
   Studies (April 1972).
Berliner, Joseph. "Soviet Economy-discussion." *American Economic*   I G
   Review (May 1966).
Bonhelles, Joseph T. *Economic Development of Communist*   II T
   Yugoslavia. Stanford, Calif.: 1968.
Cohn, Stanley H. "Soviet Growth Retardation: Trends in Resources   III T
   Availability and Efficiency." *New Directives in the Soviet*
   Economy pt. II A. U. S. Congress, Washington, D. C.
   (1966): 99-132.
Dryll-Gutkowska, I. "The Polish United Workers' Party District   III C
   Committee's Directive Role with Regard to Industry."
   Polish Sociological Bulletin 16, no. 2 (1967).
Fallenbuchl, Z. M. "Collectivization and Economic Development."   II T
   The Canadian Journal of Economics and Political Science
   33, no. 1 (February 1967).
———. "The Communist Pattern of Industrialization." *Soviet Studies*   II T
   (Glasgow) (April 1970).
Feshbach, Murray. "Manpower in the USSR: A Survey of Recent   I T
   Trends and Prospects." *New Directions in the Soviet*
   Economy pt. 3. Washington, D.C., U.S. Congress Joint
   Economic Committee, U. S. Government Printing
   Office, 1966.

Feshbach, Murray, and Stephen Rapawy. "Labor Constraints in the   II T
    Soviet Economic Prospects for the Seventies. U. S. Congress,
    Joint Economic Committee, Washington, D. C., U. S.
    Government Printing Office, 1973, pp. 485-563.
Galbraith, John Kenneth. *The New Industrial State.* New York: I C
    Houghton-Mifflin, 1967.
Gill, Richard Rockingham. "A Case for Economic Convergence."   II T
    Studies in Comparative Communism (April 1969) pp.: 34-47.
Gorlin, Alice C. "The Soviet Economic Associations." *Soviet Studies*   I C
    26, no. 1 (January 1974): 3-27.
Gregory, Paul. *Socialist and Non-Socialist Industrialization Patterns.*   II G
    New York: Praeger, 1970.
Halm, G. "Miscs, Lange, Libermann: Allocation and Motivation in the   II G
    Socialist Economy." *The Journal of Economic Abstracts*
    6, no. 3 (1968).
Heymann, H. Jr. *The Objectives of Transportation in Economic Develop-*   III T
    ment (Trans-planning in USSR). RAND P-2836, 1968.
Hough, Jerry F. *The Soviet Prefects: The Local Party Organs in Indus-*   II S
    trial Decision-making. Cambridge: Harvard University Press, 1969.
Liberman, G. *Economic Methods and the Effectiveness of Production.*   II T
    Translated by Arlo Schultz. White Plains, N. Y.: International
    Arts and Sciences Press, 1972.
Pryor, Frederic. *Property and Industrial Organization in Communist*   II T
    and Capitalist Nations (IDRCSD, No. 7). Bloomington: Indiana
    University Press, 1975.
"Resolution on Industrial Associations." *The Current Digest of the*   II T
    Soviet Press (CDSP) 25, no. 14 (2 May 1973).
Schroeder, Gertrude E. "The Reform of the Supply System in Soviet   II T
    Industry." *Soviet Studies* 24, no. 1 (July 1972).
Ward, Benjamin N. *The Socialist Economy: A Study of Organiza-*
    tional Alternatives. New York: Random House, 1967.
Wilczynski, J. *Profit, Risk and Incentives under Socialist Economic*   II G
    Planning. London: Macmillan, 1973.

2. POST-INDUSTRIAL SOCIETY: POLITICAL STABILITY AND SOCIAL CHANGE DURING THE SECOND INDUSTRIAL REVOLUTION

Nature of Socialism

Academy of the Socialist Republic of Romania. *The Revolution in*   III T
    Science and Technology and Contemporary Social Development.

Bucharest: Editura Academie Republicii Socialiste Romania, 1974.

Adams, Jan S. "Peoples' Control in the Soviet Union." *The Western*   II G
Political Quarterly (December 1967).

Altayer, O. A. "Samizdat: Intelligentsia and Pseudo-Culture."   II C
Survey 19, no. 1 (Winter 1973).

Ames, Kenneth. "Reform and Reaction." *Problems of Communism*   II C
(November-December 1968).

Aury, Phyllis. "The Origins of National Communism in Yugoslavia."   II C
Government and Opposition (Spring 1969).

Avineri, Shlomo. *The Social and Political Thought of Karl Marx.*   II G
London: Cambridge University Press, 1968.

Bakaric, Vladimir. "The Kind of League We Need." *Socialist Thought*   I C
and Practice no. 28 (October-December 1967): 48-67.

Billington, James H. *The Icon and the Axe.* New York: Alfred A.   II G
Knopf, 1966.

Brown, J. F. *The New Eastern Europe: The Khrushchev Era and*   II G
After. New York: Praeger, 1966.

————. "East Europe: The Soviet Grip Loosens." *Survey* no. 57   II G
(October 1965): 14-25.

Brzezinski, Zbigniew. *The Soviet Bloc: Unity and Conflict.*   II G
3d ed. Cambridge: Harvard University Press, 1967.

Ceausescu, N. *Rumania on the Way of Building up a Multilaterally*   II G
Developed Society. Bucharest: Meridiane Publishing House,
1973.

Childs, David. *East Germany.* New York: Praeger, 1969.   I G

Davies, R. W. "A Note on Defence Aspects of the Ural-Kuznetsk   II T
Combine." *Soviet Studies* 26, no. 2 (April 1974): 272-73.

Eissenstat, Bernard W. *Lenin and Leninism: State, Law and*   II C
Society. Lexington, Mass.: Lexington Books, 1971.

Friedrich, Carl J. and Zbigniew Brzezinski. *Totalitarian Dictator-*   II C
ship and Autocracy. 2d ed. Cambridge: Harvard University
Press, 1965.

Friedrich, Carl J. "Totalitarianism Recent Trends." *Problems of*   I C
Communism 17, no. 3 (May-June 1968).

Gilison, Jerome M. *The Soviet Image of Utopia.* Baltimore: Johns   I G
Hopkins Press, 1975.

Golan, Galia. *The Czechoslovak Reform Movement: Communism*   II G
in Crisis, 1962-1968. London: Cambridge University
Press, 1971.

————. *Reform Rule in Czechoslovakia.* London: Cambridge   II G
University Press, 1973.

————. "The Road to Reform." *Problems of Communism*   I G
20, no. 3 (May-June 1971).

_____ "The Short-Lived Liberal Experiment in Czechoslovak   I G
Socialism." *Orbis.* Philadelphia (Winter 1970).

Granick, David. "The Orthodox Model of the Socialist Enterprise in   III C
the Light of Romanian Experience." *Soviet Studies* 26, no. 2
(April 1974): 205-23.

Hale, Julian. *Ceaucescu's Romania.* London: Harrays, 1971.   I G

Harnhardt, Arthur M., Jr. *The German Democratic Republic.*   II G
Baltimore: The Johns Hopkins Press, 1968.

Harris, Chauncy D. *Cities of the Soviet Union, Studies in their*   III T
Functions, Size, Density and Growth. Skokie, Ill.: Rand
McNally, 1970.

Hook, Sidney. "Fifty Years After." *Problems of Communism*   I C
(March-April 1967).

Horecky, Paul G., ed. *Russia and the Soviet Union.* Bibliography.   II G
Chicago: University of Chicago Press, 1965.

Horelick, A. L. *The Soviet Union in 1970.* RAND P 4583   II T
(February 1971).

Hudson, G. F. *Fifty Years of Communism: Theory and Practice*   II G
1917-1967. New York: Basic Books, Inc., 1968.

Ignotus, Paul. *Hungary.* New York: Praeger, 1972.   I G

Joravsky, David. "The Debacle of Lysenkoism." *Problems of*   I G
Communism 14 (November-December 1965).

_____ *The Lysenko Affair.* Cambridge: Harvard University   II G
Press, 1970.

Jowitt, Kenneth. "The Concepts of Liberalization and Rationali-   II T
zation in Eastern Europe." *Studies in Comparative Communism*
(April 1971): 79-91.

_____ "More on Liberalization, Rationalization, and Integration: II G
A Rejoinder." *Studies in Comparative Communism* (April
1971): 108-18.

Kassof, Allen. "The Administered Society: Totalitarianism Without   II T
Terror." *World Politics* 16, no. 4 (July 1969).

Kassof, Allen, ed. *Prospects for Soviet Society.* New York: II G
Praeger, 1967.

Katz, Zev. "Sociology in the Soviet Union." *Problems of Communism*   II C
(May-June 1971): 22-40.

Kirsch, Leonard Joel. *Soviet Wages: Changes in Structure and*   I S
Administration Since 1956. Cambridge: MIT Press, 1972.

Koutassoff, Elisabeth. *The Soviet Union.* London: Ernest Benn,   I G
1971.

Kroszewski, Z. Anthony. *The Oder-Nesse Boundary and Poland's*   II T
Modernization: The Socio-economic and Political Impact.
New York: Praeger, 1972.

Levi, Arrigo. "The Evolution of the Soviet System." *Problems of*   I G
    Communism 16 (January-February 1967).
Levine, Issac Don. "Within Russia? The Crisis Ahead." *Problems of*   I G
    Communism 16 (January-February 1967).
Lindemann, Albert S. *The Red Years: European Socialism Versus*   I G
    Bolshevism, 1919-1921. Berkeley: University of California
    Press, 1974.
London, Kurt L., ed. *The Soviet Union.* Baltimore: Johns Hopkins   II G
    Press, 1968.
Ludz, Peter C. "Discovery and Recognition of East Germany: Recent   II G
    Literature on the GDR." *Comparative Politics* 2, no. 4
    (1969-70).
_____. *The German Democratic Republic from the Sixties to the*   II G
    Seventies. Cambridge: Harvard Center for International
    Affairs, 1970.
Manescu, Corneliu. "Romania in the Concept of Nations." *Inter-*   I G
    national Affairs (January 1969).
Marczewski, Jan. *Crisis in Socialist Planning: Eastern Europe and the*   II G
    USSR. New York: Praeger, 1974.
Matley, Ian M. *Romania: A Profile.* New York: Praeger, 1970.   I G
Mayer, Robert; Robert Monroney; and Robert Morris. *Centrally*   III C
    Planned Change: A Re-examination of Theory and Experience.
    Urbana: University of Illinois Press, 1974.
McNeal, Robert H., ed. *International Relations among Communists.*   I G
    Englewood Cliffs, N. J.: Prentice-Hall, 1967.
Medneden, Roy A. *Let History Judge: The Origins and Consequences*   I G
    of Stalinism. New York: Alfred A. Knopf, 1971.
Meduedev, Roy. *On Socialist Democracy.* New York: Alfred A. Knopf,   I G
    1975.
Meier, Victor. "Rumania's Way." *Swiss Review of World Affairs*   I G
    15, no. 4 (July 1965).
Mickiewicz, Ellen. *Handbook of Soviet Social Science Data.*   II S
    New York: The Free Press, 1973.
Miller, J. D. B. and T. H. Rigby, eds. *Communist Divergencies and*   I G
    the World. Canberra: ANV, 1965.
Miller, Jack. *Life in Russia Today.* New York: G. P. Putnam's Sons,   II G
    1969.
"Models and Issues in the Analysis of Soviet Society." *Survey*   II G
    60 (July 1966).
Morrison, James F. *The Polish People's Republic.* Baltimore: I G
    Johns Hopkins Press, 1968.
Murarka, Dev. *The Soviet Union.* New York: Walker and Company,   I G
    1971.

Nansal, R. "Along the Path of Socialism, Friendship and Fraternity."   I G
    International Affairs no. 2 (February 1975): 16-23.
Pauo, Nicholas C. *The People's Republic of Albania.* Baltimore: I G
    The Johns Hopkins Press, 1968.
Pethybridge, Roger. *The Social Prelude to Stalinism.* London: II G
    Macmillan, 1974.
Pospielovsky, Dmitry. "Restalinization or Destalinization? *The Russian*   II G
    Review 27, no. 3 (July 1968).
Pounds, Norman J. G. *Eastern Europe.* Chicago: Aldine Publishing   I G
    Company, 1969.
Rezler, Julius. "The Rebirth of Sociology in Hungary." *East European*   I G
    Quarterly 7, no. 2 (June 1974).
Riddell, D. "Social Self-government: The Background of Theory and   III C
    Practice in Yugoslavia Socialism." *British Journal of*
    Sociology (March 1968).
Roberts, Henry L. *Eastern Europe: Politics, Revolution and Diplo-*   II G
    macy. New York: Alfred A. Knopf, 1970.
Robinson, T. *Systems Theory and the Communist Orbit.* RAND   III C
    P-3812, 1968.
Robinson, William F. *The Pattern of Reform in Hungary: A Political*   II T
    Economic and Cultural Analysis. New York: Praeger, 1973.
Rubinstein, Alvin Z. "Reforms, Non-alignment and Pluralism."   II G
    (Yugoslavia). *Problems of Communism* 17 (March-April
    1968).
Seton-Watson, H. "The Evolution of Communist Dictatorship."   III C
    Modern World (June 1968).
Schaffer, Harry G., ed. *The Soviet System in Theory and Practice.*   III G
    New York: Appleton-Century-Crofts, 1965.
Scholz, Heinrich E.; Paul K. Urban; and Andrew I. Lebed, eds.   II G
    Who Was Who in the USSR. Metuchen, N. J.: The Scarecrow
    Press, 1972.
Spittmann. "East Germany: The Swinging Pendulum." *Problems*   I G
    of Communism 16, no. 4, 1967.
Staar, Richard F. *The Communist Regimes of Eastern Europe: An*   II G
    Introduction. Stanford, Calif.: Hoover Institution on War,
    Revolution and Peace, 1967.
Stuart, Anthony. "Ceausescu's Land." *Survey* no. 76   I G
    (Summer 1970).
Suda, Zdenek. *The Czechoslovak Socialist Republic.* Baltimore: I G
    The Johns Hopkins Press, 1969.
Szczepanski, Jan. *Polish Society.* New York: Random House, 1970.   II G

Toma, Peter A., ed. *The Changing Face of Communism in Eastern*   II G
    Europe. Tucson: University of Arizona Press, 1970.
Tornquist, David. *Look East. Look West: The Socialist Adventure in*   II G
    Yugoslavia. New York: Macmillan Co., 1966.
Triska, Jan. F., ed. *Integration and Community Building in Eastern*   II G
    Europe. Baltimore: Johns Hopkins Press, 1969.
Ulc, Otto. "On Comparing East European Political Systems:
    The Case of Czechoslovakia." *Studies in Comparative Com-*
    munism (April 1971): 47-57.
Volgyes, Ivan. *Hungary in Revolution.* Lincoln: University of   I G
    Nebraska Press, 1971.
_____ "Political Socialization in Eastern Europe." *Problems of Commu-*   I G
    nism (January-February 1974): 46-55.
Volgyes, Ivan, ed. *Political Socialization in Eastern Europe: A Com-*   II T
    parative Framework. New York: Praeger, 1975.
Vucinich, Wayne S. *Contemporary Yugoslavia: Twenty Years of*   II G
    Socialist Experiment. Berkeley: University of California
    Press, 1969.
Vucinich, Alexander. "Marx and Parsons in Soviet Sociology." *The*   II T
    Russian Review 33, no. 1 (January 1974): 1-19.
Weinberg, Elisabeth Ann. *The Development of Sociology in the*   I G
    Soviet Union. London: Routledge and Kegan Paul, 1974.
Wheeler, G. S. *The Human Face of Socialism: The Political Economy*   II G
    of Change in Czechoslovakia. New York: Lawrence Hill, 1973.
White, Stephen. "Contradiction and Change in State Socialism."   II T
    Soviet Studies 26, no. 1 (January 1974).
Wiles, P. "The Political and Social Pre-requisites for a Soviet-Type   III C
    Economy." *Journal of Economic Abstracts* (June 1967).
Zaninovich, M. George. *The Development of Socialist Yugoslavia.*   II G
    Baltimore: The John Hopkins Press, 1968.
_____ "On Comparing East European Political Systems: The Case   II G
    of Yugoslavia." *Studies in Comparative Communism*
    (April 1971): 58-70.
Zarodox, Konstantin. *Leninism and Contemporary Problems of the*   II G
    Transition from Capitalism to Socialism. Moscow: Progress
    Publishers, 1972.
Zhivkov, Todor. *Modern Bulgaria: Problems and Tasks in Building an*   II G
    Advanced Socialist Society. New York: International Publishers, 1974.
Zukin, Sharon. *Beyond Marx and Tito: Theory and Practice in*   II G
    Yugoslav Socialism. London: Cambridge University
    Press, 1975.

Social Welfare

Azrael, Jeremy. "Bringing Up the Soviet Man: Dilemmas and
  Progress." *Problems of Communism* 17 no. 3 (May-June 1968).

Field, Mark G. *Soviet Socialized Medicine: An Introduction.* New   II G
  York: Free Press, 1967.

Hanson, Philip. *The Consumer in the Soviet Economy.* Evanston,   II T
  Ill.: Northwestern University Press, 1968.

Hegedus, Andras. "On Alternatives of Social Development." RFE   II C
  Hungarian Press. *Survey* no. 1950 (1968).

Hendel, Samuel, ed. *The Soviet Crucible 1917-1967.* Princeton, N.J. :   II G
  Van Nostrand, 1967.

"Inter-regional Redistribution of Soviet Industrial Labor, 1959-1965:   II T
  The Problems of Soviet Internal Migration." Master of science
  thesis, Department of Geography, University of Wisconsin,
  Madison, 1971.

Madison, Bernice Q. *Social Welfare in the Soviet Union.* Stanford,   II T
  Calif.: Stanford University Press, 1968.

Mrozek, W. "Social Changes in the Upper Silesian Industrial District."   III T
  Polish Sociological Bulletin 15, no. 1, 1967.

Osborn, Robert J. *Soviet Social Policies: Welfare, Equality and Com-*   III G
  munity. Homewood, Ill.: The Dorsey Press, 1970.

Prybyla, Jan S. "Soviet Man in the Ninth Plan." *Current History*   I G
  (October 1971).

Simirenko, Alex. ed. *Social Thought in the Soviet Union.* Chicago: II C
  Quadrangle Books, 1969.

Zaninovich, M. George. "Party and Non-party Attitudes on Societal   III G
  Change." In Farrell R. Barry, ed. *Political Leadership in
  Eastern Europe and the Soviet Union.* Chicago: Aldine
  Publishing Company, 1970.

Individual Incentives

Kahl, Anne. "The Worker." *Problems of Communism* 14 (March-   I G
  April 1965).

Lipset, Seymour Martin. *Revolution and Counter-revolution:*   II G
  Change and Persistance in Social Structures. New York:
  Basic Books, 1968.

Nuti, D. "Material Incentive Schemes and the Choice of Techniques   III C
  in Soviet Industry." *Journal of Economic Abstracts*
  (September 1967).

Piekalkiewicz, Jaroslaw A. *Public Opinion Polling in Czechoslovakia*   II S
    1968-69. New York: Praeger, 1972.
Raitsin, V. I. *Planning the Standard of Living According to Consump-*   II G
    tion Norms. Leonard J. Kirsch, ed. White Plains, N. Y.:
    International Arts and Sciences Press, 1969.
Rudden, Bernard. "Soviet Housing and the New Civil Code." *The*   III T
    International and Comparative Law Quarterly
    (January 1966).
Schroeder, Gertrude E. "Consumer Problems and Prospects."   I G
    Problems of Communism 22 (March-April 1973).
_____. "Consumption in the USSR: A Survey." *Studies on the*   II G
    Soviet Union (Munich) 10, no. 4 (1970).
Wiles, Peter. *Distribution of Income: East and West.* Amsterdam: II T
    North Holland Publishing Co., 1974.

Mobilization Versus Modernization

Apter, David. *The Politics of Modernization.* Chicago: University   III C
    of Chicago Press, 1965.
Bakhtanov, R. and P. Volin. "People and Problems in Reform: Where   III T
    Do the Conservatives Come From?" *Current Digest of the*
    Soviet Press 19, no. 36 (September 1967).
Black, Cyril E. *The Dynamics of Modernization.* New York: Harper   II C
    & Sons, 1966.
_____. "Marxism and Modernization." *Slavic Review*   II C
    29, no. 2 (June 1970).
Blackwell, William L. *The Beginning of Russian Industrialization,*   I G
    1800-1860. Princeton: Princeton University Press, 1968.
Frolic, B. Michael. "Decision Making in Soviet Cities." *The American*   II T
    Political Science Review 66, no. 1 (March 1972): 38-52.
_____. "Municipal Administrations, Departments, Commissions and
    Organizations." *Soviet Studies* 22 (January 1971): 376-93.
Gellner, E. "The Pluralist Anti-levellers of Prague." *Government*   I G
    and Opposition 7, no. 1 (Winter 1972).
Lendvai, Paul. "Hungary: Change vs. Immobilism." *Problems of*   I G
    Communism 16 (March-April 1967).
Marsh, R. M. and W. L. Parrish. "Modernization and Communism: III C
    A Re-test of Lipset's Hypothesis." *American Sociological*
    Review (30 December 1965).
Meissner, B. ed. *Social Change in the Soviet Union. Russia's Path*   II T
    Toward an Industrial Society. Notre Dame, Ind.:
    University of Notre Dame Press, 1972.

Pirages, Dennis Clark. *Modernization and Political-Tension*   III T
     Management: A Socialist Society in Perspective: Case
     Study of Poland. New York: Praeger, 1972.
———. "Socio-Economic Development and Political in the Com-   III G
     munist System." *Stanford Studies of the Communist*
     System, research paper no. 9 (January 1966).
Powell, David E. "The Social Costs of Modernization: Ecological   II G
     Problems in the USSR." *World Politics* (July 1971).
Rustow, Dankwart A. "Modernization and Comparative Politics."   II C
     Comparative Politics 1, no. 1 (October 1968): 37-57.
———. *A World of Nations: Problems of Political Moderniza-*   II C
     tion. Washington, D. C.: The Brookings Institution, 1967.
Sefer, B. "Income Distribution in Yugoslavia." *International*   III S
     Labour Review (April 1968).
Zechowski, Z. "Urbanization Processes in the Industrial Area of   III T
     Konin." *Polish Sociological Bulletin* 14, no. 2 (1966).

Social Striations

Blobembergen, Samuel. "Personal Property: Downward Trends."   II G
     Problems of Communism 14 (March-April 1965).
Brown, Donald R. *The Role and Status of Women in the Soviet*   II T
     Union. New York: Teachers' College Press, Columbia
     University, 1968.
Bryski, Zbigniew. "The Communist Middle Class in the USSR and   II G
     Poland." *Survey* no. 73 (Autumn 1969).
Fisher, Wesley A. and Murray Yanowitch, eds. *Social Stratification*   III S
     and Mobility in the USSR. White Plains, N. Y.: International
     Arts and Sciences Press.
Krejci, Jaroslav. *Social Change and Stratification in Postwar*   II T
     Czechoslovakia. New York: Columbia University
     Press, 1972.
Lane, David. *The End of Inequality? Stratification Under State*   II G
     Socialism. Baltimore: Penguin Books, 1971.
Matejko, Alexander. *Social Change and Stratification in Eastern*   II G
     Europe. An Interpretive Analysis of Poland and Her
     Neighbors. New York: Praeger, 1974.
Matthews, Mervyn. *Class and Society in Soviet Russia.* London: II G
     Allen Lane, The Penguin Press, 1972.
Shkaratan, O. I. "The Social Structure of the Soviet Working   II S
     Class." *Current Digest of the Soviet Press* no. 12 (1968).

Vaughan, Micholina. "A Multidimensional Approach to Con-   II T
    temporary Polish Stratification." *Survey* 20, no. 1
    (Winter 1974): 62-74.
Yanowitch, Murray and N. T. Dodge. "The Social Evaluation of   III T
    Occupations in the Soviet Union." *Slavic Review*
    (Seattle) (December 1969).

3. MAN AND SOCIETY: ALIENATION, COLLECTIVIZATION AND CLASS STRUGGLE

Class Struggle

Cannon, James P. *Struggle for a Proletarian Party*. New York: II G
    Pathfinder Press, 1972.
Fejto, Francois. *A History of the Peoples Democracies: Eastern* II G
    Europe since Stalin. New York: Praeger, 1971.
Hill, Ian H. "The End of Russian Peasantry." *Soviet Studies*   I G
    27, no. 1 (January 1975): 109-27.
von Lazar, A. J. "Class Struggle and Socialist Construction: III G
    The Hungarian Paradox." *Slavic Review* 25, no. 2
    (June 1966).
Nemes, D. "The October Revolution and Hungary's Road to   II G
    Socialism." *World Marxist Review* (August 1967).
Pienkos, Donald E. "Education and Emigration as Factors in   II T
    Rural Societal Development: The Russian and Polish
    Peasantries Responses to Collectivization." *East*
    European Quarterly 7, no. 4 (January 1975): 75-95.
Wiatr, Jerzy. "Military Professionalism and Transformations of   III T
    Class Structure in Poland." *Polish Sociological Bulletin*
    16, no. 2 (1967).
Zoravomyslov, A. G., et al., eds. *Man and His Work*. (Study of   III S
    Young Working Class in Leningrad). White Plains, N. Y.:
    International Arts and Sciences Press, 1970.

Social Collectivization

Arutivnian, Yu. V. "Social Structure of the Rural Population."   III T
    Current Digest of the Soviet Press (July 13, 1966).
Aspaturian, Vernon V. "The Soviet Case: Unique and Generali-   III C
    zable Factors." In R. Barry Farrell, ed. *Approaches to*

Comparative and International Politics. Evansville, Ill.:
Northwestern University Press, 1966.

Bakst, James. *A History of Russian-Soviet Music.* New York: II T
Dodd, Mead & Co., 1966.

Baros, Victor. "Contemporary Soviet Society." *Current History*   I G
67, no. 398 (October 1974): 173-76.

Barry, Donald D. "Cities and Towns." *Problems of Communism*   II G
18, no. 3 (May-June 1969).

Bauer, Raymond. *The New Man in Soviet Psychology.*   III T
Cambridge: Harvard University Press, 1959.

Bauman, Zygmunt. "Eastern European and Soviet Social Science,   III T
A Case Study in Stimulus Diffision." Conference of the
University of Michigan Center for Russians and East
European Studies, May 1970.

Dunn, Stephen P., ed. *Sociology in the USSR: A Collection of*   III T
Readings from Soviet Journals. White Plains, N. Y.:
International Arts and Sciences Press, 1969.

Feshbach, Murray. "Observations on the Soviet Censure." *Problems*   I G
of Communism 19 (May-June 1970).

Hollander, Paul. "The Dilemmas of Soviet Sociology." *Problems*   I G
of Communism 14 (November-December 1965).

Horvat, Branko. *An Essay on Yugoslav Society.* Translated by   II S
Henry F. Mins. White Plains, N. Y.: International Arts
and Sciences Press, 1969.

Hulicka, Karel and Irene M. *Soviet Institutions: The Individual*   III C
and Society. Quincy, Mass.: Christopher Publishing
House, 1967.

Inkeles, Alex. *Social Change in Soviet Russia.* Cambridge: III T
Harvard University Press, 1968.

Johnson, Chalmers, ed. *Change in Communist Systems.* Stanford,   II G
Calif.: Stanford University Press, 1970.

Johnson, Chalmers. *Revolutionary Change.* Boston: Little,   II G
Brown, 1966.

Katz, Zev. "Sociology in the Soviet Union." *Problems of*   I G
Communism 20 (May-June 1971).

Lane, David and George Kalankiewicz. *Social Groups in Polish*   II G
Society. London: Macmillan, 1973.

Ludz, Peter C. "Sociology in Eastern Europe: East Germany."   II G
Problems of Communism 14 (January-February 1965).

Male, D. J. *Russian Peasant Organisation before Collectivization.*   II T
London: Cambridge University Press, 1971.

Miller, Wright. *Who are the Russians? A History of Russian*   I G
People. London: Faber and Faber, 1973.

Parker, W. H. *The Russians: How They Live and Work.* Newton   I G
    Abbot: David and Charles, 1973.
Rawin, S. "The Polish Intelligentsia and the Socialist Order: III C
    Elements of Ideological Compatibility."
    Political Science Quarterly (September 1968).
Szezypiorski, Andrzej. "A Feuilleton Social Integration under   II G
    Socialism." Radio Warsaw, August 18, 1968, RFE, Polish
    Press Survey no. 2148.
Tarkowski-Jacek. "A Study of Decisional Process in Rolnowe   III T
    Poviat." *Polish Sociological Bulletin* 16, no. 2 (1967).
Turowski, Jan. "Problems of Local Community in Big City."   II T
    The Polish Sociological Bulletin no. 2 (1968).

Alienation

Connor, Walter D. *Deviance in Soviet Society.* New York: Columbia   I G
    University Press, 1972.
Friedberg, Maurice. "The Alienation of Soviet Jews." *Problems*   I G
    of Communism 22 (March-April 1973).
Hollander, Paul, ed. *American and Soviet Society: A Reader in*   III T
    Comparative Sociology and Deception. Englewood Cliffs,
    N. J.: Prentice-Hall, 1969.
Ikle, F. C. *Social Forecasting and the Problem of Changing Values,*   III S
    with Special Reference to Soviet and East European
    Writings. RAND P 4550 (January 1971).
Israel, Joachim. *Alienation from Marx to Modern Sociology:*   III S
    A Macro-Sociological Analysis. Boston: Allyn and
    Bacon, 1971.
Meszaros, Istvan. *Marx's Theory of Alienation.* New York: III C
    Harper & Row, 1972.
Roberts, Paul Craig. *Alienation and the Soviet Economy: Toward*   III C
    a General Theory of Marxian Alienation, Organizational
    Principles and the Soviet Economy. Albuquerque:
    University of New Mexico Press, 1971.
Ross, Jeffrey A. "The Composition and Structure of the Alienation   II T
    of Jewish Emigrants from the Soviet Union." *Studies in*
    Comparative Communism 7, no. 2 (Spring-Summer 1974):
    107-18.
Shanin, Teodor. *The Awkward Class—Political Sociology of*   II G
    Peasantry in a Developing Society: Russia, 1910-1925.
    London: Oxford University Press, 1972.

Staats, Steven J. "Corruption in the Soviet System." *Problems*   I G
    of Communism 21 (January-February 1972).

Family

Berent, J. "Causes of Fertility Decline in Eastern Europe and   II T
    the Soviet Union." *Population Studies* 24, no. 2 (1970).
Coser, Rose L. "The Case of the Soviet Family." *In the Family:*   III T
    Its Structure and Functions. New York: St. Martins, 1964.
Geiger, H. Kent. *The Family in Soviet Russia.* Cambridge: Harvard
    University Press; and London: Oxford University Press, 1968.
Hyde, Gordon. "Abortion and Birth Rate in the USSR." *Journal*   II T
    of Biosocial Science 2, no. 3 (July 1970).
McIntyre, Robert J. "Prenatalist Programmes in Eastern Europe."   II T
    Soviet Studies 27, no. 3 (July 1975): 366-80.
Rudden, Bernard. "The Family." *Problems of Communism*   I G
    14 (March-April 1965).
Teitelbaum, M. "Fertility Effects of the Abolition of Legal   II T
    Abortions in Romania." *Population Studies* 26, no. 3
    (1972).
Valentei, Danl Kiseleva G. "The Family, Children and Society."   II G
    Current Digest of the Soviet Press (October 3, 1969).

Minorities

Gilberg, Tronel, "Ethnic Minorities in Romania Under Socialism."   I T
    East European Quarterly (January 1974): 135-58.
King, Robert. *Minorities under Communism: Nationalities as a*   II G
    Source of Tension Among Balkan Communist States.
    Cambridge: Harvard University Press, 1973.
Kochan, Lionel. *The Jews in Soviet Russia since 1917.* 2d ed.   I G
    Institute of Jewish Affairs. London: OUP, 1972.
Korey, William. *The Soviet Cage: Anti-Semitism in Russia.* New   I G
    York: The Viking Press, 1973.
Massell, Gregory J. *The Surrogate Proletariat: Moslem Women*   II T
    and Revolutionary Strategies in Soviet Central Asia
    1919-1929. Princeton: Princeton University Press, 1974.
Shaeffer, Harry G. *The Soviet Treatment of Jews.* New York: I G
    Praeger, 1974.
Shanin, T., ed. *Peasants and Peasant Societies.* Harmondsworth,   I G
    England: Penguin, 1971.

Vago, Bela and George L. Mosse, eds. *Jews and Non-Jews in*   I G
    Eastern Europe. New York: Halsped Press, 1975.

4. COMMUNIST ELITES: REVOLUTIONARIES, BUREAUCRATS, TECHNOCRATS, COMPOSITION AND AUTHORITY

Bureaucracy

Adizes, Ichak. *Industrial Democracy Yugoslavia Style.* New York: II G
    Free Press, 1971.

Armstrong, John A. "Sources of Administrative Behavior: Some   III T
    Soviet and Western European Comparisons." *The American
    Political Science Review* 59, no. 3 (September 1965).

_____. "Tsarist and Soviet Elite Administrators." *Slavic Review*   III G
    31, no. 1 (March 1972).

Azrael, Jeremy. "The Managers." In R. Barry Farrel, ed. *Political*   II G
    Leadership in Eastern Europe and the Soviet Union.
    Chicago: Aldine Publishing Company, 1970.

Beck, Carl. "Bureaucratic Conservatism and Innovation in Eastern   II G
    Europe." *Comparative Political Studies* 1 (July 1968).

Blackwell, Robert E., Jr. "Career Development in the Soviet OBKOM   III T
    Elite: A Conservative Trend." *Soviet Studies* 24, no. 1 (July 1972).

Chrypinski, V. C. "Poland's Parliamentary Committees." *East*   III T
    Europe 14, no. 2 (January 1965).

Denitch, B. "Elite Interviewing and Social Structure: An Example   II S
    from Yugoslavia." *Public Opinion Quarterly* 36, no. 2
    (Summer 1972).

Deutsch, Karl A. *The Nerves of Government.* New York: The Free   III G
    Press, 1966.

Donaldson, Robert H. "The 1971 Soviet Central Committee: An   III S
    Assessment of the New Elite." *World Politics* 24, no. 3
    (April 1972).

Dornberg, John. *The New Tsars: Russia Under Stalin Heirs.* Garden   I G
    City, N. Y.: Doubleday, 1972.

Downs, Anthony. *Inside Bureaucracy.* Boston: Little, Brown, 1967.   II G

Edinger, Lewis J., ed. *Political Leadership in Industrialized*   II C
    Societies: Studies in Comparative Analysis. New York:
    Krueger, 1967.

Fleron, Frederick. "Representation of Career Types in the Soviet   III S
    Political Leadership." In R. Barry Farrell, ed. *Political*

Leadership in Europe and the Soviet Union. Chicago:
Aldine Publishing Company, 1970.

Galli, Giorgio. "A Bureaucracy Under Fire." *Problems of*   II G
Communism (September-October 1966).

Gamarnikow, Michael. "The End of the Party Hack." *East Europe*   I G
14, no. 11 (November 1965).

Garson, G. C. *On Democratic Administration and Socialist Self*   III T
Management: A Comparative Survey Emphasizing the
Yugoslav Experience. Beverly Hills: Sage Publica-
tions, 1974.

Hollander, Paul. "Observations on Bureaucracy, Totalitarianism,   II C
and the Comparative Study of Communism." *Slavic*
Studies (June 1967).

———. "Politicized Bureaucracy, The Soviet Case." *Newsletter*   II G
on Comparative Studies of Communism 4, no. 3 (May 1971).

———. "Soviet Bureaucracy: The Pursuit of Efficiency and   II G
Political Control." *American Political Science Associ-*
ation, New York, 1968.

Joravsky, David. "Bosses and Scientists." *Problems of Communism*   II G
16, no. 1 (January-February 1967).

Korbonski, Andrzei. "Bureaucracy and Interest Groups in Communist   II G
Societies: The Case of Czechoslovakia." *Studies in Comparative*
Communism (January 1971): 57.

Label, Andrei. "The Soviet Administrative Elite: Selection and   III T
Deployment Procedures." *Studies in the Soviet Union*
(Munich) 5, no. 2 (1965).

Laird, Roy D. *The Soviet Paradigm, An Experiment in Creating a*   III G
Monohierachial Polity. New York: The Free Press, 1971.

Lodge, M. "Soviet Elite Participatory Attitudes in the Post-Stalin   III C
Period." *American Political Science Review* (September 1969).

Narkiewicz, Olga A. *The Making of the Soviet State Apparatus.*   II G
Manchester: The University Press, 1970.

Odom, William E. *The Soviet Volunteers: Modernization and*   I G
Bureaucracy in a Public Mass Organization. Princeton:
Princeton University Press, 1973.

Piekalkiewicz, Jaroslaw. "Communist Administration in Poland   III S
within the Framework of Input-output Analysis." A paper
at Mid-west Association for Advancement of Slavic Studies,
March 30, 1968, published in *East Slavic Quarterly* 6, no. 2
(June 1972).

Pirages, Dennis. "Modernization: New Decisional Models in Socialist   II G
Society." In R. Barry Farrell, ed. *Political Leadership in*   II G

Eastern Europe and the Soviet Union. Chicago: Aldine
Publishing Company, 1970.

Rigby, T. H. "Bureaucracy and Democracy in the USSR." *The*   II G
Australian Quarterly (March 1970).

Schwartz, Donald V. "Decision-making Administrative Decentrali-   III C
zation and Feedback Mechanisms: Comparisons of Soviet and
Western Models." *Studies in Comparative Communism*
(Spring-Summer 1974): 146-83.

_____. "Recent Soviet Adaptations of Systems Theory to Adminis-   II T
trative Theory." *Journal of Comparable Administration*
5, no. 2 (August 1973).

Sik, Ota. *Czechoslovakia: The Bureaucratic Economy.* White Plains,   II G
N. Y.: International Arts and Sciences Press, 1972.

Stewart, Philip D. *Political Power in the Soviet Union: A Study*   III T
of Decision-making in Stalingrad. New York: The Bobbs-
Merrill Co, Inc., 1968.

Taubmann, William. *Governing Soviet Cities: Bureaucratic Policies*   II T
and Urban Development in the USSR. New York: Praeger, 1973.

Wilensky, Harold. *Organizational Intelligence: Knowledge and*   III T
Policy in Government and Industry. New York: Basic Books,
1967.

Zawadzka, B. "Personnel and Councillors of People's Council."   II T
Polish Sociological Bulletin 16, no. 2 (1967).

Technocrats/Specialists

Azrael, J. R. *Managerial Power and Soviet Politics.* Cambridge: II G
Harvard University Press, 1966.

Beck, Carl. "Career Characteristics of East European Leadership."   III T
In R. Barry Farrell, ed., *Political Leadership in East Europe*
and the Soviet Union. Chicago: Aldine Publishing Company,
1970.

Deacon, Richard. *History of the Russian Secret Service.*   I G
N. Y.: Taplinger Publishing Company, 1972.

Document. "Appeal of Soviet Scientists to the Party-Government   I C
Leaders of the USSR." *Survey* no. 76 (Summer 1970).

Edinger, Lewis J. and D. D. Searing. "Social Background in Elite   III S
Analysis." *The American Political Science Review* 61 (June
1967).

Farkas, R. P. *Yugoslav Economic Development of Political Change:*   II T
The Relationship between Economic Managers and Policy
Making Elites. New York: Praeger, 1975.

Gill, Richard Rockingham. "Recent Developments in Soviet Science   II T
and Technology." *Current History* (November 1969).
Graham, Loren R. *The Soviet Academy of Sciences and the Commu-*   III T
nist Party 1927-1932. Princeton: Princeton University Press,
1967.
Hangen, Welles. *The Muted Revolution: East Germany's Challenge*   II G
to Russia and the West. New York: Alfred A. Knopf, 1966.
Harvey, Rose L.; Leon Govre; and Vladimir Prokofieff. *Science*   II G
and Technology as an Instrument of Soviet Policy. Center
for Advanced International Studies, University of Miami,
1972.
Hough, Jerry. "The Soviet Elite: In Whose Hands the Future?"   II G
Problems of Communism 16, no. 2 (1967).
Lowenhardt, John. "The Tale of the Torch: Scientists-   I T
Entrepreneurs in the Soviet Union." *Survey* 20,
no. 4 (Autumn 1974): 113-21.
Miller, R. F. "The New Science of Administration in the USSR."   II G
Administrative Science Quarterly 16, no. 3 (September 1971).
Parry, Albert. *The New Class Divided: Science and Technology*   II G
Versus Communism. New York: Macmillan, 1966.
Shelton, William. "The Russian Scientist Today." *RR*   II G
(January 1970).
Wiatr, Jerzy J. and Krzysztof Ostrowski. "Political Leader-   II T
ship: What Kind of Professionalism?" *Studies in the
Polish Political System.* Warsaw: Polish Academy of
Sciences Press, 1967.

Party Cadre

Akhimov, H. "The Activities of a Soviet Leader." *Bulletin*   II G
of the Institute for the Study of the USSR 13 (1966).
Barton, Allen H.; Bogdan Denitch; and Charles Kadushin,   I G
eds. *Opinion-making Elites in Yugoslavia.* New York:
Praeger, 1973.
Baylis, Thomas A. *The Technical Intelligentsia and the East*   II T
*German Elite: Legitimacy and Social Change in Mature
Communism.* Berkeley: University of California Press,
1974.
Beck, Carl, et al. *Comparative Communist Political Leader-*   II G
ship. New York: McKay, 1972.

Beck, Carl and John T. McKechnie. *Political Elites: A Select Computerized Bibliography*. Cambridge: MIT Press, 1968.   III S

Bilinsky, Yaroslav. "Changes in the Central Committee Communist Party of the Soviet Union, 1961-1966." The Social Science Foundation and Graduate School of International Studies, University of Denver, *Monograph Series in World Affairs* 4, no. 4 (1966-67).   III S

_____. "The Rulers and the Ruled." *Problems of Communism* (September-October 1967).   II G

Cattell, David T. "Collective or Personal Rule in the USSR?" *Current History* (October 1971).   II G

Farrell, R. Barry. *Political Leadership in Eastern Europe and the Soviet Union*. Chicago: Aldine Publishing Company, 1970.   II G

Fleron, Frederick. "Towards a Reconceptualization of Political Change in the Soviet Union: The Political Leadership System." *Comparative Politics* (January 1969).   II C

Gehlen, Michael P. "The Educational Backgrounds and Career Orientations of the Members of the Central Committee of the CPSU." *The American Behavioral Scientist* 9, no. 8 (April 1966).   III S

_____. "The Soviet Apparatchiki." In R. Barry Farrell, ed., *Political Leadership in East Europe and the Soviet Union*. Chicago: Aldine Publishing Company, 1970.   III S

_____. "The Soviet Central Committee: An Elite Analysis." *American Political Science Review* (December 1968).   III S

Hodnett, Gary. "The Obkov First Secretaries." *Slavic Review* 24, no. 4 (December 1965).   II T

Jacobs, E. M. "The Composition of Local Soviets, 1959-69." *Government and Opposition* 7, no. 4 (Autumn 1972).   II S

Jowitt, K. "A Comparative Analysis of Leninist and National Elite Ideologies and Nation-building Strategies." *Mimeo*. Berkeley, Calif. (1968): 1.   III S

Leites, Nathan C. *Operational Codes of the Politburo*. New York: Greenwood Press, 1972.   III T

Levytsky, Boris. *The Soviet Political Elite*. Stanford, Calif.: Hoover Institute on War, Revolution and Peace, 1970.   II G

Ludz, Peter C. *The Changing Party Elite in East Germany*. Cambridge: The MIT Press, 1972.   II G

Nicolaevsky, Boris I. *Power and the Soviet Elite*. New York: Praeger, 1965.   II G

Popovic, Nenad. *Yugoslavia: The New Class in Crisis*. Syracuse, N. Y.: Syracuse University Press, 1968.   III G

Rigby, T. H. "The CPSU Elite: Turnover and Rejuvenation   III S
from Lenin to Khrushchev." *The Australian Journal of
Politics and History* 16, no. 1 (April 1970).
————. "New Light on the Soviet Elite." *Problems of Communism* (November-December 1974).
Schindzielorz, Hubert L. *Elite Transformation: An Analysis*   III T
of the East German Political Elite. Ph. D. dissertation,
University of Pittsburgh, EPD, 1969.
Simirenko, Alex. "Ersatz Charisma: A Sociological Interpre-   III G
tation of Socialist Countries." *Newsletter on Compar-
ative Studies of Communism* (Buffalo) (August 1971).
Triska, Jan. "Party Apparatchiks at Bay." *East Europe* 16, no.   II G
12 (December 1967): 2-8.

Interest Groups

Armstrong, John. "Party Bifurcation and Elite Interests."   III G
Soviet Studies 17 (April 1966): 417-30.
Barton, Allen; Bogdan Denitch; Charles Kadushin, eds. *Opinion-*   I G
making Elites in Yugoslavia. New York: Praeger, 1973.
Bass, R. "East European Communist Elites: Their Character   II G
and History." *Journal of International Affairs* 20 (1966).
Bender, Peter. "Inside the Warsaw Pact." *Survey* nos. 74-75   II G
(Winter-Spring 1970).
Breyere, Siegfried. "Warsaw Pact: Landing Craft." *Military*   II T
Review 47, no. 5 (May 1967) 106-08. (Translated from
Soldat und Technik, December 1966.)
Bryant, Christopher. "Prague Summer: 1968." *East Europe*   I G
(September 1968).
Churchward, L. G. *Soviet Intelligentsia: An Essay on the Social*   II T
*Structure and Roles of Soviet Intellectuals During the
60's.* Boston: Routledge and Kegan Paul, 1973.
Gallagher, Matthew A. "Red Army's Arms Lobby." The   I G
Washington *Post* (February 9, 1969).
Gamarnikos, Michael. "Poland: Political Pluralism in a One-   II T
Party State." *Problems of Communism* 16, no. 7
(January-February 1967): 1-14.
Gardner, Michael. *A History of the Soviet Army.* New York: I G
Praeger, 1966.
Garthoff, Raymond L. "The Military Establishment." *East*   II G
Europe (September 1965).

_____. *Soviet Military Policy: A Historical Analysis.* New York: I G
Praeger, 1966.

Green, Barbara B. "Soviet Politics and Interest Groups." *Current*   II G
History 57, no. 302 (October 1966): 213-17.

Haigh, Patricia. "Reflections on the Warsaw Pact." *World Today*   I G
24, no. 4 (April 1968).

Haimson, Leopold H., ed. *The Mensheviks: From the Revolution of*   I G
1917 to the Second World War. Chicago: University of
Chicago Press, 1975.

Herrick, R. Waring. "Warsaw Pact Restructuring Strengthens Prin-   I G
ciple of National Control." *Radio Liberty Research Bulletin*
no. 10 (1540), March 11, 1970.

Hough, Jerry. "Groups and Individuals." *Problems of Communism*   II G
16, no. 1 (January-February 1967).

_____. "The Soviet Elite: Groups and Individuals." *Problems of*   II G
Communism 16, no. 1 (January-February 1967).

Kelley, D. R. "Interest Groups in the USSR: The Impact of Political   II G
Sensitivity on Group Influence." *Journal of Politics* 34, no. 3
(August 1972).

Kolkowicz, Roman. *A General and the Apparatchikis.* RAND   III G
P-3298 (1960).

_____. *Political Controls in the Red Army: Professional Autonomy*   III G
Versus Political Integration. Santa Monica, The Rand Corporation, P-3402 (July 1966).

_____. *The Soviet Military and the Communist Party.* Princeton,   II G
N. J.: Princeton University Press, 1967.

Langsam, David E., and David W. Paul. "Soviet Politics and the   II G
Group Approach: A Conceptual Note." *Slavic Review* 31,
no. 1 (March 1972).

Lebed, A. I.; H. E. Schulz; S. S. Taylor, eds. *Who's Who in the*   I G
USSR. 2d ed. Montreal: Intercontinental Book and Pub-
lishing Co., 1966.

Lodge, M. "Groupism in the Post-Stalin Period." *Midwest Journal*   III C
of Political Science (August 1968).

Ploss, Sidney I. "Interest Groups." In Allen Kossof, ed., *Prospects*   II C
for Soviet Society. New York: 1968.

Schopflin, George. "Hungarian Intellectuals under Pressure."   II G
The World Today 30, no. 2 (February 1974): 73-79.

Schwartz, J. "Group Influence and the Policy Process in the Soviet   II C
Union." *American Political Science Review* (September 1968).

Schwartz, Joel J. and William R. Keech. "Group Influence and the   II T
Policy Process in the Soviet Union." *American Political*
Science Review 62, no. 3 (September 1968): 840-51.

Skilling, H. Gordon. "Interest Groups and Communist Politics."   II G
  World Politics 17, no. 3 (April 1966).

Skilling, H. Gordon and Franklyn Griffiths, eds. *Interest Groups*   II G
  in Soviet Politics. Princeton: Princeton University Press,
  1971.

Stewart, Philip D. "Soviet Interest Groups and the Policy Process,   III T
  The Repeal of Production Education." *World Politics*
  22, no. 1 (October 1969).

Szczepanski, Jan. "The Policy Intelligentsia: Past and Present."   II T
  World Politics 14, no. 3 (April 1962).

Vasilyev, Lt. Col. N. "Brotherhood in Arms." *Soviet Military*   I G
  Review 61, no. 1 (January 1970): 30-34.

Wesson, Robert G. "The Military in Soviet Society." *RR*   II G
  (April 1971).

Wiatr, Jerzy. "Elements of the Pluralism in the Polish Poli-   II C
  tical System." *The Polish Sociological Bulletin* no. 1
  (1966).

Wolfe, Thomas W. *Soviet Military Policy Trends Under the*   II G
  Brezhnev-Kosygin Regime. Santa Monica, Calif.: The
  Rand Corporation, P-3556 (May 1967).

_____. *The Soviet Military Scene, Institutional and Defense*   II G
  Policy Considerations. Santa Monica, Calif.: The Rand
  Corporation, RM-4913-PR (June 1966).

_____. "Are the Generals Taking Over." *Problems of Communism*   I G
  17 (July-October 1969).

5. COLLECTIVE LEADERSHIP AND INSTITUTIONAL INTEREST GROUPS: CENTRALISM AND INFLUENCE MANIPULATION

Leading Role of Party

Akhminov, Herman. "On Methods of Analyzing Soviet Politics."   II C
  Bulletin of the Institute for the Study of the USSR 14,
  no. 10 (October 1967).

Almond, Gabriel A. "Toward A Comparative Politics of Eastern   III G
  Europe." *Studies in Comparative Communism* (April
  1971): 71-78.

Anderson, Stephen S. "Soviet Relations with East Europe."   II G
Current History 51, no. 302 (October 1966): 200-05.

Armstrong, John A. "Comparative Politics and Communist   III C
Systems: Concluding Remarks." *Slavic Review* (March
1967).

Arzael, Jeremy R. "The Party and Society." In Kassof, ed.,   II G
Prospects for Soviet Society. New York: Praeger, 1968.

Aspaturian, Vernon V. *Process and Power in Soviet Foreign*   II G
Policy. Boston: Little, Brown and Co., 1971.

_____ *The Soviet Union in the World Communist System.*   II G
Stanford, Calif.: Hoover Institution, 1966.

Autorkhanos, Abdurakhman G. *The Communist Party Apparatus.*   II G
Chicago: Regnery, 1966.

Aversperg, P. "The Pre-congress Platform of Czechoslovakia."   III T
World Marxist Review (April 1966).

Baiter, Albert. "The Three Generations of the CPSU." Radio   I G
Liberty Research, Munich, May 9, 1968.

Bialer, Seweryn. "The Coup and After." *Problems of Communism*   I G
(July-August 1965).

Biszku, Bela. "The Party of Hungarian Communists: Fifty   I G
Years Old." *World Marxist Review* (December 1968).

Bromke, Adam and Teresa Rakowska-Harmstone, eds. *The*   II G
Communist States in Disarray. Minneapolis: University of Minnesota Press, 1972.

Bromke, Adam. "History and Politics in Poland." *Problems*   II G
of Communism 15 (September-October 1966).

_____ *Poland's Politics: Idealism vs. Realism.* Cambridge: II G
Harvard University Press, 1967.

Brown, J. F. *Bulgaria Under Communist Rule.* New York: II G
Praeger, 1970.

_____ "Rumania Today I: Towards Integration." *Problems*   III G
of Communism 17, no. 1 (January-February 1969).

_____ "Rumania Today II. The Strategy of Defiance."   III G
Problems of Communism 17, no. 2 (March-April
1969).

Brzezinski, Zbigniew, ed. *Dilemmas of Change in Soviet*   II G
Politics. New York: Columbia University Press, 1969.

Brzezinski, Zbigniew. "Reflections on the Soviet System."   II G
Problems of Communism 17, no. 3 (May-June 1968).

_____ "The Soviet Past and Future." *Encounter.*   I G
London, March 1970.

———. "The Soviet Political System: Transformation or   II G
Degeneration." *Problems of Communism* 15, no. 1
(January-February 1966).

———. "What Future for Soviet Power." *Encounter.* London,   I G
March 1970.

Brzezinski, Zbigniew and Samuel P. Huntington. *Political*   II G
Power: USA-USSR. New York: The Viking Press, 1967.

Burks, R. V. "The Communist Politics of Eastern Europe."   III G
In James N. Rosenau, ed., *Linkage Politics: Essays on*
the Convergence of National and International Systems.
New York: Free Press, 1969.

———. *The Decline of Communism in Czechoslovakia.* Santa   II G
Monica, The Rand Corporation, P-3939 (September
1968).

———. *The Removal of Rantiovic: An Early Interpretation*   III T
of the July Yugoslav Party Plenum. RAND RM-5132-PR
(1966).

———. "The Rumanian National Deviation: An Accounting."   III C
In Kurt London, ed., *Eastern Europe in Transition.*
Baltimore: 1966.

———. "Yugoslavia: Has Tito Gone Bourgeois?" *East Europe*   III C
14, no. 8 (August 1965).

Burton, John W. *Conflict and Communications.* London: I G
Macmillan, 1969.

———. *Systems, States, Diplomacy, and Rules.* London: I G
Cambridge University Press, 1968.

"Can the Party Change its Spots." *The Economist.* London,   I G
August 19, 1967.

Cattell, David T. "Politics in Soviet Russia." *Current History*   I G
55, no. 327 (November 1968).

Chamberlain, William Henry. "New Books on Fifty Years of   II G
Soviet Rule." *RR* (April 1968).

Charakchiev, A. "Bulgarian Party Congress." *World Marxist*   II G
Review (December 1966).

Cocks, Paul. "Politics of Party Control: The Historical and   III G
Institutional Role of Party Control Organs in the
CPSU." Unpublished Ph. D dissertation. Cambridge:
Harvard University, 1968.

Conquest, Robert. *The Great Terror, Stalin's Purge of the*   II G
Thirties. New York: Macmillan, 1968.

———. *Power and Policy in the USSR.* New York: Harper   II G
and Row, 1967.

Conquest, Robert; Carl A. Linden; and Michael Tata.   II G
Power in the Kremlin. New York: Viking, 1970.

Cornell, Richard, ed. *The Soviet Political System.* Englewood   II G
Cliffs, N.J.: Prentice-Hall, Inc., 1970.

Crechanowski, Jan. M. *The Warsaw Rising of 1944.* London: I G
Cambridge University Press, 1974.

Crowley, Edward L.; Andrew I. Lehed; Heinrich E. Schulz, eds.   II G
Prominent Personalities in the USSR. Metuchen, N.J.:
Scarecrow Press, 1968.

"Current Soviet Policies III: The Documentary Record of the   II G
Extraordinary 21st Congress of the CP of the S. U."
New York: Columbia University Press, 1960.

Dallin, Alexander and Alan F. Westen, eds. *Politics in the*   II G
Soviet Union: 7 Cases. New York: Harcourt, Brace
and World, 1966.

Dedyer, Vladimir. *The Battle Stalin Lost: Memoirs of*   I G
Yugoslavia, 1948-1953. New York: The Viking
Press, 1971.

Devlin, Kevin. "Interparty Relations: The Limits of Normalization."
Problems of Communism 20 (July-August 1970).

———. "The New Crisis in European Communism." *Problems*   II G
of Communism (November-December 1968).

Dinerstein, Herbert S. "The Soviet Union and the
Communist World." *Survey* 19, no. 2 (Spring
1973).

Djordjevic, Jovan. "Political Power in Yugoslavia."   II G
Government and Opposition 2, no. 2
(February 1967).

Documents of Polish-Soviet Relations 1939-1945. Edited by the   II T
General Sikorski Historical Institute. London: Heinemann,
1966.

Dornberg, John. *The Other Germany.* Garden City, N. Y.:   II T
Doubleday and Co., 1968.

Drachkovitch, Milorad M., ed. *Fifty Years of Communism in*   I G
Russia. University Park: Pennsylvania State University Press, 1968.

Dubcek, Alexander. "Czechoslovakia: Vital Problems of the   III C
Communist Party." *World Marxist Review* (June 1968).

Duevel, Christian. "The Dismantling of Party and State Control as   II G
an Independent Pillar of Soviet Power." *Bulletin* 3 (Munich)
1966: 3,18.

Ermarth, F. W. *Internationalism, Security and Legitimacy: The*   II G
Challenge to Soviet Interests in East Europe. Santa Monica, Calif.:
The Rand Corporation, RM-5909-PR (March 1969).

Ermarth, F. W. *Politics and Policy in the Brezhnev Regime: A Force*   II G
for Continuity? Santa Monica, Calif.: The Rand Corporation,
P-4755 (May 1971).

Etzioni, Amitai. *The Active Society: A Theory of Societal and*   III C
Political Processes. New York: Free Press, 1968.

Ezergailis, Andrew. "Monolithic vs. Crumbling Communism." *Problems*   I G
of Communism 19 (January-February 1970) and continued in
19 (March-April 1970).

Farlow, Robert L. "Romanian Foreign Policy: A Case of Partial   I G
Alignment." *Problems of Communism* 20, no. 6 (November-
December 1971).

Farrel, Barry. "Foreign Policy Formation in the Communist Countries   II G
of Eastern Europe." *East European Quarterly* 1, no. 1 (March
1967).

Feifer, George. *Russia Close-Up.* London: Jonathan Cape, 1973.   I G

Fischer, George. *The Soviet System and Modern Society.* New York: II G
Atherton Press, 1968.

Fischer-Galati, Stephen. *The New Rumania: From Peoples' Democracy*   II G
to Socialist Republic. Cambridge: MIT Press, 1967.

_____. *The Socialist Republic of Rumania.* Baltimore: The Johns   II G
Hopkins Press, 1969.

Fleron, Frederick J. "Cooperation as a Mechanism of Adaptation to   III C
Change." *Polity* 2 (Winter 1967): 176-201.

Fleron, Frederick J., Jr., ed. *Communist Studies and the Social*   II C
Sciences. Skokie, Ill.: Rand-McNally, 1969.

Floyd, David. *Rumania: Russia's Dissident Ally.* New York: II G
Praeger, 1965.

Frank, Peter. "Constructing a Classified Ranking of CPSU Provincial   II S
Committees." *British Journal of Science* (1974).

Gehlen, Michael P. *The Communist Party of the Soviet Union.*   I G
Bloomington: University of Indiana Press.

_____. *The Politics of Coexistence: Soviet Methods and Motives.*   III G
Bloomington: Indiana University Press, 1967.

Gillison, Jerome. "New Factors of Stability in Soviet Collective   II G
Leadership." *World Politics* 19 no. 3 (July 1967).

Gross, George. "Rumania: The Fruits of Autonomy."*Problems of*   II G
Communism 15, no. 1 (January-February 1966).

Gruliow, Leo and Charlotte Sarkowski, eds., *Current Soviet*
Policies IV: The Documentary Record of the 22nd
Congress of the Communist Party of the Soviet Union.
New York: Columbia University Press, 1962.

Hammer, Darrell P. *USSR: The Politics of Oligarchy* (Modern   I G
Comparative Politics Series). Hinsdale, Ill: The Dryden
Press, 1974.
Hill, Ronald J. "Participation in the Central Committee Plenums   III S
in Moldavia." *Soviet Studies* (October 1969).
Hodnett, Grey. "Khrushchev and Party State Control." Alexander II G
Dallin and Allan F. Westin, eds. *Politics in the Soviet Union:
7 Cases.* New York: Harcourt-Brace and World, 1966.
Hoffman, Erik P. "Communication Theory and the Study of Soviet II C
Politics." *Canadian Slavic Studies* 2, no. 4 (Winter 1968).
Horelick, A. L. *Fifty Years After October: Party and Society in* II G/S
the USSR. Santa Monica, Calif.: RAND Corporation, P-3630
(September 1967).
Hough, Jerry F. "The Soviet System: Petrification or Pluralism." I G
Problems of Communism 21, no. 2 (March-April 1972).
Huntington, Samuel P. and Clement H. Moore. *Authorization* II G
*Politics in Modern Society: The Dynamics of Established One-
Party System.* New York: Basic Books, 1970.
The Impact of the Russian Revolution 1917-1967. Royal Institute II G
of International Affairs, London, 1967.
Inkeles, Alex. "Models and Issues in the Analysis of Soviet Society." II T
Survey 60 (July 1966).
Ionescu, George. *The Politics of the European Communist States.* II G
New York: Praeger, 1967.
Ivask, Ivar, ed. *First Conference on Baltic Studies: Summary of* II G
Proceedings. Association for Advancement of Baltic
Studies, 1969.
Jones, Christopher D. "The Revolution in Military Affairs and Party- I G
Military Relations, 1965-70." *Survey* 20, no. 1 (Winter
1974): 84-100.
Juviler, Peter H., and Henry W. Morton, eds. *Soviet Policy-Making:* III G
Studies of Communism in Transition. New York: Praeger, 1967.
Kanet, Roger E. "The Rise and Fall of the 'All-People's State'." II G
Soviet Studies (July 1968).
Kolkowicz, Roman. *The Soviet Army and the Communist Party,* III G
Institutions in Conflict. Santa Monica, Calif.: RAND Cor-
poration (August 1966).
Krakhmalev, M. "Great Party Cause." *CDSP* 17, no. 36, 1965.
Lab, M. "Czechoslovakia: Impact of the Economic Reform on the III G
Party." *World Marxist Review* (December 1967).
Ludz, Peter C. "The SED Leadership in Transition." *Problems of* II G
Communism 19, no. 3 (May-June 1970).

McNeal, Robert H., ed. *Resolutions and Decisions of the Communist*   I G
  Party of the Soviet Union, 1898-1964. Four volumes.
  Toronto: University of Toronto Press, 1974.
Meyer, Alfred. *The Comparative Study of Communist Political*   II G
  Systems. New York: Randon House, 1965.
———. *The Soviet Political System—An Interpretation.* New York: II G
  Random House, 1965.
Miller, Dorothy. "Some Political Aspects of the 13th SED CC   I G
  Plenum." Radio Free Europe Research Report, June 18,
  1970.
Nettl, P. J. *The Soviet Achievement.* London: Thames and Hudson,   I G
  1968.
Nie, Norman and Kenneth Prewitt. *Economic Development and*   III G
  Political Culture. Mimeographed. Stanford University, Insti-
  tute of Political Studies, February, 1965.
"On the Comparative Study of Communism." *World Politics* 19 no. 2   II G
  (January 1967): 242.
Oxley, Andrew; Alex Pravda; Andrew Ritchie. *Czechoslovakia:*   I G
  The Party and the People. New York: St. Martin's Press,
  1973.
Ploss, Sidney I. "Soviet Party History: The Stalinist Legacy."   I G
  Problems of Communism 21 (July-August 1972).
Pravdin, A. "Inside the CPSU Central Committee." An Interview   I G
  by Mervyn Matthews. *Survey* 20, no. 4 (Autumn 1974).
Prybyla, Jan S., ed. *Communism at the Crossroads.* University Park: III G
  Pennsylvania State University Press, 1968.
Prybyla, Jan S. "The Convergence of Western and Communist   III G
  Systems: A Critical Estimate." *Russian Review* 23, no. 1
  (January 1964): 3-17.
Racz, Barnabas. "Political Changes in Hungary After the Soviet   II G
  Invasion of Czechoslovakia." *Slavic Review* (December 1970).
Radvanyi, Jonos. *Hungary and the Superpowers.* Stanford, Calif.:   II G
  Hoover Institution Press, 1972.
Randall, Francis B. *Stalin's Russia.* New York: The Free Press, 1965.   I G
Resolution of the C. P. S. U. Central Committee. "On the Further   II C
  Improvement of the Organization of Socialist Competition."
  The Current Digest of the Soviet Press 23, no. 36 (October
  5, 1971).
Rigby, T. H. *Communist Party Membership in the USSR: 1917-1967.*   II S
  Princeton: Princeton University Press, 1968.
Robinson, William F. *The Pattern of Reform in Hungary.* New York: I T
  Praeger, 1973.
Schapiro, Leonard. *The Communist Party of the Soviet Union.*   II G
  2d ed. London: Eyred Spottswoode, 1970.

_____ . "The Concept of Totalitarianism." *Survey* no. 73 (Autumn   II C
1969): 98.

_____ . "Reflections on the Changing Role of the Party in the Totali-   IIC
tarian Polity." *Studies in Comparative Communism* (April
1969): 1-13.

_____ . "The Twenty-third Congress of the CPSU (I)." *Survey*   II G
no. 60 (July 1966).

Schwartz, M. "Czechoslovakia's New Political Model: A Design for   II G
Renewal." *Journal of Politics* (November 1968).

Schwartz, Morton. "Czechoslovakia: Toward One-party Pluralism?"   II C
Problems of Communism 16, no. 1 (January-February 1967):
21-27.

Segal, Gerald. "Automation, Cybernetics, and Party Control."   I T
Problems of Communism (March-April 1966).

_____ . "The 24th Congress: Personalities and Issues." *Survey*   II G
17, no. 2 (Spring 1971).

Seton-Watson, Hugh. "The Khrushchev Era." *Survey* no. 58   II G
(January 1966).

Shub, Anatole. "One Hundred Days." *Encounter*. July 1968.   I G

Stankovic, Slobodan. "The Crisis of the One-party System in   III G
Yugoslavia." Radio Free Europe Research Department,
June 5, 1967.

Staron, Staniskaw. "Political Developments in Poland: The Party   II G
Reacts to Challenge." *Orbis* (Winter 1970).

Stehle, Hansjakob. *The Independent Satellite: Society and Politics   II G
Since 1945*. New York: Praeger, 1965.

Stern, Carola. *Ulbricht: A Political Biography*. New York: I G
Praeger, 1966.

Strayer, Joseph R. "Problems of Dictatorship: The Russian Experi-   I G
ence." *Foreign Affairs* (January 1966).

Symposium (6 articles on the Comparative Study of Communist   II G
Systems). *Slavic Review* 26, no. 1 (March 1967).

Toma, Peter A. "On Comparing East European Political Systems: II G
The Case of Hungary." *Studies in Comparative Communism*
(April 1971): 43-46.

"Totalitarianism." *International Encyclopedia of the Social Sciences*.   I C
New York: 1968.

"Twenty-Fourth Congress of the CPSU." *Info. Bulletin* 9, nos.   II G
7 - 8. Prague: Peace and Socialism Publishers, 1971.

Triska, Jan F., ed. *Communist Party-States*. New York: Bobbs-   II G
Merrill Co., 1969.

Triska, Jan F. "On Comparing East European Political Systems: II G
Introduction." *Studies in Comparative Communism* (April
1971): 30-35.

Tucker, Robert. "The Dictator and Totalitarianism." *World*   I C
Politics 17, no. 4 (July 1965).

Tucker, Robert C. *The Soviet Political Mind.* New York: W. W.   II C
Norton and Co., 1971.

U. S. Department of State. Bureau of Intelligence and Research.   III T
World Strength of Communist Party Organizations
(January 1968).

Wightman, G. and A. H. Brown. "Changes in the Levels of Member-   II G
ship and Social Composition of the Communist Party of
Czechoslovakia, 1945-73." *Soviet Studies* 27, no. 3 (July
1975): 396-417.

Wolfe, Bertram D. *An Ideology in Power: Reflections On the*   II G
Russian Revolution. New York: Stein and Day, 1969.

Political Succession and Accretion of Power

Alexander, Hunter. "Khrushchev's Removal." Unpublished confer-   I G
ence paper. Southern Slavic Conference, Lexington, Ky.,
1966.

Barghoorn, Frederick C. "Analytic Framework: Soviet Politics."   II G
Comparative and Historical Contexts 4, nos. 3-4 (July-
October 1971): 42-57.

———. "Changes in Russia: The Need for Perspectives." *Problems*   II G
of Communism 15 (March-April 1966).

———. "Trends in Top Political Leadership in USSR." In R.   III T
Barry Farrell, ed., *Political Leadership in Eastern Europe
and the Soviet Union.* Chicago: Aldine Publishing
Company, 1970.

Baylis, Thomas A. "In Quest of Legitimacy." *Problems of*   II G
Communism 21, no. 2 (March-April 1972).

———. "Political Change in East Germany." *Problems of*   II G
Communism 21, no. 6 (November-December 1972).

Beck, Carl; Frederick Fleron, Jr.; Milton Lodge; Derek Waller;   II G
William Welsh; George Zaninovich. *Comparative
Communist Political Leadership.* New York: David
McKay Co., 1973.

Brinkley, George A. "Khrushchev Reremembered: On the Theory   I G
of Soviet Statehood." *Soviet Studies* (January 1973).

Bromke, Adam and John Strong, eds. *Gierik's Poland.* New   I G
York: Praeger, 1973.

Brzezinski, Zbigniew, et al. "Five Years After Khrushchev."   II G
Survey no. 72 (Summer 1969).

Burkes, R. V. *Technological Innovations and Political Change in*   III T
   Communist East Europe. RAND RM-6051-PR (1969).
Chamberlin, William Henry. "The Trend After Khrushchev: Immo-   II G
   bolism." *The Russian Review* 25 (January 1966): 3-9.
Cohen, Stephen F. *Bukharin and the Bolshevik Revolution: A*   II G
   Political Biography 1888-1938. New York: Alfred A.
   Knopf, 1973.
Constantinescu, Radu. "Why Patrascanu was Rehabilitated." *East*   III C
   Europe (August 1968).
Conquest, Robert. "After the Fall: Some Lessons." *Problems of*   I G
   Communism 14 (January-February 1965).
_____ *Russia After Khrushchev*. New York: Praeger, 1966.   I G
Croan, Melvin. "After Ulbricht: The End of an Era." *Survey*   II G
   17, no. 2 (Spring 1971).
Dean, Robert W. "Glerek's Three Years: Retrenchment and Reform."   II G
   Survey 20, no. 2-3 (Spring-Summer 1974): 59-75.
Djilas, Milovan. "After Tito—A Weaker Yugoslavia." New York *Times*   I C
   (October 30, 1970).
Dornberg, John. *Brezhnev: The Masks of Power*. New York: Basic   I G
   Books, 1974.
Duevel, Christian. "The Central Committee and the Central Auditing   III G
   Commission Elected by the 23rd CPSU Congress: A Study of
   the Political Survival of Their Members and a Profile of Their
   Professional and Political Composition." *Radio Liberty*
   Research Paper No. 6. New York: Radio Liberty Com-
   mittee, 1966.
Etzioni, Amitai. *Political Unification: A Comparative Study of Leaders* III C
   and Forces. New York: 1965.
Fainsod, Merle. "Khrushchevism in Retrospect." *Problems of Commu-*   I G
   nism 14 (January-February).
_____ "Whither Russia? Roads to the Future." *Problems of Communism*   I G
   16 (July-August 1967).
Farrell, R. Barry. "Top Political Leadership in Eastern Europe." In   II S
   R. Barry Farrell, ed., *Political Leadership in Europe and the*
   Soviet Union. Chicago: Aldine Publishing Company, 1970.
Gilberg, Trond. "Ceausescu's Romania," *Problems of Communism*   I G
   (July-August 1974): 29-43.
Ginsburgs, George. "The Kremlin Scene: Politics in a Cul-de-Sac,"   I G
   Current History (October 1969).
Haugh, Jerry F. "Enter N. S. Khrushchev." *Problems of Communism*   I G
   (July-August 1964).
Hingley, Ronald. *Joseph Stalin: Man and Legend*. New York: I G
   McGraw-Hill, 1974.

Hyland, William and Richard Wallace Shryock. *The Fall of Khrushchev.*   I G
New York: Funk and Wagnalls, 1969.

Jancar, Barbara Wolf. *Czechoslovakia and the Absolute Monopoly of*   II G
Powers: A Study of Political Power in a Communist System.
New York: Praeger, 1971.

Johnson, A. Ross. *The Polish Riots and Gomulka's Fall.* Santa   II G
Monica, The Rand Corporation, P-4615 (April 1971).

———. *The Power Struggle in the Polish Communist Leadership:*   II G
The "March Events"—End of an Era. The Rand Corporation, P-4238 (November 1969).

———. "Poland: End of an Era?" *Problems of Communism* 19, no. 1   I G
(January-February 1970).

———. "Polish Perspectives, Past and Present." *Problems of*   I G
Communism (July-August 1971).

Larson, Thomas B. "What Happened to Stalin?" *Problems of Com-*   I G
munism 16, no. 2 (March-April 1967).

Leonhard, Wolfgang. "The Day Stalin Died." *Problems of Communism*   I G
16 (July-August 1967).

Liebman, Marcel. *Leninism under Lenin.* London: Cape, 1975.   I G

Linden, Carl A. *Khrushchev and the Soviet Leadership.* Baltimore: II G
Johns Hopkins Press, 1966.

———. "No Room for Radicalism." *Problems of Communism* 14   I G
(May-June 1965).

Lowenthal, Richard. "The Coup and After." *Problems of Commu-*   I G
nism (July-August 1965).

Ludz, Peter C. "Continuity and Change Since Ulbricht." *Problems*   II G
of Communism 21, no. 2 (March-April 1972).

Marko, Kurt. "Ghosts Behind the Ghost—Stalin under Revision."   II G
Survey no. 60 (July 1966).

Mlynar, Z. "Problems of Political Leadership and the New Economic   II C
System." *World Marxist Review.* Prague, December 1965.

Organski, A. F. K. *The Stages of Political Development.* New York: II G
1965.

Page, Martin. *The Day Khrushchev Fell.* New York: Hawthorne, 1965.   I G

Page, Martin and David Burg. *Unpersonned: The Fall of Nikita*   I G
Sergeyevich Khrushchev. London: Chapman and Hall, 1966.

Rigby, T. H. "The Soviet Leadership: Towards a Self-Stabilizing   II C
Oligarchy?" *Soviet Studies* (October 1970).

———. "The Soviet Politburo: A Comparative Profile 1951-71."   II G
Soviet Studies 24, no. 1 (July 1972).

Roberts, Henry L. "The Succession to Khrushchev in Perspective."   III G
Proceedings of the Academy of Political Science 27 (1 April
1965).

Rose, Richard. "Dynamic Tendencies in the Authority of Regimes."
World Politics 21, no. 4 (July 1969): 627-28.

Rothenberg, Joshua. "The Status of Cults." *Problems of Communism* I G
(September-October 1967).

Rush, Myron. "After Khrushchev: Problems of Succession in the Soviet II G
Union." *Studies in Comparative Communism* (July-October 1969):
79-94.

_____. "Brezhnev and the Succession Issue." *Problems of Communism* I G
20 (July-August 1970).

_____. *How Communist States Change Their Rulers.* Ithaca: Cornell I G
University Press, 1974.

_____. *Political Succession in the USSR.* New York: Columbia Uni- II G
versity Press, 1965.

Schapiro, Leonard. "Collective Lack of Leadership." *Survey* nos. II G
70-71 (Winter-Spring 1969).

Shapiro, Jane P. "Rehabilitation Policy Under the Post-Khrushchev I G
Leadership." *Soviet Studies* (April 1969).

Shawcross, William. *Crime and Compromise: Janos Kadar and the I G
Politics of Hungary Since Revolution.* New York: Dutton,
1974.

Smolinski, Leon. "Khrushchevism without Khrushchev." *Problems of I G
Communism* 14 (May-June 1965).

Sobel, Lester A. *Russia's Rulers: The Khrushchev Period.* New York: I G
Facts on File, Inc., 1971.

Steward, Philip D. and others. "Political Mobility and the Soviet II G
Political Process: A Partial Test of Two Models." *The
American Political Science Review* 66, no. 1.

Swearer, Howard R. "The Politics of Succession in the USSR." II G
Journal of Politics 28 (1 February 1966).

Talbott, Strobe. *Khrushchev Remembers: The Last Testament.* I G
Boston: Little, Brown and Co., 1974.

Tucker, Robert. *Stalin as Revolutionary, 1879-1929: A Study I G
in History and Personality.* New York: W. W. Norton, 1973.

Ulam, Adam. "Another Crisis." *Problems of Communism* 14 I G
(May-June 1965).

Ulam, Adam B. *Stalin: The Man and His Era.* New York: I G
Viking, 1973.

"The USSR Since Khruschchev." Symposium. *Survey* (Summer II G
1969).

Wolfe, T. W. *The Soviet Union Six Months After Khruschev's Fall.* III G
Santa Monica, Calif.: RAND Corporation, P-3120 (April 1965).

Wynot, Edward D., Jr. *Polish Politics in Transition: The Camp*   II G
of National Unity and the Struggle for Power. Athens:
University of Georgia Press, 1974.

Governing Process—Legislation Versus Direction

Almond, G.; S. C. Glanagan; R. J. Mundt, eds. *Crisis, Choice and*   I G
Change: Historical Studies of Political Development.
Boston: Little, Brown and Co., 1973.
Barron, John. *KGB: The Secret Work of Secret Soviet Agents.*   I G
Pleasantville, N. Y.: Readers Digest Press, 1974.
Benes, Vaclav; Andrew Gyorgy; and George Stanbak. *Eastern*   I G
European Government and Politics. New York: Harper &
Row, 1966.
Bierzanck, R. "Parliamentary Control over Administration in   III T
Poland." *Polish Round Table* (January 1967).
Brown, A. H. *Soviet Politics and Political Science, Studies in*   I G
Comparative Politics. London: Macmillan, 1974.
Brzezinski, Z. *Dilemmas of Change in Soviet Politics.* New York: I G
Columbia University Press, 1969.
Churchward, L. G. *Contemporary Soviet Government.* New York: II G
American Elsevier Publishing Co., 1968.
Colton, Timothy J. "Civil-Military Relations in Soviet Politics."   I G
Current History 67, no. 398 (October 1974): 160-63.
Costello, Michael. "Political Prospects." *Survey* 17, no. 3   I G
(Summer 1971).
Crowe, Barry. *Concise Dictionary of Soviet Terminology, Insti-*   II G
tutions and Abbreviations. Oxford: Pergamon Press, 1969.
Frank, Peter. "The CPSU Ohkom First Secretary." *The British*   II T
Journal of Political Science 1 (April 1971): 173-90.
Gati, Charles, ed. *Political Modernization in Eastern Europe:*   II G
Testing the Soviet Model. New York: Praeger, 1974.
George A. *The "Op Code": A Negated Approach to the Study*   III S
of Political Leaders and Decision-Making. RAND
RM-5427-PR (1967).
Gilbert, Trond. "Political Leadership at the Regional Level in   II G
Romania: The Case of the Judet Party 1968-1973."
East European Quarterly 9, no. 1 (Spring 1975):
97-112.
Golan, Galia. *Reform Rule in Czechoslovakia: The Dubcek Era*   I G
1968-1969. London: Cambridge University Press, 1973.

Groth, Alexander J. *Peoples Poland: Government and Politics.*   II G
Scranton, Pa.: International Textbook Co., 1972.

Gripp, Richard C. *Patterns of Soviet Politics.* Homewood, Ill.:   II C
Dorsey Press, 1967.

Grzylowski, K. and J. L. Alder. "Legislative Trends." *Problems of*   I T
Communism 14 (March-April 1965).

Hough, Jerry F. "The Soviet Concept of the Relationship between   III G
the Lower Party Organs and the State Administration."
Slavic Review (June 1965).

Jowitt, Kenneth. "Political Innovation in Romania." Background   II G
to the 11th Party Congress. *Survey* 26, no. 4 (Autumn
1974): 132-51.

Krisch, Henry. *German Politics under Soviet Occupation.* New York: I G
Columbia University Press, 1974.

_____. *The Changing Role of the Standing Commissions of the USSR*   II T
Supreme Soviet 1966-1971. Paper for Annual APSA Meeting.
Chicago (September 1971).

Kohler, Foy D. and Mose L. Harvey, eds. *The Soviet Union: Yes-*   II G
terday, Today, Tomorrow. A Colloquy of American Long-
Timers in Moscow. Washington: Center for Advanced
International Studies, University of Miami, 1975.

Little, Richard D. "Soviet Parliamentary Committees After   II G
Khrushchev: Obstacles and Opportunities." *Soviet*
Studies 24, no. 1 (July 1972).

Lowenstein, James C. "Yugoslavia: Parliamentary Model?" *Problems*   II G
of Communism 14, no. 2 (March-April 1965).

Matthews, Mervyn, ed. *Soviet Government: A Selection of Official*   II T
Documents on Internal Policies. New York: Taplinger, 1974.

Metzl, Lothar. "Reflections on the Soviet Secret Police and   I T
Intelligence Services." *Orbis* 18, no. 3 (Fall 1974):
917-30.

Minagawa, Shugo. "The Functions of the Supreme Soviet Organs   II T
and Problems of their Institutional Development." *Soviet*
Studies 27, no. 1 (January 1975): 46-70.

Mitchell, R. Judson. "Soviet Politics: Stability or Immobilism."   II G
Current History 67, no. 398 (October 1974): 155-59.

Moroz, Valentin. *Report from the Beria Reserve.* Edited and   II G
translated by John Kolasky. Chicago: Cataract Press, 1974.

Morton, H. and R. Tokes, eds. *Soviet Politics and Society in the*   II G
1970's. New York: The Free Press, 1974.

Osborn, Robert. *The Evolution of Soviet Politics.* Homewood,   I G
Ill: Dorsey Press, 1974.

Piekalkiewicz, Jaroslaw. *Communist Local Government: A Study*   I G
of *Poland.* Athens: Ohio University Press, 1975.
Regional Party Leadership and Policy-Making in the USSR. New York   II G
Praeger, 1974.
Selucky, Radoslav. *Czechoslovakia: The Plan that Failed.* London: I G
Thomas Nelson and Sons, 1970.
Smith, Hedrick. "Soviet's Internal Security Eased Since Stalinist   I G
Era." New York *Times* (January 13, 1974).
Ulc, Otto. *Politics in Czechoslovakia.* San Francisco: W. H. Freeman   I G
and Reading, 1974.
Wesson, Robert G. *The Russian Dilemma: A Political and Geopoli-*   II G
tical View. New Brunswick, N. J.: Rutgers University Press,
1974.

Election Process—Representation

Bromke, Adam. "A New Political Style. *Problems of Communism*   II G
21, no. 5 (September-October 1972).
Gilson, J. "Soviet Elections as a Measure of Dissent: The Missing One   II S
Percent." *American Political Science Review* (September 1968).
Gostkowski, Z. "Analysis of the Panel Effect in the Study of an   III G
Election Campaign in Poland." *Polish Sociological Bulletin*
15, no. 1 (1967).

Interest Aggregation

Brown, A. H. "Pluralistic Trends in Czechoslovakia." *Soviet*   I G
Studies 17, no. 4 (April 1966).
_____. "Political Change in Czechoslovakia." *Government and*   II C
Opposition (Spring 1969).
_____. "Problems of Interest Articulation and Group Influence in   III G
the Soviet Union." *Government and Opposition* 7, no. 2
(Spring 1972).
Castles, Francis G. "Interest Articulation: A Totalitarian Paradox."   II G
Survey no. 73 (Autumn 1969).
Deakin, F. W. *The Embattled Mountain.* New York: Oxford Univer-   I G
sity Press, 1971.
Dean, Robert W. "Czechoslovakia: Consolidation and Beyond."   II G
Survey 17, no. 3 (Summer 1971).
Jacobs, Everett M. "Soviet Local Elections: What They Are, and   II G
What They Are Not." *Soviet Studies* (July 1970).

Jankowski, Jerzy. "Problems of Eastern Europe at Three European   III G
    Congresses." *The Central European Federalist* (June 1968).
Kautsky, John H. *The Political Consequences of Modernization.*   I T
    New York: Wiley, 1972.
King, Robert R. "Reorganization in Rumania." *Osteuropa* (January   I G
    1974): 37-46.
Klein, Ota and Jindrich Zeleny. "Dynamics of Change: Leadership,   II T
    The Economy, Organizational Structure, and Society." In R.
    Barry Farrell, ed., *Political Leadership in East Europe and the
    Soviet Union.* Chicago: Aldine Publishing Co., 1970.
Kolkowicz, Roman K. "Generals and Politicians: Uneasy Truce."   II G
    Problems of Communism 17, no. 3 (May-June 1968).
Krucky, Josef. "Democratic Upsurge in Czechoslovakia." *East   I G
    Europe* (September 1968).
Kuusinen, Aino. *The Rings of Destiny: Inside Soviet Russia From   I G
    Lenin to Brezhnev.* New York: Morrow, 1974.
Morton, Henry W., ed. *Soviet Policy Making: Studies of Communism   II G
    in Transition, 1966.*
Neal, Fred Warner. *Titoism in Action: The Reforms in Yugoslavia   I G
    after 1948.* Berkeley: University of California Press, 1958.
New Trends in Kremlin Policy. Washington, D. C., Center for   II G
    Strategic and International Studies, Georgetown
    University, 1970.
Oliver, J. H. "Citizen Demands and the Soviet Political System."   II G
    American Political Science Review (June 1969).
Palmer, Alan. *Russia in War, in Peace.* London: Weidenfield and   II G
    Nicolson, 1972.
Ploss, Sidney I. *Conflict and Decision-making in Soviet Russia.*   III G
    Princeton, N. J.: Princeton University Press, 1965.
_____. "Politics in the Kremlin." *Problems of Communism*   I G
    19, no. 3 (May-June 1970).
Ploss, Sidney I., ed. *The Soviet Political Process: Aims, Techniques*   III G
    and Examples of Analysis. Boston: Ginn and Co., 1971.
Polonsky, Antony. *Politics in Independent Poland, 1921-1939.*   III T
    New York: Oxford University Press, 1972.
Reshetar, John S., Jr. *The Soviet Polity, Government and Politics*   II G
    in the USSR. New York: Dodd, Mead and Co., 1971.
Roberts, Walter R. *Tito, Mihailovic and the Allies 1941-1945.*   I G
    New Brunswick, N. J.: Rutgers University Press, 1973.
Schapiro, Leonard. *Government and Politics in the Soviet Union.*   II G
    Revised edition. New York: Random House, 1965.
_____. "Keynote-Compromise." *Problems of Communism* (July-   II G
    August 1970).

Schwartz, Morton. "Czechoslovakia's New Political Model: A Design   II G
for Renewal." *Journal of Politics* 30, no. 1, (1968): 966-84.
Shanor, Donald Z. *Soviet Europe.* New York: Harper & Row, 1975.   I G
Simon, Gerhard. *Church, State and Opposition in the USSR.*   I G
London: C. Hurst, 1974.
Skilling, H. Gordon. "Leadership and Group Conflict in Czechoslovakia."   II G
In R. Barry Farrell, ed,, *Political Leadership in Eastern Europe
and the Soviet Union.* Chicago: Aldine Publishing Co., 1970.
Steele, Jonathan, ed. *Eastern Europe Since Stalin.* New York: Crane,   I G
Russak, 1974.
Strong, John W., ed. *The Soviet Union under Brezhnev and Kosygin:*   II G
The Transition Years. New York: Van Nostrand.
Tata, Michael. *Power in the Kremlin.* New York: Viking Press, 1969.   II G
Thornton, Richard C. "The Structure of Communist Politics." *World*   II G
Politics 24, no. 4 (July 1972).
Ward, Benjamin. "Political Power and Economic Change in Yugoslavia."   III C
American Economic Review. May 1968.
Wesson, Robert G. *The Russian Dilemma: A Political and Geopolitical*   II G
View. New Brunswick, N. J.: Rutgers University Press, 1974.
_____. *The Soviet Russian State.* New York: John Wiley and Sons, 1972.   II G
Wolfe, T. W. *Policymaking in the Soviet Union: A Statement with*   III G
Supplementary Comments. Santa Monica, Calif.: RAND
Corporation P-4194 (September 1969).

6. IDEOLOGY AND POLITICAL CULTURE: REVOLUTIONARY AND TRADITIONAL VALUES

Traditional Values

Aptheker, Herbert, ed. *Marxism and Christianity, A Symposium.*   I C
New York: Humanities Press, 1968.
Aron, Raymond. *Democracy and Totalitarianism; A Theory of*   II G
Political Regimes. New York: Praeger, 1969.
_____. *Industrial Society.* New York: 1967.   II T
Bennigsen, Alexandre and Chantal Lemercier-Quelquejay. *Islam in*   II G
the Soviet Union. New York: Praeger, 1967.
De George, Richard T. "Marxism and Anti-Marxism." *Studies in*   II C
Comparative Communism (January 1971): 37.
Demaitre, Edmund. "An Inconclusive Dialogue." *Problems of*   I C
Communism 20 (September-October 1971).

Devlin, Kevin. "The Catholic-Communist Dialogue." *Problems of*   II C
    Communism (May 1966).
Feaver, George. "Popper and Marxism." *Studies in Comparative*   III C
    Communism 4, nos. 3-4 (July-October 1971): 3-24.
Fitszman, Hoseph R. *Revolution and Tradition in Peoples Poland:*   II S
    Education and Socialization. Princeton, N. J.: Princeton
    University Press, 1972.
Gruenwald, Oskar. "Marxist Humanism." *Orbis* 18, no. 3 (Fall   I G
    1974): 888-916.
Kline, G. L. *European Philosophy Today.* Chicago, 1965.   II C
Klugman, James, ed. *Dialogue of Christianity and Marxism.*   II C
    London: 1968.
Kolawkowski, Leszek. "Karl Marx and the Classical Definition of   III C
    Truth." *Marxism and Beyond.* London: 1969, p. 64.
_____ *Towards a Marxist Humanism: Essays on the Left Today.*   I G
    New York: Grove Press, 1969.
Leonhard, Wolfgang. *Three Faces of Marxism: The Political Concepts*   III C
    of Soviet Ideology, Maoism and Humanist Marxism. New York:
    Holt, Rinehart and Winston, 1974.
MacIntyre, Alasdair. *Marxism and Christianity.* New York: Schocken,   II C
    1968.
Marcuse, Herbert. *Reason and Revolution: Hegel and the Rise of*   II C
    Social Theory. London: Oxford University Press, 1969.
McInnes, Neil. "The Christian Marxist Dialogue." *Survey* no. 67   II G
    (April 1968).
McClellan, David. *Marx Before Marxism.* New York: Harper &   II C
    Row, 1970.
Meisel, James H. *Counter-Revolution.* New York: 1966.   II C
Mitchell, R. Judson. "The Sino-Soviet Conflict and the Marxist-
    Leninist Theory of Development." *Studies in Comparative*
    Communism 7, no. 2 (Spring-Summer 1974): 119-45.
Moore, Barrington, Jr. *Social Origins of Dictatorship and Democracy.*   II C
    Boston: Harvard University Press, 1966.
Morgenthau, Hans J. "Alternatives for Change." *Problems of*   I G
    Communism (September-October 1966).
Nagy-Talavera, Nicholas M. *The Green Shirts and the Others:*   II G
    A History of Fascism in Hungary and Rumania. Stanford,
    Calif.: Stanford University, Hoover Institution Press, 1970.
Osborn, R. J. *The Evolution of Soviet Politics.* Homewood, Ill.:   I G
    Dorsey Press, 1974.
Parsons, H. L. *Humanistic Philosophy in Contemporary Poland*   II G
    and Yugoslavia. New York: American Institute for Marxist
    Study, 1966.

Rejai, M.; W. L. Mason; and D. C. Beller. "Political Ideology: III C
    Empirical Relevance of the Hypothesis of Decline." *Ethics*
    78, no. 4 (July 1968): 303-12.
Schaff, Adam. *Marxism and the Human Individual.* New York: II G
    McGraw-Hill, 1970.
Schapiro, Leonard. "Out of the Dustbin of History." *Problems of*   II C
    Communism (November-December 1967).
Zwerman, William A. *New Perspectives on Organization Theory:*   III C
    An Empirical Reconsideration of the Marxian and Classical
    Analyses. Westport, Conn.: Greenwood Publishing Corpor-
    ation, 1970.

Revolutionary Ideals

Adelmann, F. J. "Another Negation of the Negation." *Studies in*   II C
    Soviet Thought (SST) (September 1972).
Althussar, Louis. *Lenin and Philosophy.* Translated by B. Brewster.
    London: New Left Books, 1971.
The Anti-Stalin Campaign and International Communism: A   II G
    Selection of Documents. New York: Columbia Uni-
    versity Press, 1965.
Armstrong, John A. *Ideology Politics and Government in the Soviet*   I G
    Union. 3d ed. New York: Praeger, 1974.
Arnold, Bradley. "Soviet Views on Mao and Marxism." *SST*   II C
    (April 1972).
Aurich, Paul. *The Russian Anarchists.* Princeton, N. J.: Princeton   II G
    University Press. 1972.
————. *Russian Rebels.* New York: Schocken, 1972.   II G
Bachman, John E. "Recent Soviet Historiography of Russian Revolu-   III T
    tionary Populism." *Slavic Review* (December 1970).
Balinky, Alexander. *Marx's Economics: Origin and Development.*   II T
    Lexington, 1970.
Ballestrem, K. G. "Dialectical Logic." *SST* (1965)   III C
Barber, Noel. *Seven Days of Freedom: The Hungarian Uprising 1956.*   I G
    New York: Stein and Day, 1974.
Beemaus, Pierre J. "Scientific Atheism in the Soviet Union,   III G
    1917-54." *SST* (September 1967).
Bell, Daniel. "The End of Ideology in the Soviet Union?" *Marxist*   III G
    Ideology in the Modern World. Stanford, Calif.: Stanford
    University Press, 1965.
Berki, R. N. "Georg Lukacs in Retrospect: Evolution of a Marxist   *II C*
    Thinker." *Problems of Communism* 21, no. 6 (November-
    December 1972).

Berkman, Alexander. *What is Communist Anarchism?* New York: II C
    Dover, 1972.
Biszkv, Bels. "The Other Revolution and Social Progress in Hungary."   II G
    World Marxist Review (November 1967).
Bochenski, J. M. *The Methods of Contemporary Thought.* New York: II C
    Harper & Row, 1968.
Bochenski, Joseph, ed. *Guide to Marxist Philosophy: An Introduction*   II G
    Bibliography. Chicago: Swallow Press, 1972.
Bochenski, Joseph M. "Thomism and Marxism-Leninism."   III C
    SST (June 1967).
Boeselager, W. R. "Soviet Dialectical Methodology." *SST*   III C
    (June 1966).
Broido, Eva. *Eva Broido: Memoirs of a Revolutionary.* London: II C
    Oxford University Press, 1967.
Brower, Daniel, ed. *The Soviet Experience: Success or Failure.*   II C
    New York: Holt, Rinehart and Winston, 1971.
Brzezinski, Zbigniew. "Communist State Relations: The Effect   II C
    on Ideology." *East Europe* (March 1967).
Caldwell, John C. *Communism in Our World.* New York: John   I G
    Day, 1972.
Campbell, John C. "Moscow's Purposes." *Problems of Communism*   I G
    21, no. 5 (September-October 1972).
"Ceausescu's Little Cultural Revolution in Romania." *Osteuropa*   I G
    (Berlin) (October 1972): 717-28.
Chermilovsky, Z. M. "Contemporary Views of the USSR on Origins   II C
    and Role of the States." *International Social Sciences
    Journal* 22, no. 3 (1970).
Cienciala, Anna M. "Marxism and History: Recent Polish and Soviet   III C
    Interpretations of Polish Foreign Policy in the Era of
    Appeasement. An Evaluation." *East European
    Quarterly* 6, no. 1.
Cohen, Arthur A. "Thoughts on Maoism," *Studies in Comparative*   I C
    Communism (January 1971): 29.
Conquest, Robert. *V. I. Lenin.* New York: Viking Press, 1972.   I C
Cranston, Maurice. "The Ideology of Althusser." *Problems of
    Communism* 22 (March-April 1973).
Daniels, Robert V. "The Left Communists." *Problems of*   I G
    Communism (November-December 1967).
DeGeorge, Richard T. *Patterns of Soviet Thought.* Ann Arbor: II C
    University of Michigan Press, 1966.
———. *The New Marxism.* Racine, Wis.: Western Publishing   II C
    Company, 1968.

_____. *The New Marxism: Soviet and East European Marxism*　　II C
Since 1956. New York: Pegasus, 1968.

Demaitre, Edmund. "The Great Debate on National Communism."　　II C
Studies in Comparative Communism 5, nos. 2-3 (Summer-
Autumn, 1972).

_____. "The Origins of National Communism." *Studies in Compara-*　　II G
tive Communism (January 1969).

_____. "Stalin and the Era of Rational Irrationality." *Problems of*　　III C
Communism (November-December 1967).

_____. "The Wonders of Marxology." *Problems of Communism*　　II C
(July-August 1966).

Dinerstein, Herbert. "Moscow and the Third World—Power Politics　　I G
or Revolution." *Problems of Communism* 17, no. 1
(January-February, 1968).

Dirscherl, Denis, ed. *The New Russia Communism in Evaluation*.　　III G
Dayton, Ohio: Pflaum Press, 1968.

Drachkovitch, M. M. and Branko Lazitch. *The Comintern: Historical*　　I C
Highlights. New York: Praeger, 1966.

Drachkovitch, Milorad M., ed. *Marxism in the Modern World*. Palo　　II C
Alto: Stanford University Press, 1965.

Durauevskaya, Raya. "The Shock of Recognition and the Philosophic　　III C
Ambivalence of Lenin." *Telos* no. 5 (Spring 1970).

Dupre, Louis. *The Philosophical Foundations of Marxism*. New York:　　II C
Harcourt, Brace and World, 1966.

Easton, Loyd D. and Kurt H. Guddat, eds. *Writings of Young Marx*　　II C
on Philosophy and Society. New York: 1967.

Ellison, Herbert J. "The Socialist Revolutionaries." *Problems of*　　I G
Communism (November-December 1967).

Fetscher, Irving. *Marx and Marxism*. New York: Herder and Herder,　　II C
1971.

"Fidelity to Leninist Organizational Principles." *Pravda* (18　　I C
November 1964) or *GDSP* 16, no. 45.

Fiszman, Joseph. *Revolution and Tradition in Peoples' Poland,*　　II G
Education and Socialization. Princeton, N. J.:
Princeton University Press, 1972.

Fromm, Erich. *Marx's Concept of Man*. New York: Ungar, 1970.　　II C

Garaudy, Roger. *From Anathema to Dialogue*. New York: Herder　　II C
and Herder, 1966.

_____. *Marxism in the Twentieth Century*. New York: Scribners,　　II C
1970.

Gati, Charles. "History, Social Science, and the Study of Soviet　　II C
Foreign Policy." *Slavic Review* (December 1970).

Gella, Aleksander. "The Fate of Eastern Europe Under Marxism."   I G
     Slavic Review 29, no. 2 (June 1970).
Gerschenkron, Alexander. *Continuity in History and Other Essays.*   III C
     Cambridge, Mass.: Harvard University Press, 1968.
Getzler, Israel. *Martov: A Political Biography of a Russian Social*   I G
     Democrat. London: Cambridge University Press, 1967.
_____. "The Mensheviks." *Problems of Communism* (November-   I C
     December 1967).
Graham, Loren. *Science and Philosophy in the Soviet Union.*   III C
     New York: Knopf, 1972.
Gyorgy, Andrew, ed. *Issues of World Communism.* Princeton,   II C
     N. J.: Van Nostrand, 1966.
Halbrook, S. P. "Lenin's Bakuninism." *International Review of*   II C
     History and Political Science 8, no. 1 (February 1971).
Halperin, Ernst. "Beyond Libermanism." *Problems of Communism*   II C
     16 (January-February 1967).
Hammer, Darrell P. "The Dilemna of Party Growth." *Problems of*   I G
     Communism 20 (July-August 1970).
Hammond, Thomas T. *The Anatomy of Communist Takeovers.*   II G
     New Haven, Conn.: Yale University Press, 1975.
Haword, Dick. *The Development of the Marxian Dialectic.* Carbon-   II C
     dale: Southern Illinois University Press, 1972.
Hayward, Max. *On Trial.* New York: Harper & Row, 1966.   II C
Haword, Dick and Karl E. Klare, eds. *The Unknown Dimension:*   II C
     European Marxism Since Lenin. New York: Basic Books,
     1972.
Heitman, Sidney. "Nikolai Ivanovich Bukharin." *Problems of*   II C
     Communism (November-December 1967).
_____. *The Path to Socialism: Selected Works on N. I. Bukharin.*   III C
     New York: Omicron Books, 1967.
Hogan, Homer. "The Basic Perspective of Marxism-Leninism."   II C
     SST (December 1967).
Honecker, E. "The Problems of Building a Highly Developed   I C
     Socialist Society in the GDR." *World Marxist Review*
     (September 1967).
Hook, Sidney. "Marx's Second Coming." *Problems of Communism*   I C
     15 (July-August 1966).
Hopmann, P. Terry. "International Conflict and Cohesion in the   II G
     Communist System." *International Studies Quarterly*   II
     (1967): 212-36.
Huizinga, J. J. "The New Socialism: The End of an Illusion."   I G
     Problems of Communism 17 (July-October 1969).
"International Communism: The End of an Epoch." *Survey*   II G
     no. 54 (January 1965).

Ionescu, Ghita. *The Reluctant Ally, A Study of Communist*   II G
Neo-colonialism. London: Ampersand Press, 1965.

Jacobs, Dan N., ed. *The New Communisms.* New York:
Harper & Row, 1969.

Jacobs, Dan N. *The New Communist Manifesto and Related Documents.*   II C
New York: Harper & Row, 1965.

Jacobson, Julius. *Soviet Communism and the Socialist Vision.*   II C
New Brunswick, N. J.: Transaction Books, 1972.

Jameson, Fredric. *Marxism and Form: Twentieth Century Dialec-*   III C
tical Theories of Literature. Princeton, N. J.: Princeton
University Press, 1971.

Jancar, B. "The Case for a Loyal Opposition Under Communism: II C
Czechoslovakia and Yugoslavia." *Orbis* (Summer 1968).

Janus, Andrew C. and W. B. Slottman. *Revolution in Perspective,*   III C
Essays on the Hungarian Soviet Republic. Berkeley: University of California Press, 1973.

Johnson, A. Ross. *The Transformation of Communist Ideology:*   I G
The Yugoslav Case 1945-1953. Cambridge, Mass.: The M. I. T.
Press for the Center for International Studies, 1972.

Jordan, Zbigniew. *The Evolution of Dialectical Materialism.*   III C
New York: St. Martin, 1967.

Jowitt, Kenneth. "The Romanian Communist Party and the World   II C
Socialist System: A Redefinition of Unity." *World Politics*
(October 1970).

Kanet, Roger E. and Ivan Volgyes, eds. *On the Road to Communism.*   II C
Lawrence, Kans.: University of Kansas Press, 1972.

Kaplan, Frederick I. *Bolshevik Ideology and the Ethics of Soviet*   III C
Labor, 1917-1920: The Formative Years. New York:
Philosophical Library.

Kelsen, Hans. *The Political Theory of Bolshevism.* Berkeley: III C
University of California, 1948.

Kelray-Silk, Robert. *Socialism Since Marx.* New York: Taplinger,   II C
1972.

Kirchheimer, Otto. "Confining Conditions and Revolutionary   III C
Breakthroughs." *American Political Science Review* 59
(4 December 1965).

Kirschenmann, P. P. *Information and Reflection On Some Problems*   III T
of Cybernetics and How Contemporary Dialectical Material-
ism Copes with Them. New York: Humanities Press, 1970.

_____. "On the Kinship of Cybernetics to Dialectical Materialism."   III T
SST (March 1966).

_____ "Science and Its Metaphysical Interpretations." *SST* III C
(September 1971).

Kovaly, Pavel. "Is It Possible to Humanize Marxism? " *Studies* II C
in Soviet Thought (December 1971).

Kline, George L. "Georg Lukacs in Retrospect: Impressions of the I G
Man and His Ideas." *Problems of Communism* 21, no. 6
(November-December 1972).

_____ "Was Marx an Ethical Humanist." *SST* (June 1969). II C

Klinghoffer, Arthur Jay. *Soviet Perspectives on African Socialism*. I G
Rutherford, N. J.: Fairleigh Dickinson University
Press, 1969.

Koecher, Karl F. *The Marxist Scrutiny of Marxism*. RR II C
Det, 1971.

Kolakowski, Leszek. *Toward a Marxist Humanism: Essays on the* II C
Left Today. New York: Grove Press, 1968.

_____ "The Fate of Marxism in Eastern Europe." *Slavic Review* III C
29, no. 2 (June 1970).

_____ "Hope and Hopelessness." *Survey* 17, no. 3 (Summer II C
1971).

Konstantinov, P. and V. Kelle. "Historical Materialism-Marxist II C
Sociology." *Kommunist* no. 1 (January 1965): 92-93
as translated in the *Current Digest of the Soviet Press*
(CDSP) 17, no. 8 (1965): 3-8.

Korbonski, Andrzy. "Comparing Liberalization Processes in II C
Eastern Europe: A Preliminary Analysis." *Comparative*
Politics 4, no. 2 (January 1972).

Koren, Henry J. *Marx and the Authentic Man*. Pittsburgh, Pa.: II C
Duquesne University Press, 1967.

Korey, William. "Grigori Yevseevich Zinoviev." *Problems* I G
of Communism (November-December 1967).

Korsch, Karl. "Three Essays on Marxism." *Monthly Review* I G
(N. Y.) 1972.

Kortz, Paul and Suctozar Stojanovic, eds. *Tolerance and Revo-* III C
lution: A Marxist–Non-Marxist Humanist Dialogue.
Belgrade Philosophical Society of Serbia, 1970.

Kusin, Vladimir L. *The Intellectual Origins of the Prague Spring:* III T
The Development of Reformist Ideas in Czechoslovakia.
Soviet and East European Studies Series of the National
Association for Soviet and East European Studies. London:
Cambridge University Press, 1971.

Laqueur, Walter. *The Fate of the Revolution: Interpretations* II G
of Soviet History. New York: Macmillan, 1967.

Lasswell, Harald D. and Daniel Lerner. *World Revolutionary Elites.*   II G
Cambridge: MIT Press, 1966.

Laszlo, Ervin. *The Communist Ideology in Hungary.* Dordrecht/   II C
Holland: Reidel Press, 1966.

———. "Dynamics of Ideological Change in Eastern Europe."   II C
Inquiry 1, no. 1 (1966).

———. "Marxism–Leninism vs. Neurophysiology." *SST* (June 1969).   II C

———. "The Planification of Hungarian Marxism-Leninism." *SST*   II C
(December 1965).

Lazitch, Branko and Milorad M. Drachkovich. *Lenin and the Comin-*   II C
tern 1. Stanford, Calif.: Hoover Institution Press, 1972.

Lefebure, Henri. *The Sociology of Marx.* New York: Vintage   II C
Books, 1969.

Lendvai, Paul. *Eagles in Cobwebs: Nationalism and Communism in*   I G
the Balkans. London: Macdonald, 1970.

Lenin, V. I. *The State and Revolution.* Peking: Foreign   II C
Language Press, 1970.

Lewis, J. "The Uniqueness of Man and the Dialectic of History."   II C
Praxis 1-2 (Zagrck) 1970.

Lichtheim, George. *The Origins of Socialism.* New York: Praeger,   III C
1969.

———. "The Transmutation of a Doctrine." *Problems of Communism*   II G
15 (July-August 1966).

Lippmann, Heinz. "The Limits of Reform Communism." *Problems of*   I G
Communism 19, no. 3 (May-June 1970).

Lobkowicz, Nikolai. *Theory and Practice.* Notre Dame, 1967.   III C

———. "Is the Soviet Notion of Practice Marxian? " *SST*   II C
(March 1966).

———. "Historic Laws." *Studies in Soviet Thought* (December   II C
1971).

Lobkowicz, Nikolai, ed. *Marx and the Western World.* Notre Dame,   I C
Ind.: University of Notre Dame Press, 1967.

Loebl, Eugen. "Computer Socialism." *Studies in Soviet Thought*   III T
(December 1971).

Logoreci, Anton. "Albania: The Anabaptists of European Communism."   II C
Problems of Communism (May-June 1967).

Lowenthal, Richard. "The Model of the Totalitarian State." In   II C
Royal Institute of International Affairs, *The Impact*
of the Russian Revolution 1917-1967. London: 1967.

———. "The Prospects for Pluralistic Communism." *Dissent*
12, no. 1 (Winter 1965): 109.

_____ "The Revolution Withers Away." *Problems of Communism*   I C
14, no. 1 (1965).

_____ "Russia, The One Party System and the Third World."   II G
Survey no. 58 (January 1966).

Ludz, Peter. "The New Socialism: I. Philosophy in Search of   I C
Reality." *Problems of Communism* 18 (July-October
1969).

Lukacs, Georg. *History and Class Consciousness: Studies in*   III C
Marxist Dialectics: Cambridge, Mass: The MIT Press,
1971.

_____ *Lenin: A Study on the Unity of his Thought.* Cambridge,   III G
Mass.: The MIT Press, 1971.

Malinov, K. "Party Work in Residential Areas." *World Marxist*   I G
Review (December 1967).

Mandel, Ernest. *The Formation of the Economic Thought of Karl*   II C
Marx, 1843 to Capital. New York: Monthly Review Press,
1969.

_____ *Marxist Economic Theory.* New York: Monthly Review   III C
Press, 1968.

Marcuse, Herbert. *One Dimensional Man: Studies in the Ideology*   III C
of Advanced Industrial Society. Boston, Mass.: Beacon
Press, 1964.

_____ *Soviet Marxism: A Critical Analysis.* New York: Vantage   II C
Books, 1961.

Marx and Contemporary Scientific Thought. UNESCO Inter-   III C
national Social Science Council. Mouton (Hague), 1969.

Marxism-Leninism on War and Army (A Soviet View).   II T
Moscow: Progress Publishers and Washington,
D. C.: U. S. Government Printing Office, 1972.

Meiler, V. "Czechoslovakia: The Struggle for Reform." *East*
Europe 14 (8 August 1965).

Meyer, Alfred G. "Empty Formalism?" *Studies in Comparative*   II G
Communism (January 1971): 42.

_____ "Lev Davidovich Trotsky." *Problems of Communism*   I C
(November-December 1956).

Miele, Renato. "Lenin and the Revolution." *Problems of Com-*   I C
munism (November-December 1967).

Milazzo, Matteo J. *The Chetmk Movement and the Yugoslav Resis-*   I G
tance. Baltimore: Johns Hopkins Press, 1975.

Milovidov, A. S., ed. *The Philosophical Heritage of V. I. Lenin*   II T
and Problems of Contemporary War (A Soviet View).
Washington, D. C.: U. S. Government Printing Office,
1972.

Moore, B., Jr. *Social Origins of Dictatorship and Democracy.*   II G
Harmondsworth, Eng.: Penguin Books, 1967.

Niemeyer, Gerhart. "Philosophical Inquiry or Ideological System?"   III C
Studies in Comparative Communism (January 1971): 45.

O'Meara, Andrew P., Jr. *Infrastructure of the Marxist Power Seizure:*   III C
An Analysis of the Communist Models of Revolution. New
York: Vantage Press, 1973.

Ostrowski, K. "Local Leadership in Poland." *Polish Sociological*   III G
Bulletin 16, no. 2 (1967).

Parry, Albert. "On Lenin: Recent Contributions in the West."   II C
RR (October 1970).

Parry, Albert, ed. *Peter Kapitsa on Life and Science.* New York: III C
Macmillan, 1960.

Petrovic, Gaja. "Dialectical Materialism and the Philosophy of   II C
Praxis." *Boston Studies in the Philosophy of Science*
4, New York (1969): 265.

———. *Marx in the Mid-Twentieth Century.* New York: 1967.   II G

Pipes, Richard, ed. *Revolutionary Russia.* Cambridge: Harvard   I G
University Press, 1968.

Polin, Raymond. *The Marxian Foundations of Communism.* Chicago: I G
Henry Regnery, 1966.

Polonsky, Anthony. *The Little Dictators: The History of Eastern*   I G
Europe Since 1918. Boston: Routledge and Kegan Paul, 1975.

Poromarev, Boris. "The October Revolution—Beginning of the   II G
Epoch of Socialism and Communism." *World Marxist
Review.*

Pospielovsky, Dimitry. "Dogmas Under Attack: A Traveler's Report."   I C
Problems of Communism (March-April 1968).

Pyziur, Eugene. "Recent Offerings on Marxist Ideology." *RR*   II C
(October 1967).

Rankovic, Aleksander. "The Reform is Consolidating the Unity   III C
of the People." *Socialist Thought and Practice* no. 1 (1966).

Ristic, Dragisa N. *Yugoslavia's Revolution of 1941.* University Park: II G
Pennsylvania State University Press, 1966.

Rosenberg, William G. *Liberals in the Russian Revolution: The*   I G
Constitutional Democratic Party, 1917-1921. Princeton,
N. J.: Princeton University Press, 1974.

Rus, Veljko. "Institutionalization of the Revolutionary Movement."   II G
Praxis 2, no. 2 (1967).

Schaff, Adam. *Marxism and the Human Individual.* New York: II C
McGraw-Hill, 1970.

Schapiro, Leonard and Peter Reddaway, eds. *Lenin, the Man,*   II C
the Theorist, the Leader: A Reappraisal. New York: 1967.

Schart, C. Bradley. "Toward A Comparative Analysis of Workers' Movements." *Studies in Comparative Communism* 4, nos. 3-4 (July-October 1971): 105-10. II G

Schiebel, Joseph. "National-Liberation Movements, Historical Materialism and Soviet Philosophy." *SST* (June 1966). III C

———. "Changing the Unchangeable Historical Materialism and Six Versions of Eternal Laws of Historical Development." *SST* (December 1967). III C

Schwartz, Harry, ed. *Prague's 200 Days.* New York: Praeger, 1969. II G

Sherman, Howard. "The Marxism of Ernest Mandel." *Problems of Communism* 21, no. 6 (November-December 1972). II C

Sirkov, D. "Bulgarians in the October Revolution (Party Work in Bulgaria)." *World Marxist Review* (December 1967). II G

Skolimowski, Henry K. "Are There No Consequences of Open Marxism?" *Studies in Comparative Communism* (January 1971): 48. II C

———. "Logos and Praxis." *Studies in Comparative Communism* (April 1970): 25-30. II C

———. "Open Marxism and Its Consequences." *Studies in Comparative Communism* (January 1971): 23. II C

Sommerville, John. *The Philosophy of Marxism.* New York: Random House, 1967. III C

Staar, Richard F. *Aspects of Modern Communism.* Columbia: University of South Carolina Press, 1968. II C

Tokes, Rudolph L. *Bela Kun and the Hungarian Soviet Republic: The Origins and Role of the Communist Party of Hungary in the Revolutions of 1918-1919.* New York: 1967. II G

Treadgold, Donald W., ed. *Soviet and Chinese Communism: Similarities and Differences.* Seattle: University of Washington Press, 1967. II C

Tsapanov, A. Loshchakov Y. "Socialist Countries Ideological Cooperation." *International Affairs* no. 2 (February 1975): 24-33. I G

Tucker, Robert C. "The Deradicalization of Marxist Movements." *American Political Science Review* 61, no. 2 (June 1967): 343-58. II C

———. *The Marxist Revolutionary Idea.* New York: W. W. Norton, 1969. II G

"Unity of Action of the World Communist Movement." *World Marxist Review* 8, no. 4 (April 1965). II G

Urban, G. R. "Removing the Hyphen." *Studies in Comparative Communism* (July-October 1968): 1-6. II G

Valentinov, N. *Encounters with Lenin*. New York: Oxford   I G
University Press, 1968.

Vardys, Stanldy. "The Baltic Nations in Search of Their Own   I G
Political Systems." *East European Quarterly* 7, no. 4
(1973).

Vigor, P. H. *A Guide to Marxism and Its Effects on Soviet*   I G
Development. New York: Humanities Press, 1966.

Walker, Franklin A. "P. L. Lavrov's Concept of the Party."   II C
The Western Political Quarterly (June 1966): 235.

Weeks, Albert L. "The First Bolshevik." *Problems of Communism*
16 (November-December 1967).

Wesson, Robert G. "Soviet Ideology: The Necessity of Marxism."   II G
Soviet Studies (July 1969).

Wetter, Gustav A. "Freedom of Thought and Ideological Coexis-   II C
tence." *SST* (December 1966).

_____. *Soviet Ideology Today*. New York: Praeger, 1966.   II G

Wolfe, Bertram D. *Marxism: One Hundred Years in the Life of*   II C
a Doctrine. New York: Dial Press, 1965.

Solfenstein, E. Victor. *The Revolutionary Personality*. Princeton: III T
Princeton University Press, 1972.

Zeitlin, I. M. *Marxism: A Re-examination*. Princeton, N. J.:   II C
Van Nostrand Reinhold Co., 1970.

Zhivkov, Z. "People's Democracy—Tried and Tested Road to   II G
Socialism." *World Marxist Review* 8, no. 6 (June 1965).

Zieleniec, L., and A. Charakchiev "Milestone in the March of   I G
History." *World Marxist Review* 8, no. 5 (May 1965).

Individual Motivation

Cole, Michael. "Psychology: A Checkered Course." *Problems of*   II T
Communism 14 (November-December 1965).

Dechert, C. R. "Cybernetics and the Human Person." *Inter-*   III C
national Philosophical Quarterly 4, (1964).

Fromm, Erich. *Socialist Humanism: An International Symposium*.   III C
New York: Doubleday, Anchor (paper), 1965.

Gyaurov, K. "The Intelligentsia, True Helpers of the Communists."   II G
World Marxist Review (December 1968).

"Individual Liberty and Czechoslovakia's Freedom." Documents   I G
in *Problems of Communism* 17, no. 3 (May-June 1969).

Petrov, Vladimir. *Escape from the Future: The Incredible Adven-*   I G
tures of a Young Russian. Bloomington: Indiana University
Press, 1973.

Education

Ablin, Fred, ed. *Contemporary Soviet Education, A Collection*   III G
  of Readings from Soviet Journals. White Plains, N. Y.:
  International Arts and Sciences Press, 1969.

Blakeley, Thomas J. "Current Soviet Views on Existentialism."   II C
  SST (December 1967).

_____. "Soviet Philosophical Method: The Case of B. M. Kedrov."   III C
  SST (March 1966).

_____. *Soviet Philosophy.* Dordrecht/Holland: Reidel Press, 1964.   III C

_____. *Soviet Theory of Knowledge.* Dordrecht: D. Reidel Co.,   III C
  1964.

Bochenski, Joseph M. "On Partignost in Philosophy." *SST*, June 1965.   III C

Brickman, William W. "Academic Adventures in East Germany."   II T
  Educational Forum (May 1971): 467-69.

Chauncey, Henry, ed. *Soviet Preschool Education Vol. I: Program*   II T
  of Instruction. New York: Holt, Rinehart, and Winston, 1969.

Coleman, James S. *Education and Political Development.* Princeton,   II G
  N. J.: Princeton University Press, 1965.

"Colleges Curbed in East Germany." New York *Times* (January   III G
  8, 1969).

Drapela, Victor J. "Educational Guidance in the United States and   II G
  Czechoslovakia: A Comparative Study." *East European*
  Quarterly 8, no. 3 (1974): 295-305.

Fischer, George, ed. *Science and Ideology in Soviet Society.*   II S
  New York: Atherton, 1967.

Fitzpatrick, Sheila. *The Commisariat of Enlightenment: Soviet*   III T
  Organization of Education and the Arts Under Lunacharsky,
  October 1917-1921. London: Cambridge University
  Press, 1970.

Finiasov, B. "The All Union Scientific Research Institute of State   II S
  Patent Review." *JPRS, News of Soviet Scientific Organiza-*
  tion no. 37,087 (August 18, 1966).

Frolic, B. Michael. "The Soviet Study of Soviet Cities." *Journal*   III T
  of Politics 32 (August 1970): 675-95.

Grant, Nigel. *Society, Schools and Progress in Eastern Europe.*   II T
  London: Pergamon Press, 1969.

Hahn, Walter. "Education in East and West Germany—A Study of   III S
  Similarities and Contrasts." *Studies in Comparative Commu-*
  nism 5, no. 1 (Spring 1972).

Hübener, Theodore. "History as Taught Through East German   III T
  Textbooks." *School and Society* 99 (January 1971): 56-59.

Jacoby, Susan. *Inside Soviet Schools.* New York: Hill and Wang, 1974.   I G

Johnson, William H. E. *Russia's Educational Heritage.* New York: II G
     Octagon Books, 1969.
Keep, John. "Current Soviet Historiography." *Survey* 19, no. 1   III T
     (Winter 1973).
Laszlo, Erwin. "Trends in East European Philosophy." *SST*   III C
     (June 1967).
Little, Richard. "The Academy of Pedagogical Sciences: Its Political   II G
     Roles." *Soviet Studies* 19, no. 3 (January 1968).
Mazour, Anatole G. *The Writing of History in the Soviet Union.*   II G
     Stanford, Calif.: The Hoover Institution Press, 1971.
Medvedev, Zhores A. *The Medvedev Papers. The Plight of Soviet*   II G
     Science Today. New York: St. Martin's Press, 1971.
_____. *The Rise and Fall of T. D. Lysenko.* New York: Columbia   II G
     University Press, 1969.
Micjievicz, Ellen, ed. *Handbook of Soviet Social Science Data*   III S
     New York: Free Press, 1973.
Mickiewicz, Ellen Propper. *Soviet Political Schools: The Communist*   III G
     Party Adult Instruction System. New Haven: Yale University
     Press, 1967.
Mills, R. M. "One Theory in Search of Reality: The Development of   II C
     United States Studies in the Soviet Union." *Political Science*
     Quarterly 87, no. 1 (March 1972).
Muller-Markus, S. "Soviet Discussion on General Relativity Theory."   III T
     SST (September 1965).
Nettl, J. P. "The Early Marx and Modern Sociology." *Studies in*   III T
     Comparative Communism (April 1969): 48-73.
Noah, Harold J. *Financing Soviet Schools.* New York: New York   II G
     Teachers' College Press, Columbia University, 1966.
Parsons, Talcott. "An American Impression of Sociology in the Soviet   II G
     Union." *American Sociological Review* (February 1965).
Payke, T. R. "The 'Brain-Psyche' Problems in Soviet Psychology."   III C
     SST (June 1967).
_____. "On the Theoretical Foundations of Soviet Psychology."   III C
     SST (June 1966).
Pennor, Joan; Ivan J. Bakolo; and George Z. F. Bereday. *Moderni-*   III S
     zation and Diversity in Soviet Education with Special
     Reference to Nationality Groups. New York: Praeger,
     1971.
Redl, Helen B. and Fritz, eds. *Soviet Education on Soviet Education.*   II T
     New York: The Free Press, 1964 Docs.
Revesz, Laszlo. "Political Science in Eastern Europe: Discussion   II G
     and Initial Steps." *SST* (September 1967).

Robinson, T. W. *Game Theory and Politics: Recent Soviet Views.*   *III C*
    RAND RM-5839 RR (May 1970).
Rosen, Seymour M. *Education and Modernization in the USSR.*   II G
    Reading, Mass.: Addison-Wesley, 1971.
Rosen, S. M. *Soviet Programs in International Education.* Washington   III T
    D. C.: Department of Health, Education and Welfare, Institute
    of International Studies, 1971.
Rubenstein, Alvin Z. "Lumumba University: An Assessment."   I G
    Problems of Communism 20, no. 6 (November
    December 1971).
Rudman, Herbert C. *The School and the State in the USSR.*   II G
    New York: Macmillan, 1967.
Satina, Sophie. *Education of Women in Pre-Revolutionary Russia,*   III G
    The Author. 1966.
Shimoniak, Wasyl. *Communist Education: Its History, Philosophy*   II G
    and Politics. Skokie, Ill.: Rand McNally and Co., 1970.
Silver, Brian D. "The Status of National Minority Language in   II T
    Soviet Education: An Assessment of Recent Changes."
    Soviet Studies 26, no. 1 (January 1974): 28-39.
Simirenko, Alex, ed. *Soviet Sociology.* Chicago, Ill.: Quadrangle   II T
    Books, 1966.
Taborsky, Edward. "Sociology in Eastern Europe: Czechoslovakia."   II G
    Problems of Communism 14 (January-February 1965).
Theen, Rolf, H. W. "Political Science in the USSR." *Problems of*   II G
    Communism 21 (May-June 1972).
Torkevich, John. "Soviet Science Appraised." *Foreign Affairs*   II G
    (April 1966).
Vucinich, Alexander. *Science in Russian Culture 1861-1917.*   II G
    Stanford, California: Stanford University Press, 1970.
Waitr, Jerzy, ed. *The State of Sociology in Eastern Europe Today.*   II G
    Carbondale: Southern Illinois University Press, 1971.
Wilder, Emilia. "Sociology in Eastern Europe: Poland." *Problems*   II G
    of Communism 14 (January-February 1965).
Yanowitch, M. and Dodge, N. "Social Class and Education: Soviet   II C
    Findings and Reactions." *Comparative Education Review*
    (October 1968).

Youth Groups

Bauman, Z. "Polish Youth and Politics." *Polish Round Table,*   III G
    1967.
Cornell, Richard. *Youth and Communism.* New York: Walker and   II G
    Co., 1965.

Dasbacn, Anita. "Czechoslovakia's Youth." *Problems of Communism*   I G
18, no. 2 (March-April 1969).
Deutscher, Issac. "The Old Party and the Young People." *The Nation*   II G
202 (May 2, 1966): 517-20.
DeWitt, Nicholas. *Education and Professional Employment in the USSR.*   III S
National Science Foundation, 1961.
Georgeoff, Peter John. *The Social Education of Bulgarian Youth.*   II T
Minneapolis: University of Minnesota Press, 1968.
Golan, Galia. "Youth and Politics in Czechoslovakia." *Journal of*   I G
Contemporary History 1 (London), 1970.
Kassof, Allen. *The Soviet Youth Program: Regimentation and*   II T
Rebellion. Cambridge, Mass.: Harvard University Press,
1965.
Lewytzkyj, Barys. "Generations in Conflict." *Problems of Communism*   I G
16, no. 1 (January-February 1967).
Neuberg, Paul. *The Hero's Children: The Post-War Generation in*   II G
Eastern Europe. New York: Morrow, 1973.
Rutkevich, M. N., ed. *The Career Plans of Youth.* Translated by Murray   II S
Yanowitch. White Plains, N. Y.: International Arts and
Sciences Press, 1969.
Skrzypek, Stanislaw. "The Political, Cultural and Social Views of   III S
Yugoslav Youth." *Public Opinion Quarterly* 29, no. 1
(Spring 1965): 87-106.
Tomsv, I. "Party Guidance of the Young Communist League."   II T
World Marxist Review (December 1967).
Ulc, Otto. "The Communist Party of Czechoslovakia and the Young   II G
Generation." *East European Quarterly* 6, no. 2 (June 1972).
Weaver, Kitty D. *Lenin's Grandchildren: Preschool Education*   III S
in the Soviet Union. New York: Simon and Schuster, 1971.

7. CULTURE AND SOCIALIST MORALITY: PERSONAL EXPRESSION AND SOCIETAL RESPONSIBILITY

Censorship Control/Artistic Policy

Adams, Jan S.; Michael W. Curran; J. Patrick Lewis, eds. *The USSR*   I G
Today, Current Readings from the Soviet Press, 1973 to 1975.
"Appeal of Evangelical Christians-Baptists in Kiev to Soviet   III C
Government." *RCDA* 6, no. 10 (May 24, 1966).
Barooshian, Vahan D. "The Politics of the Avant-Garde." *Problems*   I G
of Communism (March-April 1970).

Bernstein, Robert L., et al., eds. *Book Publishing in the USSR.*   II T
Cambridge, Mass.: Harvard

Blake, Patricia. "Freedom and Control in Literature, 1962-1963."   II T
In Dallin and Westin, eds., *Politics in the Soviet Union:
Seven Cases.* New York: Harcourt, Brace and World, 1966.

⎯⎯⎯. "New Voices in Russian Writing." *Encounter* (London)   I T
(April 1963).

Blakely, T. J. "On Lies; Big, Little and Soviet." *Studies in Soviet*   I G
Thought (September 1969).

Borome, Joseph A. "The Bolshoi Theater and Opera." *RR*   I G
(January 1965).

Brown, Deming. "The Art of Andrei Sinyavsky." *Slavic Review*   II G
(December 1970).

Brown, J. F. "Frost and Thaw in Bulgarian Culture." *Studies in*   II T
Comparative Communism (July-October 1969): 95-120.

Burg, David and George Feifer. *Solzhenitsyn.* London: Hoddard   I G
Stoughton, 1972.

Buzek, Antony. *How the Communist Press Works.* New York: III T
Praeger, 1964.

⎯⎯⎯. "Studies on the Soviet Union: The Soviet Censorship."   III G
New Series 11, no. 2, (1971).

Constantine, Mildred and Alan Fem. *Revolutionary Soviet Film*   I T
Posters. Baltimore: Johns Hopkins Press, 1974.

Dallin, Alexander and George W. Breslauer. *Political Terror in*   I G
Communist Systems. Stanford, Calif: Stanford University Press, 1970.

Delany, Joan. "Krushchev's Anti-Religious Policy and Campaign   II G
of 1954." *Soviet Studies* (January 1973).

Dewhirst, Martin and Robert Farrell, eds. *The Soviet Censorship.*   I G
Metuchen, N. J.: The Scarecrow Press, 1973.

Durham, F. Gayle. *Radio and Television in the Soviet Union.*   II G
Center for International Studies, MIT (June 1965).

Egbert, Donald D. "Politics and the Arts in Communist   II G
Bulgaria." *Slavic Review* 26, no. 2 (June 1967).

Ehrenburg, Elya. *Men, Years–Life.* 6 vols. London: MacGibbon   II G
and Kee, 1961-66.

Fanger, Donald. "Solzhenitsyn: Art and Foreign Matter."   I G
Problems of Communism 21 (May-June 1972).

Friedberg, Maurice. "What Price Censorship? " *Problems of*   I G
Communism 17, no. 5 (September-October 1968).

Gebrian, George. *Soviet Russian Literature in English.* A check-   II S
list bibliography. Ithaca, N. Y.: Cornell University, 1967.

Grimstead, Patricia K. "Archives in the Soviet Union: Their   II T
Organization and the Problem of Access." *The
American Archivist* 34 (1971).

Grossman, Jean Delaney. "Leadership of Anti-Religious   II T
Propaganda in the Soviet Union." *Studies in Soviet
Thought* (September 1972).

Hingley, Ronald. "Defeat at Tannenberg." *Problems of   I G
Communism* 21, no. 6 (November-December 1972).

———. "Home Truths on the Farm: The Literary Mirror."   I G
Problems of Communism 14, no. 3 (May-June 1965).

Hollander, Gayle Durham. *Soviet Political Indoctrination: II G
Developments in Mass Media and Propaganda Since
Stalin.* New York: Praeger, 1972.

Hopkins, Mark W. *Mass Media in the Soviet Union.* New York:
Pegasus, 1970.

Johnson, Priscilla. *Khrushchev and the Arts: The Politics of   II G
Soviet Culture, 1962-1964.* Cambridge: MIT Press, 1965.

Koehler, Ludmilla. "New Trend in Soviet Literary Criticism."   II C
RR (January 1968).

Liehm, Antonin J. *Closely Watched Films: The Czechoslovak   I G
Experience.* White Plains, N. Y.: International Arts
and Sciences Press, 1974.

———. *The Politics of Culture.* New York: Grove Press   II G
1972.

Maguire, Robert A. *Red Virgin Soil: Soviet Literature in the   II T
Twenties.* Princeton, N. J.: Princeton University
Press, 1968.

Majstorvic, Steven. *Cultural Policy in Yugoslavia.* New York: I G
Unipub, Inc., 1972.

Makanowitzky, Barbara. "Music to Serve the State." *RR*   II T
(July 1965).

McClure, T. "The Politics of Soviet Culture, 1964-1967."   II G
Problems of Communism (March-April 1967).

McLean, Hugh. "Et Resurrexerunt: How Writers Rise from   I G
the Dead." *Problems of Communism* 19, no. 2
(March-April 1970).

Merritt, Richard L. "Politics, Theater and the East-West   II G
Struggle: The Theater as a Cultural Bridge in
West Berlin, 1948-1967." *Political Science
Quarterly* no. 2 (June 1965): 186-215.

Mickiewicz, Ellen. "The Modernization of Party Propaganda   II G
in the USSR." *Slavic Review* 30, no. 2 (June 1971).

Monas, Sidney. "In Defense of Socialist Realism." *Problems*   I C
    of Communism (March-April 1967).
Mork, Gordon R. "The Archives of the German Democratic   III T
    Republic." *Central European History* 2 (1969).
Orlovsky, Serge. "Moscow Theaters, 1917-1941." *Soviet*   II T
    Theaters: 1917-1941. Research Program on the
    USSR, New York, 1954.
Paull, Burton. *Radio and Television Broadcasting in Eastern*   I G
    Europe. Minneapolis: University of Minnesota Press,
    1974.
Piekalkiewicz, Jaroslaw A. *Public Opinion Polling in*   I T
    Czechoslovakia 1968-1969. Results and
    Analysis of Surveys Conducted During
    the Dubcek Era. New York: Praeger, 1972.
Piper, Donald G. B. *U. A. Kaverin: A Soviet Writer's Response*   II C
    to the Problem of Commitment. Pittsburgh, Pa.:
    Duquesne University Press, 1970.
Ploss, Sidney. *Political Conflict and the Soviet Press.* American   II S
    Political Science Association (Chicago) September 1972.
Pohribny, Arsen. "Art and Artists of the Underground." *Problems*   I G
    of Communism (March-April 1970).
Rice, Martin P. *Valery Brivsor and the Rise of Russian Symbolism.*   II G
    Ann Arbor, Mich.: Ardis Publishers, 1975.
Shapiro, Jane P. "Soviet Historiography and the Moscow Trials: II G
    After Thirty Years." *RR* (January 1968).
_____. "The Soviet Press and the Problem of Stalin." *Studies*   I G
    in Comparative Communism (July-October 1971).
_____. "The Soviet Press and the Problem of Stalin." *Studies in*   II G
    Comparative Communism 4, nos. 3-4 (July-October 1971):
    177-209.
Sjeklocha, Paul. "Modern Art and the Shackles of Dogma." *Problems*   II C
    of Communism 14 (November-December 1965).
Sjeklocha, Paul and Igor Mead. *Unofficial Art in the Soviet*   I G
    Union. Chicago, Ill.: University of Chicago Press, 1967.
Slonim, Marc. "Writers and Communism." *RR* (January 1971).   II G
Struve, Gleb. *Russian Literature Under Lenin and Stalin*   III T
    1917-1953. Norman, Okla.: University of Oklahoma
    Press, 1971.
Taylor, Pauline B. "Underground Soviet Broadcasting." *RR*   II T
    (April 1972).
Turkevich, Ludmilla B. "Culture Under Lenin and Stalin."   II G
    Problems of Communism 22 (March-April 1973).

Viereck, Peter, et al. "Creativity in the Soviet Union." *Tri-*　　III C
Quarterly. Northwestern University (Spring 1965).

Wedgewood, Benn. "New Thinking in Soviet Propaganda."　　II G
Soviet Studies (July 1969).

Dissent

Aczel, Tamas. "Budapest 1956–Prague 1968: II Spokesman　　II C
of Revolution." *Problems of Communism* 18 (July-
October 1969).

———. *Ten Years After–The Hungarian Revolution in the*　　II C
Perspective of History. New York: Holt, Rinehart and
Winston, 1966.

Amalrik, Andrei. *Involuntary Journey to Siberia.* New York:　　I C
Harcourt-Brace-Jovanovich, 1970.

———. "I Want to be Understood Correctly." *Survey*　　I C
(Winter-Spring 1970).

———. "Will the USSR Survive Until 1984?" *Survey*　　I C
no. 73 (Autumn 1969).

Anonymous. "Samizdat: Reply to Altayev." *Survey* 19, no. 1　　I G
(Winter 1973).

The Anti-Jewish Campaign in Present Day Poland. London:　　I G
Institute of Jewish Affairs, 1968.

Barry, Donald D. "Dissident Intellectuals: Views from Moscow."　　I G
Survey nos. 70-71 (Winter-Spring 1969).

Biddulph, Howard L. *Public Opposition in the USSR*　　I G
(forthcoming).

———. "Public Protest in the Soviet Political System: The　　I G
Strategy of Policy Opposition." (forthcoming).

———. "Soviet Intellectual Dissent as a Political Counter-　　II G
Culture." *The Western Political Quarterly* 25, no. 3
(September 1972): 222.

Bienen, Henry. *Violence and Social Change.* Chicago: University　　III G
of Chicago Press, 1968.

Bingham, J. B. and Seymour Halpern. "Recent Soviet Immigration　　II T
to Israel." Report of Special Study Mission to Austria and
Israel, April 2-8, 1972, Committee on Foreign Affairs,
House, Washington, 1972.

Bird, Christopher. "Psychiatry to Silence: Dissent." *RR*　　III T
(April 1972).

Bociurkiw, Bohdan R. "Political Dissent in the Soviet Union."　　III G
Studies in Comparative Communism (April 1970): 74-105.

_____. "Soviet Nationalities Policy and Dissent in the Ukraine."   II T
   The World Today 30, no. 5 (May 1974): 214-26.

_____. "The Voices of Dissent and the Visions of Gloom."   II G
   RR (July 1970).

Boiter, Albert. "Samizdat: Primary Source Material in Study of   III C
   Current Soviet Affairs." *RR* (July 1972).

Bonavia, David. *Fat Sasha and the Urban Guerilla: Protest and*   I T
   Conformism in the Soviet Union. New York: Atheneum, 1973.

Bourdeaux, Michael. *Faith on Trial in Russia.* New York: Harper   I G
   & Row, 1971.

_____. "Reform and Schism." *Problems of Communism*   II C
   (September-October 1967).

_____. *Religious Ferment in Russia: Protestant Opposition*   II T
   to Soviet Religious Policy. London, 1968.

Brumberg, Abraham. " Dissent in Russia." *Foreign Affairs*   I G
   52, no. 4 (July 1974): 181-98.

Brumberg, Abraham, ed. *In Quest of Justice: Protest and Dissent*   II G
   in the Soviet Union Today. New York: Praeger, 1970.

Cattell, David T. "Dissent and Stability in the Soviet Union."   II G
   Current History (October 1970).

Cohen, Richard, ed. *Let My People Go!* New York: Popular   I G
   Library, 1971.

Connor, Walter D. "Dissent in a Complex Society: The Soviet   II C
   Case." *Problems of Communism* 22 (March-April 1973).

Cuiic, K. F. "A Pro-Soviet Plot in Yugoslavia." *The World Today*   I G
   30, no. 11 (November 1974): 445-48.

Dahl, Robert A., ed. *Regimes and Oppositions.* New Haven: II C
   Yale University Press, 1973.

Decter, Moshe, ed. *Redemption! Jewish Freedom: Letters from*   I G
   Russia. New York: Macmillan, 1970.

Document. "Chronicle of Current Events." *Survey* nos. 74-75   I G
   (Winter-Spring 1970).

Document. "Protest from 170 Parishioners of St. Nicholas'   I G
   Church in Moscow." *Problems of Communism*
   (July-August 1968).

Durasoff, Steve. *The Russian Protestants: Evangelicals in the*   II T
   Soviet Union 1944-1964. Rutherford, N.J.: Fairleigh
   Dickinson University Press, 1969.

Ello, Paul, compiler. *Czechoslovakia's Blueprint for "Freedom":*   III G
   "Unity, Socialism and Humanity." Dubcek's Statements—
   The Original and Official Documents Leading to the
   Conflict of August 1968. Washington, D. C.:
   Acropolis Books, 1969.

Elwood, Ralph Carter. *Russian Social Democracy in the Under-*   II G
Ground: A Study of the RSDRP in the Ukraine. Assen:
Van Gorcum, 1974.

Eshliman and Iakunin. *A Cry of Despair from Moscow Churchmen.*   II G
New York: 1966.

———. *Religion in Communist Dominated Areas* (New York)   III G
5, nos. 15-16 (1966).

Feuer, Lewis S. "The Intelligentsia in Opposition." *Problems of*   II G
Communism 19, no. 6 (November-December 1970).

Fletcher, William B. "Religious Dissent in the USSR in the   II T
1960s." *Slavic Review* 30, no. 2 (June 1971).

Friedberg, Maurice. "The Plight of Soviet Jews." *Problems of*   II G
Communism 19, no. 6 (November-December 1970).

Glenny, Michael and Bohdan R. Bociurkew. "Dissent in the   II C
USSR." Commentary and Documents. *Studies in Com-*
parative Communism 3, no. 2 (April 1970).

Glenny, Michael, ed. *"Novy Mir."* A Selection 1925-1967.   I G
London: Jonathan Cape, 1972.

Glazov, Yuri. "Samizdat: Background to Dissent." *Survey*   I G
19, no. 1 (Winter 1973).

Gosztony, Peter I. "General Maleter: A Memoir." *Problems*   I G
of Communism 15 (March-April 1966).

Gorbatov, General A. V. *Years Off My Life.* Translated by   I G
Gordon Clough and Anthony Cash. New York: W. W.
Norton, 1965.

Grigorunko, P. G. and I. Yakhimovich. "Individual Liberty   I G
and Czechoslovakia's Freedom." *Problems of Com-*
munism 18 (May-June 1969).

Harris, Jonathan. "The Dilemna of Dissidence." *Survey* 16, no. 1   II C
(Winter 1971).

Hawson, Donald W. and Robert B. Fowler. *Obligation and*   II C
Dissent. Boston: 1971.

Hayward M. and W. C. Fletcher, eds. *Religion and the Soviet*   II G
State: A Dilemma of Power. New York: 1969.

Hulicka, K. and I. M. Hulicka. "Problems of Socialist Morality   II S
in Czechoslovakia." *International Journal of Compara-*
tive Sociology 7, no. 2 (April 1971).

"In Quest of Justice: Protest and Dissent in the USSR."   I G
Problems of Communism 17 (July-August and
September-October 1968).

Kline, George L. *Religious and Anti-Religious Thought in*   I C
Russia. Chicago: University of Chicago Press, 1969.

Kovacs, Inre, ed. *Facts about Hungary: The Fight for Freedom.*   I G
    N. Y.: The Hungarian Committee, 1966.
Kusin, Vladimir V. "A Note on K 231." *Soviet Studies*   II G
    24, no. 1 (July 1972).
_____. *Political Grouping in the Czechoslovak Reform Move-*   II T
    ment. New York: Columbia University Press, 1972.
Landsberger, Henry A., ed. *Rural Protest: Peasant Movements*   I T
    and Social Change. New York: Barnes and Noble, 1975.
Lendvai, Paul. *Anti-Semitism Without Jews.* New York: I G
    Doubleday and Co., 1971.
Lengyel, Jozsef. *Confrontation.* London: Peter Owen, 1973.   I G
Littell, Robert, ed. *The Czech Black Book.* New York: II G
    Praeger, 1969.
Litvinov, Pavel. *The Demonstration in Pushkin Square.*   I G
    Boston: Gambit, 1969.
Marchenko, Anatol. *My Testimony.* New York: E. P. Dalton, 1969.   I G
Markowski, Stefan. "Mr. Gomulka's Economic Legacy: The Roots   II G
    of Dissent." *The World Today* (London) February 1971.
Menges, C. *Prague Resistance, 1968: The Ingenuity of Conviction.*   II C
    Santa Monica: The Rand Corporation, P-3930,
    (September 1968).
Meyer, Alfred G. "Political Change Through Civil Disobedience   II C
    in the USSR and Eastern Europe." In Chapman, W. and
    S. Roland Pennock, eds., *Political and Legal Obligation:*
    Nomos XII. New York: Atherton Press, 1970.
Monas, Sidney. "Engineers or Martyrs: Dissent and the   I G
    Intelligentsia." *Problems of Communism* 17, no. 5
    (September-October 1968).
Oppenhiem, Samuel A. "Rehabilitation in the Post-Stalinist   I G
    Soviet Union." *The Western Political Quarterly*
    (March 1967).
Petrovich, Michael B. "Yugoslavia: Religion and the Tensions of   II G
    a Multi-National State." *East European Quarterly*
    6, no. 1 (March 1972).
Piekalkiewicz, Jaroslaw. *Public Opinion Polling in Czechoslovakia,*   I S
    1968-69—Results and Analysis of Surveys Conducted During
    the Dubcek Era. New York: Praeger, 1972.
Pospielovsky, Dimitry. *Russian Police Trade Unionism,*   II C
    Experiment or Provocation? London: Weidenfield
    and Nicolson, 1971.
Powell, D. E. "Controlling Dissent in the Soviet Union."   II G
    Government and Opposition 7, no. 1.

Rayuonny, S. "Political Forces in the CPSU" (Samizdat). *Survey*   II G
    17, no. 2 (Spring 1971).
Reddaway, Peter, ed. *Uncensored Russia, The Human Rights*   II G
    *Movement in the Soviet Union. The Annotated Text of
    the Unofficial Moscow Journal. "A Chronicle of Current
    Events," (nos. 1-11).* London: Jonathan Cape, 1972.
_____. *Uncensored Russia: Protest and Dissent in the Soviet*   II G
    Union. Translation with commentary of *Chronicle of
    Current Events* of April 1968-December 1969. New
    York: American Heritage Press, 1972.
Rothberg, Abraham. *The Heirs of Stalin, Dissidence and the*   II G
    Soviet Regime. Ithaca: Cornell University Press, 1972.
Sakharov, Andrei D. *Progress, Coexistence and Intellectual*   I C
    Freedom. N. Y.: Norton, 1968.
Saunders, George, ed. *Samizdat: Voices of the Soviet Opposition.*   II G
    N. Y.: Monad Press—distributed by Pathfinder Press (for
    the Anchor Foundation), 1974.
Sawczuk, Konstantyn. "Opposition in the Ukraine: Seven Versus   I G
    the Regime." *Survey* 20, no. 1 (Winter 1974): 36-46.
Scanmell, Michael, ed. *Russia's Other Winters: Selections from*   I G
    Samizdat Literature. New York: Praeger, 1969.
Scanmell, Michael. "Soviet Intellectuals Soldier On." *Survey*   II G
    16, no. 1 (Winter 1971).
Seton-Watson, H. "Czechoslovakia—1938, 1948 and 1968."   I G
    Government and Opposition (Spring 1969).
Simon, Gerhard. *Church, State and Opposition in the USSR.*   I T
    Berkeley: University of California Press, 1974.
Singleton, F. "The Roots of Discord in Yugoslavia." *The World*   I G
    Today (April 1972).
Sinyavski, Andrei. *For Freedom of Imagination.* New York: II C
    Holt Rinehart and Winston, 1971.
Skilling, H. Gordon. "Background to the Study of Opposition   II G
    in Communist East Europe." *Government and Opposi-
    tion* 3, no. 3 (Summer 1968): 294-324.
Smith, Paul A., Jr. "Protest in Moscow." *Foreign Affairs*   I G
    47, no. 1 (October 1968).
Soronani, Pietro. "Dissidence in Moscow." *Survey* 17, no. 2   II G
    (Spring 1971).
Sperber, Manes. "On Terror." *Survey* no. 72 (Summer 1969).
"Stalin and Stalinism." Letters and Documents. *Problems of*   II G
    Communism 18 (July-October 1969).

Starobin, J. "1956–A Memoir." *Problems of Communism*   I G
    15 (November-December 1966).
Sylvester, Anthony. "Intellectual Ferment in Yugoslavia." *Survey*   II G
    62 (January 1967).
"Text of Appeal Denouncing Trial of Four Russians." New York   I G
    Times (January 1967).
Tikos, Laszlo M. "Eugene Varga: A Reluctant Conformist." *Problems*   II C
    of Communism 14 (January-February 1965).
Tokes, Rudolf L., ed. *Dissent in the USSR: Politics, Ideology*   II G
    and People. Baltimore: Johns Hopkins Press,
    1975.
Tucker, Robert C. and Stephen F. Cohen, eds. *The Great Purge*   I G
    Trial. New York: Grosset and Dunlap, 1965.
Ulc, Otto. "Pilsen: The Unknown Revolt." *Problems of Communism*   II G
    14 (May-June 1965).
Vaculik, Ludvik. "2,000 Words: A Statement of Democratization."   I G
    East Europe (August 1968).
"Writers in Prison." *Problems of Communism* 16 (March-   I G
    April 1966).
Vakir, P. "An Open Letter to Amalvik." *Survey* (Winter-Spring 1970).   I G
Yakushev, Alexei A. "The Samizdat Movement in the USSR: II G
    A Note on Spontaneity and Organization." *The Russian*
    Review 34, no. 2 (April 1975): 186-93.
Zacek, Judith Cohen. "The Russian Bible Society and the Catholic
    Church." *Canadian Slavic Studies* 5, no. 1 (Spring).

Nationalities, Russification, Minorities

Allworth, Edward, ed. *Central Asia: A Century of Russian Rule*.   II G
    New York: Columbia University Press, 1967.
_____ *The Nationality Question in Soviet Central Asia*.   II T
    New York: Praeger, 1973.
_____ *Soviet Nationality Problems*. New York: Columbia   II G
    University Press, 1971.
Altschuler, Mordechai, ed. *Russian Publications on Jews and*   III T
    Judaism in the Soviet Union. Jerusalem: Society for
    Research on Jewish Communities and the Historical
    Society of Israel, 1970.
Ami, Ben. *Between Hammer and Sickel*. Philadelphia: The Jewish   I G
    Publication Society of America, 1967.
The Anti-Jewish Campaign in Present Day Poland. London: II G
    Institute of Jewish Affairs, 1968.

Bacon, Elizabeth E. *Central Asians Under Russian Rule: A Study*   II T
of Cultural Change. Ithaca, N. Y.: Cornell University
Press, 1966.

Barghoorn, Frederick C. *Soviet Russian Nationalism.*   III G
New York: 1956.

Bauman, Zygmund. "The End of Polish Jewry—A Sociological   II S
Review." *Bulletin on Soviet and East European Jewish
Affairs* (London) June 1969.

Browne, Michael, ed. *Ferment in the Ukraine: Documents by V.*   III T
*Chornovil, I. Kandyba, L. Lukyanenko, V. Moroz and
Others.* New York: Praeger, 1971.

Burks, R. V. *The National Problem and the Future of Yugoslavia.*   II T
Santa Monica, Calif.: RAND Corporation, P-4761
(October 1971).

Caroe, Olaf. *Soviet Empire, The Turks of Central Asia and*   III G
Stalinism. New York: St. Martin's Press, 1967.

Clem, Ralph S., ed. *The Soviet West: Interplay Between Nation-*   II G
ality and Social Organization. New York: Praeger, 1975.

Conolly, Violet. "The Yakuts." *Problems of Communism*   III G
(September-October 1967).

Conquest, Robert. *The Nation Killers: The Soviet Deportation*   II G
of Nationalities. New York: Macmillan, 1970.

Conquest, Robert, ed. *Soviet Nationalities Policy in Practice*   I G
(Soviet Studies Series). London: The Bodley Head, 1967.

Dadrian, V. N. "Signs of Armenian Unrest." *Problems of Com-*   I G
munism (September-October 1967).

Davis, H. B. "Lenin and Nationalism: The Redirection of the Marxist   I G
Theory of Nationalism." *Science and Society* (Spring 1967).

Dzyuba, Ivan. *Internationalism or Russification.* New York: II T
Humanities Press, 1968.

———. *Internationalism or Russification? A Study of the Soviet*   II G
Nationalities Problem. New York: Monad Press, 1975.

———. *Internationalism or Russification.* London: Weidenfeld   II C
and Nicholson, 1968.

Fisher, Jack C. *Yugoslavia: A Multi-National State.* San Fran-   II T
cisco: Chandler Publishing Company, 1966.

Gilboa, Yeoshua A. *The Black Years of Soviet Jewry, 1939-1953.*   II G
Boston: Little, Brown and Co., 1971.

Gitelman, Zvi. "The Jews." *Problems of Communism* 16   I G
(September-October 1967).

———. *Jewish Nationality and Soviet Politics.* Princeton, N. J.:   II G
Princeton University Press, 1972.

Goldhagen, Erich, ed. *Ethnic Minorities in the Soviet Union.*   II G
    New York: Praeger, 1968.
Gregory, James S. *Russian Land–Soviet People.* London: II G
    Marmp, 1968.
Janos, Andrew C. "Ethnicity, Communism and Political Change   II S
    in Eastern Europe." *World Politics* 23, no. 3 (April 1971).
Jews in Eastern Europe 3, no. 5 (October 1966).   I G
Jowitt, Kenneth. *Revolutionary Breakthroughs and National*   II G
    Development: The Case of Rumania "1944-65".
    Berkeley, Calif.: University of California
    Press, 1971.
Kirby, E. Stuart. *The Soviet Far East.* New York: Macmillan, 1971.   II G
Kochan, Lionel, ed. *The Jews in Soviet Russia Since 1917.*   II G
    2d ed. London: Oxford University Press for the
    Institute of Jewish Affairs, 1972.
Kutz, Zev; Rosemarie Rogers; and Fredric Harned, eds. *Handbook*   I T
    of Major Soviet Nationalities. New York: Macmillan,
    The Free Press, 1975.
Labachko, Ivan S. *Belorussia Under Soviet Rule, 1917-1957.*   II G
    Lexington, Ky.: University of Kentucky Press, 1972.
Lendvai, Paul. *Eagles in Cobwebs: Nationalism and Communism*   II G
    in the Balkans. New York: Doubleday, 1969.
Lewis, E. Glyn. *Multilingualism in the Soviet Union: Aspects*   II T
    of Language Policy and Its Implementation. The Hague:
    Mouton, 1971.
Luckyjm, George. "Turmoil in the Ukraine." *Problems of*   I G
    Communism (July-August 1968).
Matossian, Mary. "The Armenians." *Problems of Communism*   I G
    (September-October 1967).
Medvedev, Roy. "Jews in the USSR." Document. *Survey*   II G
    17, no. 2 (Spring 1971).
Nove, A. "History, Hierarchy and Nationalities: Some Observa-   II G
    tions on the Soviet Social Structure." *Soviet Studies*
    (July 1969).
Palmer, Stephen E., Jr. and Robert R. King. *Yugoslav Communism*   II T
    and the Macedonian Question. Hamden, Conn: Archon
    Books, 1971.
Perovic, Radasav. "Religious Communities." *Yugoslav Survey*   II G
    11, no. 3 (August 1970).
Pipes, Richard. "'Solving' the Nationality Problem." *Problems of*   I G
    Communism (September-October 1967).
Pospielovsky, Dimitry. "Russian Nationalism in Samizdat."   II G
    Survey 19, no. 1 (Winter 1973).

Rakowska-Harmstone, Teresa. *Russia and Nationalism in Central*   III G
     Asia: The Case of Tadzhikistan. Baltimore: Johns
     Hopkins Press, 1970.
Remeikis, Thomas. "The Evolving Status of Nationalities in the   II G
     Soviet Union." *Canadian Slavic Studies* 1, no. 3 (Fall 1967).
Riveles, Stanley. "Slovakia: Catalyst of Crisis." *Problems of*   II G
     Communism 17, no. 3 (May-June 1968).
Rubin, Ronald J., ed. *The Unredeemed: Anti-Semitism in the*   II G
     Soviet Union. Chicago: Quadrangle Books, 1968.
Sabaliunas, Leonas. *Lithuania in Crisis: Nationalism to Communism.*   III G
     Bloomington: Indiana University Press, 1972.
Schapiro, Leonard. *Rationalism and Nationalism in Russian*   II C
     Nineteenth Century Political Thought. New Haven: Yale
     University Press, 1967.
Schoepflin, George. "Croatian Nationalism." *Survey* 19, no. 1   III G
     (Winter 1973).
_____. "Rumanian Nationalism." *Survey* 20, nos. 2-3 (Spring-   I G
     Summer 1974): 77-104.
Shoup, Paul. *Communism and the Yugoslav National Question.*   III C
     New York: Columbia University Press, 1968.
_____. "The Evolution of a System." *Problems of Communism*   II G
     (July-October 1969).
_____. "The National Question in Yugoslavia." *Problems of*   II G
     Communism (January-February 1972).
Singleton, F. "The Roots of Discord in Yugoslavia." *World*   II G
     Today 28, no. 4 (April 1972).
Smolar, Boris. *Soviet Jewry, Today and Tomorrow.* New York: II G
     Macmillan, 1971.
Steiner, Eugen. *The Slovak Dilemma.* New York: Cambridge   III G
     University Press, 1973.
_____. *The Slovak Dilemma.* London: Cambridge University   I G
     Press. Center for International Studies, London School
     of Economics and Politics, 1973.
Struve, N. *Christians in Contemporary Russia.* New York: 1967.   II G
Sullivant, Robert S. "The Ukranians." *Problems of Communism*   II G
     (September-October 1967).
Symonenko, R. H. "Ukrainian Bourgeois Nationalism—Instrument   II T
     of Contemporary Anticommunism." *Soviet Analyst* 2, no. 2
     (June 7, 1973); no. 4 (February 15, 1973); no. 6
     (August 2, 1973).
Taagepera, Rein. "The 1970 Soviet Census: Fusion or Crystal-   II S
     lization of Nationalities?" *Soviet Studies* (October 1971).

Tillett, Lowell R. "Nationalism and History." *Problems of*   II G
    Communism (September-October 1967).
Tobias, Henry J. *The Jewish Bund in Russia. From Its Origins*   II G
    to 1905. Stanford, Calif.: Stanford University Press, 1972.
Vaidyanath, R. *The Formation of the Soviet Central Asian*   III T
    Republics: A Study in Soviet Nationalities Policy
    1917–1936. New Delphi: People's Publishing
    House, 1967.
Van Haxthausen, August. *Studies on the Interior of Russia.*   II G
    University Press, 1972.
Vardys, Stanley V. "The Baltic Peoples." *Problems of Communism*   III G
    (September-October 1967).
––––––. "The Case of the Crimean Tartars." *RR* (April 1971).   II G
––––––. *Soviet Nationalities Policy Since the XXII Party Con-*   I T
    gress. RR (October 1965).
Vardys, V. Stanley, ed. *Lithuania Under the Soviets.* New York: III G
    Praeger, 1965.
Volgin, L. M. "Friendship of Peoples." Pages from a Notebook.   II G
    Problems of Communism (September-October 1967).
Wheeler, G. "National and Religious Consciousness in Soviet   III G
    Islam." *Survey* no. 66 (January 1968).
Wheeler, Geoffrey. "The Muslims of Central Asia." *Problems*   III G
    of Communism (September-October 1967).
Wiesel, Elie. "Will Soviet Jewry Survive?" *Commentary*   I G
    (February 1967).
Wolf, John B. "Islam in the Soviet Union." *Current History*   II G
    (March 1969).

Socialist Morality

Bociurkiw, Bahdan. "Religion and Soviet Society." *Survey*   II G
    60 (July 1966).
––––––. "The Shaping of Soviet Religious Policy." *Problems of*   III G
    Communism 22 (May-June 1973).
Bourdeaux, Michael. "Dissent in the Russian Orthodox Church."   II G
    RR (1969).
––––––. *Opium of the People: The Christian Religion in the*   I G
    USSR. Indianapolis: Bobbs-Merrill Co., 1966.
––––––. *Patriarch and Prophets: Persecution of the Russian*   II G
    Orthodox Church Today. London: Macmillan, 1969.
Chalidze, Valery. *To Defend These Rights: Human Rights and*   I G
    the Soviet Union. Translated by Guy Daniels, New York:
    Random House, 1974.

Conner, Walter D. *Deviance in Soviet Society: Crime, Delin-*   III S
    quency, and Alcoholism. New York: Columbia
    University Press, 1972.
Conquest, Robert, ed. *The Politics of Ideas in the USSR.*   I G
    New York: Praeger, 1967.
_____. *Religion in the USSR.* London: 1968.   I G
DeGeorge, Richard T. *Soviet Ethics and Morality.* Ann Arbor,   II C
    Mich.: University of Michigan Press, 1969.
Demaitre, Edmund. "In Search of Humanism." *Problems of*   I C
    Communism 14 (September-October 1965).
Fletcher, William C. and A. J. Strover, eds. *Religion and the*   II C
    Search for New Ideals in the USSR. New York: 1967.
Fletcher, William C. *Nikolai, Portrait of a Dilemma.* New   II C
    York: Macmillan, 1968.
_____. *The Russian Orthodox Church Underground, 1917-1970.*   I G
    London: Oxford University Press, 1971.
_____. *A Study of Survival: The Church in Russia 1927-1943.*   I G
    New York: Macmillan, 1965.
Gaer, Felice D. "The Soviet Film Audience: A Confidential   I G
    View." *Problems of Communism* (January-February
    1974): 56-70.
Grossman, Joan Delaney. "Krushchev's Anti-religious Policy   II G
    and the Campaign of 1954." *Soviet Studies* (January
    1973).
Hayward, Max and William C. Fletcher, eds. *Religion and the*   II G
    Soviet State: A Dilemma of Power. London: 1969.
Jennes, Linda. *Feminism and Socialism.* New York: Pathfinder   II G
    Press, 1972.
Kalnins, Bruno. "Communist Oppression in Eastern Europe."   I C
    Socialist International Information (September 1966).
Koucky, V. "Comprehensive Development of Socialism in   II C
    Czechoslovakia." *World Marxist Review* (August
    1966).
Kurganov, I. A. *Women and Communism.* Available from the   I G
    author, 147 Jasmine, One Flushing, New York,
    11355 (1968).
Lennon, Lotta. "Women in the USSR." *Problems of Communism*   I G
    20 (July-August 1970).
Mandic, O. "A Marxist Perspective on Contemporary Religious   III T
    Revivals." *Social Research* 37, no. 2, (Summer 1970).
Marshall, Richard H., Jr., et al., eds. *Aspects of Religion in the*   II G
    Soviet Union, 1917-1967. Chicago: The University of
    Chicago Press, 1971.

Rathenburg, Joshua. *Synagogues in the Soviet Union*. Woltham,   II T
    Mass.: Institute of East European Jewish Studies, Brandeis
    University, 1966.

Schuster, Alice. "Woman's Role in the Soviet Union: Ideology and   II G
    Reality." *RR* (July 1971).

Sicinski, A. "Peace and War in Polish Public Opinion." *Polish*   II S
    Sociological Bulletin 16, no. 2 (1967).

"Religion in the USSR." Special Issue. *Survey* no. 66 (January 1968).   II G

Stroyen, William B. *Communist Russia and the Russian Orthodox*   III G
    Church, 1943-1962. Washington, D.C.: Catholic University of
    America Press, 1967.

Teodorovich, N. "Monasteries of the Russian Orthodox Church."   I G
    Institute for the Study of the USSR. *Bulletin* 13, no. 9
    (March 1966).

Vrcan, S. "Religion and Irreligion in a Socialist Society: Dilemmas   III S
    of the Sociological Approach." *Social Compass* 19: no. 2
    (1972).

Zamyatin, Yevgeny. *A Soviet Heretic: Essays*. Chicago: Univer-   III G
    sity of Chicago Press, 1970.

Zenkovsky, Serge. "Islam in Russia Today." *RR* (July 1968).

8. LAW AND PUBLIC DISCIPLINE: THE DEVELOPMENT OF CITIZENS' RIGHTS AND THE ROLE OF CONTRACTS

Source of Law—Legislative Process

Berman, Harold J. and John B. Quigley, eds. and translators.   III G
    Basic Laws on the Structure of the Soviet State.
    Cambridge, Mass.: Harvard University Press, 1969.

Berman, Harold J. and Peter B. Maggs. *Disarmament Inspection*   II T
    under Soviet Law. Dobbs Ferry: Oceana Publications, 1967.

Berman, Harold J. "What Makes 'Socialist Law' Socialist?"   II G
    Problems of Communism 20 (September-October 1971).

Bloembergen, S. "The Union Republics: How Much Autonomy."   II T
    Problems of Communism (September-October 1967).

Butler, William E. *The Law of Soviet Territorial Waters: A Case*   II T
    Study of Maritime Legislation and Practice. New York:
    Praeger, 1967.

Conquest, Robert, ed. *Justice and the Legal System in the USSR*.   I G
    New York: Praeger, 1968.

150   CURRENT RESEARCH IN COMPARATIVE COMMUNISM

Denisov, A. "Some Theoretical Problems of the Constitutional   II C
Structure of the Soviet State." *Soviet Law and Government* no. 4 (Spring 1967).

Feldbrugge, F. J. M. *Encyclopedia of Soviet Law.* Dobbs Ferry,   II T
N. Y.: Oceana Publications, 1973.

Fisk, Winston M. and A. Z. Rubenstein. "Yugoslavia's Constitu-   II G
tional Court." *East Europe* (July 1966).

Fisk, Winston M. "The Constitutionalist Movement in   II G
Yugoslavia." *Slavic Review* 30, no. 2 (June 1971).

"Fundamental Principles of Labor Law." *Current Digest of the Soviet Press* 22, no. 34 (September
22, 1970).

Gawenda, J. A. B. *The Soviet Domination of Eastern Europe in   II T
the Light of International Law.* M. P. Richmond, Surrey:
Foreign Affairs Publishing Co., 1974.

Gertsenzon, A. "Biology Has Nothing to Do With It." *Current   II C
Digest of the Soviet Press* 19, no. 4 (February 15, 1967).

Gilison, Jerome M. "Krushchev, Brezhnev, and Constitutional   I G
Reform." *Problems of Communism* 21, no. 5
(September-October 1972).

Grigoryan, Levon and Yari Dolgopolov. *Fundamentals of Soviet   III C
State Law.* Moscow: Progress Publishers, 1971.

Hazard, J., ed. *Soviet Legal Philosophy.* Translated by J. Babb.   III C
Cambridge, Mass.: Harvard University Press, 1951.

Hazard, John N. *Communists and Their Law. A Search for the   II G
Common Core of the Legal Systems of the Marxian
Socialist States.* Chicago: The University of Chicago
Press, 1969.

———. "Simplicity and Popularity: Early Dreams." *Problems of   I G
Communism* 14 (March-April 1965).

———; Isaac Shapiro; and Peter B. Maggs. *The Soviet Legal   III T
System. Contemporary Documentation and
Historical Commentary.* Revised edition.
Dobbs Ferry, N. Y.: Oceana Publishing
Co., 1969.

———. *The Soviet System of Government.* Fourth Edition revised.   II G
Chicago: University of Chicago Press, 1968.

Hoskins, Geoffrey A. *The Russian Constitutional Experiment   II T
Government of Duma, 1907-1914.* New York: Cambridge
University Press, 1973.

Johnson, E. L. *An Introduction to the Soviet Legal System.* New   II G
York: Barnes and Noble, 1973.

Kelsen, Hans. *The Communist Theory of Law.* New York: II C
Praeger, 1955.
Lafaue, Wayne R., ed. *Law in the Soviet Society.* Urbana, Ill.:   II G
University of Illinois Press, 1965.
Lapenna, Ivo. *State and Law: Soviet and Yugoslav Theory.* New   II C
Haven, Conn.: Yale University Press, 1964.
"Law and Legality in the USSR." Special Issue. *Problems of*   II G
Communism 14, no. 2 (March-April 1965).
Meissner, B. "Party Supremacy: Some Legal Questions." *Problems*   II G
of Communism 14, no. 2 (March-April 1965).
Meyer, Alfred G. "Authority in Communist Political Systems."   III S
In Lewis Edinger, ed. *Political Leadership in Industrial-*
ized Societies. New York: Kirjeger, 1967.
"New Criminal Legislation in Romania." *The Review: Inter-*   III T
national Commission of Jurists 4 (December 1969):
21-24.
Revesz, Laszlo. "Open Questions in Contemporary Soviet Philosophy   III C
of Law and State." *SST* (September 1966).
Rumann, T. "GDR's Socialist Constitution." *World*   II G
Marxist Review (April 1968).
Schapiro, Leonard. "Prospects for the Rule of Law." *Problems of*   II C
Communism 14 (March-April 1965).
Triska, Jan F., ed. *Constitutions of the Communist Party States*   II T
(Publication Ser. No. 70). Stanford, Calif.: Hoover
Institution Press, Stanford University, 1968.
Ulc, Otto. "The Vagaries of Law." *Problems of Communism*   II G
(July-October 1969).
Weiner, Stephen. "Socialist Legality on Trial." *Problems of Commu-*   II G
nism 17, no. 4 (1968).
Zile, Zigurds; Robert Sharlet; Jean C. Love. *The Soviet Legal System* II T
and Arms Inspection: A Case Study in Policy Implementation.
New York: Praeger, 1972.

Judicial System

Barry, Donald D. "The USSR Supreme Court: Recent Develop-   II T
ments." *Soviet Studies* (April 1969).
Berman, Harold J. *Justice in the USSR.* Cambridge: Harvard   II T
University Press, 1963.
Brill, E. J. *The Organs of Soviet Administration of Justice: Their*   II G
History and Operation. Leiden: Leiden University Press, 1970.

Brumberg, Abraham. "In Quest of Justice." *Problems of Communism*   I G
17 (July-August 1968).

———. "When Comrades Sit in Judgement." *Problems of*   I G
Communism 14 (March-April 1965).

Conquest, Robert, ed. *The Soviet Police System.* The Contem-   II T
porary Soviet Union Series. New York: Praeger, 1968.

Critchlow, James, tr. "Amalrik's Trial Excerpts from the Chronicle   III G
of Current Events." *RR* (October 1971).

Kucherov, Samuel. *The Organs of Soviet Administration of Justice:*   II T
Their History and Operation. Leiden: E. J. Brill, 1970.

"Scientific-Methodological Conference of USSR Supreme Court."   III T
Soviet Law and Government 5, no. 4 (Spring 1967).

Ulc, Otto. *The Judge in a Communist State: A View from Within.*   II G
Athens: Ohio University Press, 1972.

Unger, A. L. "Stalin's Renewal of the Leading Stratum: A Note on   II G
the Great Purge." *Soviet Studies* (January 1969).

Criminal Process

Berman, Harold J. *Soviet Criminal Law and Procedure: The*   III G
RSFSR Codes. Cambridge, Mass.: Harvard University
Press, 1967.

———. *Soviet Criminal Law and Procedure: The RSFSR Codes.*   II T
Cambridge, Mass.: Harvard University Press, 1972.

Connor, Walter D. *Deviance in Soviet Society: Crime, Delinquency*   II G
and Alcoholism. New York: Columbia University Press, 1972.

Dewar, Hugo. "Murder Revisited: The Case of Sergei Mironovich   I G
Kirov." *Problems of Communism* 14 (September-
October 1965).

Grzbowski, Kazimierz. "Soviet Criminal Law." *Problems of*   I G
Communism 14 (March-April 1965).

Lepenna, Ivo. *Soviet Penal Policy.* Chester Springs, Pa.: Defour   III T
Editions, 1968.

Noble, John. *I Was a Slave in Russia.* New York: Devin-Adair   I G
Co., 1968.

"Principles of Corrective Labor Legislation" and "Preventive   III T
Detention in Custody." *Current Digest of the Soviet
Press* 21, no. 29 (August 13, 1969).

Reddaway, Peter. *Trial of the Four: The Case of Ginzberg,*   II G
Cqalanskov, Lashkova and Dobrovski. New York:
Viking Press, 1972.

Rudzinski, Aleksander W. "The New Communist Civil Codes of   III T
    Czechoslovakia and Poland." *Indiana Law Journal* 41
    (Fall 1965).
Solomon, Peter Jr. "A New Soviet Administrative Ethos—Example   III G
    from Crime Prevention." Paper for Northeastern Slavic
    Conference, Montreal 1971.
_____. *Soviet Criminology*. University of Cambridge Institute of   III T
    Criminology, Bibliographic Series No. 4. Cambridge: 1969.

Social Correction

Anashkin, G. Z. "The Role of Law Consciousness and Public Opinion   III T
    in Setting Punishment." *Current Digest of the Soviet Press*
    19, no. 9 (March 22, 1967).
Bilinsky, Andreas. "The Lawyer and Soviet Society." *Problems of*   II T
    Communism 14 (March-April 1965).
Boiter, Albert, Dr. "Comradely Justice: How Durable Is It?" *Problems* II T
    of Communism 14 (March-April 1965).
_____. "A New Orientation in Soviet Law Enforcement." Radio   II T
    Liberty Research Paper, no. 11 (1966).
Chloror, A. M. *Yugoslav Civil Law: History, Family, Property*.   II T
    Oxford: Clarendon Press, 1970.
Ginsburgs, George. "Rights and Duties of Citizens." *Problems of*   I G
    Communism 14 (March-April 1965).
_____. *Soviet Citizenship Law*. Leyden, The Netherlands: II G
    A. W. Sijthoff, 1968.
Gray, Whitmore. "Scholarship on Soviet Family Law in Perspective." III G
    Columbia Law Review (February 1970).
Hayward, Max, ed. *On Trial: The Soviet State Versus "Ahram Tertz"* III G
    and "Nikolai Arzhak." Revised edition. 1967.
Kamenka, Eugene. "The Soviet View of Law." *Problems of Commu-*   III T
    nism 14, no. 2 (March-April 1965).
Rudden, Bernard. *Soviet Insurance Law*. Leyden, The Netherlands: III T
    A. W. Sijthoff, 1966.
"Some Causes of Juvenile Delinquency in the USSR and Measures   II T
    to Prevent It." *Current Digest of the Soviet Press* 18, no. 30
    (August 17, 1966).
Taylor, Pauline B. "Sectarians in Soviet Courts." *RR* (July 1965).   II T
Vogel, Ezra. "Voluntarism and Social Control." In Donald W.   III C
    Threadgold, ed., *Soviet and Chinese Communism*.
    Seattle, Washington: 1967.

Walter, Eugene V. *Terror and Resistance.* London: Oxford Univer- II G
sity Press, 1972.

Wolfe, Bertram D. "Dress Rehearsals for the Great Terror." *Studies* II G
in Comparative Communism (April 1970).

Resolution of Conflicts of Interest

Brunner, George. "Bylaws of the Elite: The Party Statute." *Problems* II G
of Communism 14 (March-April 1965).

Butler, William E. *The Soviet Union and the Law of the Sea.* Balti- II T
more: The Johns Hopkins Press, 1971.

Duevel, Christina. "Chesnokov Undermines the 'All-People's State' II G
of the CPSU Program." Radio Liberty Despatch (March
31, 1967).

Feuerle, Peter. "State Arbitration in Communist Countries: The III T
Differentiation of Functions." *Studies in Comparative*
Communism 4, nos. 3-4 (July-October 1971).

Fox, Irving, K., ed. *Water Resources Law and Policy in the Soviet* II C
Union. Madison, Wis.: University of Wisconsin Press, 1971.

Reddaway, Peter. "Freedom of Worship and the Law." *Problems* II G
of Communism (July-August 1968).

9. AGRICULTURE: PROPERTY RELATIONSHIPS AND INVESTMENT PRIORITIES

Ownership

DePauw, John W. "The Private Sector in Soviet Agriculture." *Slavic* II G
Review 28, no. 1 (March 1969).

Feiwel, G. R. *The Economics of a Socialist Enterprise: A Case Study* III T
of the Polish Firm. New York: Praeger, 1965 and 1968.

Hammen, O. J. "Marx and the Agrarian Question." *American* II C
Historical Review 77, no. 3 (June 1972).

Laird, Roy D. and Edward L. Crowley. *Soviet Agriculture: The* II S
Permanent Crisis. New York: Praeger, 1965.

Male, D. J. *Russian Peasant Organization Before Collectivization:* III G
A Study of Commune and Gathering 1925-30. New York:
Cambridge University Press, 1971.

Osofsky, Stephen. *Soviet Agricultural Policy: Toward the Abolition* I G
of Collective Farms. New York: Praeger, 1974.

Thorner, Daniel and Basile Kierblay, eds. *A. V. Chayanou, Theory*   III C
    of Peasant Economy. Homewood, Illinois: 1966.
Wädckin, Karl Eugen. *The Private Sector in Soviet Agriculture.*   II T
    Berkeley: University of California Press, 1973.

Organization

Adams, A. E. and J. S. Men. *U. S. Systems—Agriculture in the USSR,*   II G
    Poland, Czechoslovakia. Urbana: University of Illinois
    Press, 1971.
The Agricultural Situation in Communist Areas. U. S. Department of   II G
    Agriculture, Economic Research Service, Washington,
    D. C., 1971.
Biggart, John. "The Collectivisation of Agriculture in Soviet Lithuania."   I T
    East European Quarterly 9, no. 1 (Spring 1975): 53-75.
Bradley, Michael E. "Prospects for Soviet Agriculture." *Current*   II G
    History (October 1970).
Domar, E. "The Soviet Collective Farm as a Producer Cooperative."   III T/S
    Journal of Economic Abstracts (September 1966).
Heady, Earl O., ed. *Economic Models and Quantative Methods for*   II T
    Decisions and Planning in Agriculture. Proceedings of an
    East West Seminar. Ames: Iowa State University Press, 1971.
Horvath, Janos. "Agriculture: Which Path." *Problems of Communism*   I G
    14 (May-June 1965).
Hough, Jerry F. "A Hare-brained Scheme in Retrospect." *Problems of*   I G
    Communism 14, no. 4 (July-August 1965).
Jackson, W. A. Douglas. "Wanted: An Effective Land Use Policy and   II T
    Improved Reclamation." *Slavic Review* 29, no. 3
    (September 1970).
Johnson, D. Gale. "The Soviet Grain Shortage: A Case of Rising   I T
    Expectations." *Current History* 68, no. 406 (June 1975).
Karcz, Jerzy F., ed. *Soviet and East European Agriculture.* Berkeley: I G
    University of California Press, 1967.
Kiss, Sandor. "Hungarian Agriculture Under the NEM." *East*   III G
    Europe (August 1968).
Korbonski, Andrezej. *Politics of Socialist Agriculture in Poland*   II G
    1945-1960. New York: Columbia University Press, 1965.
Kostiowicki, Jerry and Roman Szczesny. *Polish Agriculture:*   II T
    Characteristics, Types and Regions. Hungarian Academy
    of Sciences, 1972.
Miller, Robert F. *One Hundred Thousand Tractors: The MTS and the*   III T
    Development of Control in Soviet Agriculture. Cambridge, Mass.:
    Harvard University Press, 1970.

156   CURRENT RESEARCH IN COMPARATIVE COMMUNISM

Nimitz, Nancy. "The Lean Years." *Problems of Communism*   II G
14, no. 3 (May-June 1965).
Osofsky, Stephen. "The Soviet Grain Problem in Perspective."   II G
RR (April 1973).
Salzmann, Z. and V. Scheufler. *Komárov: A Czech Farming*   I T
Village. New York: Holt, Rinehart and Winston, 1974.
"Socialist Transformation of Polish Agriculture." A Nine Part   II T
Series. *Zycic Gospordarcze* (29 October 1972-18
February 1973).
Strauss, Erich. *Soviet Agriculture in Perspective.* London: Allen   II G
and Unwin, 1969.
———. "The Soviet Dairy Economy." *Soviet Studies*   III G
(January 1970).
Stuart, Robert C. *The Collective Farm in Soviet Agriculture.*   III G
Lexington, Mass.: Lexington Books, D. C. Heath and
Co., 1972.
Symons, Leslie. *Russian Agriculture: A Geographic Survey.*   I G
London: Bell and Sons, 1972.
———. *Russian Agriculture: A Geographic Survey.* New York: I T
John Wiley, 1972.
Volin, Lazar A. *A Century of Russian Agriculture: From Alexander*   II G
II to Khrushchev. Cambridge, Mass.: Harvard University
Press, 1970.
Wadekin, Karl-Eugen. "Manpower in Soviet Agriculture—Some   II G
Post-Khrushchev Developments and Problems."
Soviet Studies (January 1969).

Management

Autorkhanov, Abdurakhman G. "A New Deal for Collective   II T
Farmers?" Institute for the Study of the USSR. Analysis
of Current Developments in the Soviet Union, no. 452,
Munich (April 25, 1967).
Bornstein, Morris. "The Soviet Debate on Agricultural Price and   III T
Procurement Reforms." *Soviet Studies* (July 1969).
Bradley, Michael E. and Clark M. Gardner. "Supervision and   III T
Efficiency in Socialized Agriculture." *Soviet Studies*
(January 1972).
Davies, R. W. "A Note on Grain Statistics." *Soviet Studies*   II T
(January 1970).
Hahn, Werner G. *Politics of Soviet Agriculture, 1960-1970.*   II G
Baltimore: Johns Hopkins Press, 1972.

Jackson, Douglas W. A. *Agrarian Policies and Problems in*   II T
   Communist Countries. Seattle: University of
   Washington Press, 1971.

Johnson, D. "The Environment for Technological Change in Soviet   II G
   Agriculture." *American Economic Review* (May 1966).

Karcz, Jerzy F. "Some Major Persisting Problems in Soviet   II S
   Agriculture." *Slavic Review* 29, no. 3 (September 1970).

_____. "Thoughts on the Grain Problem." *Soviet Studies*   II S
   17, no. 4 (April 1967).

Laird, Roy D. "Agriculture Under Khrushchev." *Survey*   II G
   no. 65 (1965).

_____. "New Trends and Old Remedies." *Problems of*   I G
   Communism (March-April 1966).

Luxenburg, Norman. "Soviet Agriculture Since Khrushchev."   II G
   RR (January 1971).

Millar, James R. "The Agricultural Surplus Hypothesis: A Reply   II G
   to Alec Nove." *Soviet Studies* (October 1971).

_____. "Soviet Rapid Development and the Agricultural Surplus   II G
   Hypothesis." *Soviet Studies* (July 1970).

Nove, Alec. "The Agricultural Surplus Hypothesis: A Comment   II G
   on James R. Millar's Article." *Soviet Studies*
   (January 1971).

_____. "Soviet Agriculture Under Brezhnev." *Slavic Review*   I G
   29, no. 3 (September 1970).

Schwarz, Solomon. "Agriculture: The Curtain Is Lifted." *Problems*   II G
   of Communism (March-April 1966).

Sulemezov, S. "Bulgaria's New Agricultural Management System."   II T
   World Marxist Review (January 1968).

Tikmakoff, George. "Stolypin's Agrarian Reform: An Appraisal."   I G
   RR (April 1971).

Investment

Conklin, David W. *An Evaluation of the Soviet Profit Reforms:*   III S
   With Special Reference to Agriculture. New York:
   Praeger, 1970.

Dibb, Paul. *Soviet Agriculture Since Khrushchev—An Economic*   III S
   Appraisal. Occasional paper no. 4. Canberra: Australian
   National University, Department of Political Science,
   Research School of Social Sciences, 1969.

Folke, Dovring. "Soviet Farm Mechanization in Perspective."   III T
   Slavic Review 25, no. 2 (June 1966).

Laird, Roy D. "Prospects for Soviet Agriculture." *Problems of*   I G
    Communism 20, no. 5 (September-October 1971).
Mills, Richard M. "The Formation of the Virgin Lands Policy."   II G
    Slavic Review 29, no. 1 (March 1970).
Owen, Wyn F. "The Double Developmental Squeeze on Agriculture."   II G
    American Economic Review 56, no. 1 (March 1966).

Social Conditions and Incentives

Belov, Fedor. *The History of a Soviet Collective Farm.* New
    York: Praeger, 1955.
Celt, Marek. "Another Round: Peasant and Party in Poland."   II G
    East Europe (February 1968).
Conquest, Robert, ed. *Agricultural Workers in the USSR.*   II G
    New York: Praeger, 1969.
Dunn, Stephen P. and Ethel Dunn. *The Peasants of Central Russia.*   II G
    New York: Holt, Rinehart and Winston, 1967.
Fallenbuchl, Z. "Collectivization and Economic Developments."   II G
    Journal of Economic Abstracts (June 1967).
Jackson, George D. *Comintern and Peasant in East Europe, 1919-*   I G
    1930. New York: Columbia University Press, 1966.
Jasny, Naum. *Khrushchev's Crop Policy.* Glasgow: Outram and   II T
    Co., 1965.
Kucherov, Samuel. "The Peasant." *Problems of Communism*   I G
    14 (March-April 1965).
Laird, Roy D. "Prospects for Soviet Agriculture." *Problems of*   I G
    Communism 20 (September-October 1971).
"Soviet Agriculture in 1973 and Beyond in Light of U. S. Perfor-   II T
    mance." *The Russian Review* 33, no. 4 (October
    1974): 373-85.
Laird, Roy D. and Betty A. *Soviet Communism and Agrarian*   II G
    Revolution. Harmondsworth, Middlesex, England:
    Pelican Original, 1970.
Lewin, M. *Russian Peasants and Soviet Power: A Study of Col-*   III T
    lectivization. New York: Norton, 1975.
Lipset, S. M. *Agrarian Socialism.* Garden City, New York: II C
    Doubleday Anchor Books, 1968.
Millar, James R., ed. *The Soviet Rural Community.* Urbana, Ill.:   II G
    University of Illinois Press, 1971.
Miller, R. F. *Socialism and Agricultural Cooperation: The Soviet*   II T
    and Yugoslav Cases. Canberra: Australian National
    University, 1974.

Potichnyi, Peter. *Soviet Agricultural Trade Unions 1917-1970.*   I T
    Toronto: University of Toronto Press, 1972.
Powell, David E. "Soviet Society in Flux: The Rural Exodus."   I T
    Problems of Communism (November-December 1974):
    1-13.
Wodekin, Karl Eugen. "Income Distribution in Soviet Agriculture."   II T
    Soviet Studies 27, no. 1 (January 1975): 3-26.
Wright, Arthur W. "Systemic Ills in Soviet Agriculture." *Problems of*   II T
    Communism (January-February 1975): 51-55.

LAWRENCE L. WHETTEN is Director of the German Graduate Program in International Relations, University of Southern California, in Munich, West Germany. From 1963 to 1970 he was Senior Political Analyst with the United States Air Force in Europe. He is the author of *Germany's Ostpolitik, Contemporary American Foreign Policy,* and *The Canal War: Four Power Conflict in the Middle East.* He is also a frequent contributor to numerous journals of international affairs. Dr. Whetten holds a Ph.D. from New York University.

PERIODICAL PUBLICATIONS ON THE SOCIALIST
COUNTRIES: A New Annotated Index of English-
Language Materials for Europe, Asia, and Latin America
                                    Harry G. Shaffer

CHANGE AND ADAPTATION IN SOVIET AND
EAST EUROPEAN POLITICS
                        edited by Peter J. Potichnyj and
                        Jane P. Shapiro

POLITICAL DEVELOPMENT IN EASTERN EUROPE
                        edited by Jan F. Triska and
                        Paul M. Cocks

IMPLEMENTATION OF SOVIET ECONOMIC
REFORMS: Political, Organizational, and Social
Processes
                        Karl W. Ryavec

INPUT-OUTPUT ANALYSIS AND THE SOVIET
ECONOMY: An Annotated Bibliography
                        Vladimir G. Treml

THE SOCIAL STRUCTURE OF EASTERN EUROPE:
Transition and Process in Czechoslovakia, Hungary,
Poland, Romania and Yugoslavia
                        edited by Bernard Lewis Faber